In Defense of Reason After Hegel

In Defense of Reason After Hegel

Why We Are So Wise

Richard Dien Winfield

ANTHEM PRESS

Anthem Press
An imprint of Wimbledon Publishing Company
www.anthempress.com

This edition first published in UK and USA 2025
by ANTHEM PRESS
75–76 Blackfriars Road, London SE1 8HA, UK
or PO Box 9779, London SW19 7ZG, UK
and
244 Madison Ave #116, New York, NY 10016, USA

First published in the UK and USA by Anthem Press in 2022

Copyright © Richard Dien Winfield 2025

The author asserts the moral right to be identified as the author of this work.

All rights reserved. Without limiting the rights under copyright reserved above,
no part of this publication may be reproduced, stored or introduced into
a retrieval system, or transmitted, in any form or by any means
(electronic, mechanical, photocopying, recording or otherwise),
without the prior written permission of both the copyright
owner and the above publisher of this book.

British Library Cataloguing-in-Publication Data
A catalogue record for this book is available from the British Library.

Library of Congress Control Number: 2025936615

ISBN-13: 978-1-83999-638-2 (Pbk)
ISBN-10: 1-83999-638-2 (Pbk)

Cover image: Friedrich Nietzsche, 1887. By Everett Collection / Shutterstock.com

This title is also available as an eBook.

In memory of William Maker, defender of reason

CONTENTS

Acknowledgments   xi

Introduction   1

1. Why We Are So Wise: Hegelian Reflections on whether Reason Can Be Enhanced   7
    Challenge to the Improvers of Reason   7
    The Natural Enabling Conditions of Reason   9
    The Psychological Prerequisites of Thinking   12
    Universality, Self-Determination, and Rational Autonomy   15
    The Effect of Terrestrial and Extraterrestrial Evolution upon the Life of the Mind   17
    Can Technology and Artificial Intelligence Augment Our Wisdom?   18

2. Self-Determination in Logic and Reality   23
    Overcoming the Logical Challenge to Self-Determination   25
    Self-Determination and Conceptual Determination   32
    Overcoming the Psychological Challenge to Self-Determination   35
    Overcoming the Practical Challenge to Self-Determination   41

3. Hegel's Overcoming of the Overcoming of Metaphysics   47
    The Repudiation of Foundational Ontology and Its Hegelian Critique   47
    The Repudiation of Synthetic a priori Knowledge and Its Hegelian Critique   49
    Hegel and the Future of Metaphysics   56

4. On Contradiction: Hegel versus Aristotle, Sextus Empiricus, and Kant   59
    Aristotle on Contradiction   60
    Sextus Empiricus and the Principle of Contradiction   63
    Hegel's Account of Determinacy as the Thoroughgoing Refutation of the Principle of Contradiction   66
    Why Hegel Addresses Contradiction and Its Principle in the Logic of Essence   68

	The Logic of the Concept and Emancipation from the Principle of Contradiction	71
5.	Overcoming Actuality: How Hegel Frees Us from the Prison of Modality	75
	The Prison of Actuality	75
	Putting Actuality in Its Proper Place	75
	Why Actuality Falls in the Logic of Determined Determinacy	76
	From Substance to Modality	81
	From Modality to Causality	85
	From Causality to Freedom	86
	Self-Determination and the Concept	88
6.	Time and Reason	91
	The Inscrutable Ubiquity of Time	91
	The Attempt to Root Time in Motion	92
	The Attempt to Root Time in Mind	94
	From Space to Time	96
	The Concrete Material Determination of Space–Time	97
	The Psychological and Historical Determinations of Time	100
7.	Hegel and the Problem of Consciousness	103
	Philosophy and the Opposition of Consciousness	103
	From the Modern Philosophy of Mind to Hegel's Systematic Account of Consciousness	104
	Hegel's Account of Prediscursive Self-Consciousness	107
	From Consciousness to Intelligence	109
8.	Hegel and the Origin of Language	113
	The Puzzle of the Origin of Language	113
	The Three Dogmas Barring Comprehension of the Origination of Language	116
	The Origin of the Basic Element of Language	118
	The Move from Names to Discourse	123
9.	The Logic of Right	127
	Philosophy, Logic, and Ethics	127
	Logic per se versus the Logic of *Realphilosophie*	132
	Self-Determination in Logic versus Self-Determination in Ethics	134
	Is the Threefold Division of Abstract Right, Morality, and Ethical Community Valid?	139
	Are Family, Civil Society, and the State the Exhaustive Differentiations of Ethical Community?	142

10. A Dream Deferred: From the US Constitution to the Universal Declaration of Human Rights	147
Rights and the Constitution	147
The Narrow Focus of the US Constitution	149
The Promise of the Preamble	150
Liberty versus Self-Determination	153
The Limitation of Rights in the Articles of the US Constitution	162
Prepolitical Rights in Article I	162
Prepolitical Rights in Article II	166
Prepolitical Rights in Article III	167
Prepolitical Rights in Articles IV–VII	167
Prepolitical Rights in the Bill of Rights	169
Prepolitical Rights in the Other Amendments	170
Is the US Constitution Incomplete?	172
FDR's Call for a New Social Bill of Rights	173
The Additional Rights of the Universal Declaration of Human Rights	176
The Abiding Challenge	179
11. World Spirit on the Campaign Trail in Georgia: Can the Philosophy of Right Be a Guide to Social Reform?	181
Contesting the Enslavement of Theory to Practice	181
From the Practical Conditioning of Knowing to the General Impasse of Transcendental Philosophy	182
The Unification of Theory and Practice in Systematic Logic	183
From the System of Right to the History of Right	185
The Philosophy of Right's Challenge to the US Democracy	189
World Spirit on the Campaign Trail in Georgia	192
12. The Classical Nude and the Limits of Sculpture	197
The Constitutive Limits of Figurative Sculpture	198
The Affinity between Sculpture and Classicism	203
Form and Content in the Classical Nude	205
Sculpture and Modernity	210
Bibliography	213
Index	217

ACKNOWLEDGMENTS

The following chapters incorporate text that was previously published and/or delivered at conference meetings.

Chapter 1 incorporates text published as "Why I Am So Wise: Hegelian Reflections on whether Reason Can Be Enhanced," in *Creolizing Hegel*, ed. Michael Monahan (Lanham, MD: Rowman & Littlefield, 2017), 79–91.

Chapter 2 incorporates text delivered as my Presidential Address at the 66th Annual Meeting of the Metaphysical Society of America, at the University of Georgia, Athens, Georgia, on April 18, 2015, and published as "Self-Determination in Logic and Reality," *Review of Metaphysics*, vol. 69, no. 3, issue no. 275 (March 2016), 467–94.

Chapter 3 incorporates text delivered at the 23rd Biennial Conference of the Hegel Society of America, at Northwestern University, Evanston, IL, on October 31, 2014, and published as "Hegel's Overcoming of the Overcoming of Metaphysics," in *Hegel and Metaphysics: On Logic and Ontology in the System*, ed. Allegra de Laurentiis (Berlin/Boston: De Gruyter, 2016), 59–70.

Chapter 4 incorporates text delivered at the 24th Biennial Meeting of the Hegel Society of America, at Concordia University, Montreal, on November 15, 2016, and published as "On Contradiction: Hegel versus Aristotle, Sextus Empiricus, and Kant," in *Hegel and Ancient Philosophy: A Re-Examination*, ed. Glenn Magee (New York: Routledge, 2018), 147–60.

Chapter 5, "Overcoming Actuality: How Hegel Frees Us from the Prison of Modality," was delivered at the *Conference Examining Hegel's Idea of Self-Determination: From Actuality to Concept*, University of Warwick, UK, June 7, 2019.

Chapter 6 incorporates text delivered at the Collaborations Conference at Southern Illinois University, Carbondale, Illinois, on March 20, 2015, and published in expanded form as "Time and Reason: How Unveiling the Mystery of Time Certifies Rational Autonomy," in *Plí: The Warwick Journal of Philosophy*, vol. 31 (2019), 95–103.

Chapter 7 incorporates text published as "Hegel and the Problem of Consciousness," in *Consciousness and the Great Philosophers*, ed. Stephen Leach and James Tartaglia (London: Routledge, 2017), 125–32.

Chapter 8 incorporates text delivered at the Society for Systematic Philosophy group meeting, American Philosophical Association Eastern Division Meeting, in Philadelphia, December 29, 2014, and published as "Hegel and the Origin of Language," in *Hegel's Philosophical Psychology*, ed. Susanne Herrmann-Sinai and Lucia Ziglioli (New York: Routledge, 2016), 91–103.

Chapter 9 incorporates text delivered at the Society for Systematic group meeting, American Philosophical Association Pacific Division Meeting, San Francisco, April, 2, 2016, and published as "The Logic of Right," in *Hegel's Political Philosophy: On the Normative Significance of Method and System*, ed. Thom Brooks and Sebastian Stein (Oxford: Oxford University Press, 2017), 222–38.

Chapter 12 incorporates text published as "The Classical Nude and the Limits of Sculpture," *Revue Internationale de Philosophie*, vol. 3, no. 221 (2002), 443–60.

I wish to thank the editors, journals, and publishers listed above for their permissions.

INTRODUCTION

Contempt for truth is rampant in a world whose most powerful leaders denounce the independent press as an organ of phony news, propagate "alternate facts," betray partners with abandon, and spread brazen falsehoods with neither remorse nor political cost. Compounding the mystification is the proliferation of unfiltered opinion in the web of internet connectivity, where the ceaseless dissemination of information overwhelms critical discrimination.

More insidious, however, is the attack on reason from within the philosophical community. No longer do skeptics just suspend judgment while examining whether they can counter every new truth claim with equal argument. Instead, cruder dogmatists reign, confident in the assumption that reason is empty and formal, incapable of obtaining any new truth on its own and only fit to certify the consistency of given suppositions. Thought, they tell us, can only reflect on the judgments of empirical science, our linguistic usage, our common moral intuitions, our historical conventions, or our aesthetic tastes and analyze to what degree they cohere. Alternately, we can deconstruct our knowledge, ethical, and aesthetic claims and expose the various contingent conditions that underlie them and seal their corrigible relativity. On both fronts of analysis and deconstruction, the philosophical academy propagates the disempowerment of reason, all the while completely ignoring how the denial of the independent sovereignty of reason robs that diagnosis of any global authority.

The destruction of reason by our undertakers of philosophy cannot succeed. It is pointless to use philosophy to cure us of its lure, since doing so enlists and thereby endorses its authority. The reigning orthodoxy may not have the faintest clue how reason can free itself of all juridical assumptions, overcome foundations, and achieve autonomy. Yet the philosophical tradition offers one figure, who haunts the margins of the canon but provides the path for resurrecting the unqualified promise of reason. This is Hegel, and if we stand on his shoulders and think through what he has and should have done, we can defeat the assault on philosophy by the assassins of reason.

The following investigations build upon and enlist Hegel's arguments to empower reason to conceive the categories of autonomous thought, the fundamental character of nature and mind, and the reality of freedom in which normative conduct resides.

The first chapter, "Why We Are So Wise: Hegelian Reflections on Whether Reason Can Be Enhanced," clears the way by examining how the enabling conditions of our thought cannot possibly limit what our reason knows to be true and right. Although we cannot engage in philosophical investigation without inhabiting a biosphere in which rational animals have emerged in some given linguistic community with customs of its own, none of these preconditions of thought can rob reason of the autonomy by which it alone can set its own limits. Due to this constitutive self-determination of reason, neither natural evolution nor our own bioengineering can possibly enhance our capacity for philosophical thinking. In showing why and how this is so, the first chapter refutes Nietzsche's contrary claim that he can have a special wisdom due to his particular nature.

Chapter 2, "Self-Determination in Logic and Reality," my presidential address to the 66th Annual Meeting of the Metaphysical Society of America, further explores how philosophical thought can be autonomous and how self-determination can operate in the historical world of living agents. The chapter begins by exploring the perplexities of the logic of self-determination, whose difficulties Hegel first unraveled in his *Science of Logic*. Although the autonomy of reason underlies the autonomy of action, the self-determined will presents specific challenges of its own on whose solution depends the successful working out of ethics. The chapter sketches out how a plurality of agents can achieve self-determination, bringing right into being despite all the contingencies of our natural, psychological, and historical existence.

Philosophers have variously characterized metaphysics as a first philosophy of being *qua* being, as the body of synthetic a priori knowledge and as comprehensive knowledge of things in themselves. Metaphysics in all these forms has been challenged, most notably by Kant and by Nietzsche and his followers. Their repudiations of metaphysics, however, are themselves subject to devastating critiques by arguments that Hegel develops in his *Phenomenology of Spirit* and *Science of Logic*. Chapter 3, "Hegel's Overcoming of the Overcoming of Metaphysics," considers the success and outcome of the Hegelian critique of anti-metaphysical philosophy and what it augurs for the future of metaphysics. In so doing, the chapter draws upon Hegel's insights concerning the relation of universality and individuality, conceptual determination and objectivity, and the connection of self-determination to the concept.

No principle has enjoyed more abject fealty in the annals of Western philosophy than the principle of contradiction. From Aristotle onward, almost all philosophers have invoked this hallowed principle to support their philosophical systems or to embolden skepticism of them all. Their adherence to the principle of contradiction has yielded the same outcome: reason's search for truth has been banished from the territory in which contradiction is encountered. Chapter 4, "On Contradiction: Hegel versus Aristotle, Sextus Empiricus, and Kant," examines how Aristotle, Sextus Empiricus, and Kant have embraced the principle of contradiction and how their embrace cannot be sustained. Turning to Hegel, the chapter shows how Hegel's account of determinacy provides a thoroughgoing refutation of the principle of contradiction. The chapter then examines why Hegel determines contradiction and its principle in the Logic of Essence and not in the Logic of the Concept. This provides the basis for understanding how the Logic of the Concept's identification of self-determination with universality emancipates reason from the principle of contradiction and paves the way for the autonomy of truth and right.

Since the rise of early modern Western philosophy, the modal categories of actuality have reigned supreme over almost all the philosophical academy, leaving our universe inhospitable to life, right, beauty, and reason, none of which fit the chains of necessity that actuality imposes. Hegel puts actuality in its proper place, showing how the modal categories cannot be ultimate but give way through their own working to the categories of self-determination. Chapter 5, "Overcoming Actuality: How Hegel Frees Us from the Prison of Modality," examines how this self-elimination of modal categories takes place and how it frees philosophy to address the fundamental features of human reality.

Time may be inescapable and ubiquitous, but grasping its reality is a daunting challenge. Chapter 6, "Time and Reason," exposes the fundamental dilemmas confronting all those formidable thinkers who have attempted to root time in motion (from Ptolemy to Einstein) or in mind (Augustine, Kant, Brann). Drawing upon insights of Hegel, the chapter shows how to resolve the basic paradoxes that arise in thinking time by following a completely different path. This involves first freeing thought of the formality of the principle of non-contradiction and then thinking through how space gives rise to time, how time and space give rise to matter, and how time finally acquires a new determination in the historical reality of rational animals. What is offered is not so much a textual commentary on Hegel's *Philosophy of Nature*, as an independent philosophical investigation standing on Hegel's broad shoulders.

Chapter 7, "Hegel and the Problem of Consciousness," addresses what is fundamentally revolutionary in Hegel's conception of consciousness. Most modern philosophers have tended to identify mind with consciousness and consciousness with discourse, confining knowing to the oppositional framework of conscious awareness, trapping awareness in a mind/body dualism, leaving problematic the consciousness of prerational animals and children, and rendering unintelligible the emergence of thought and language. Hegel, by contrast, conceives consciousness as one of three fundamental aspects of mind that together comprise the totality of human awareness: the preconscious psyche, consciousness, and intelligence. The chapter shows how Hegel's conception of consciousness as the intermediary sphere of mind allows him to understand how animals and young children can have psyches, as well as prelinguistic consciousness and self-consciousness, how language and thought can be acquired, and how philosophical reason can overcome the epistemological limitations of the opposition of consciousness.

Hegel has very little to say about the origin and character of language. Nonetheless, his *Philosophy of Subjective Spirit* provides certain key arguments, without which the origin of language remains an enigma. Hegel recognizes that individuals could not create language, let alone learn how to communicate in an already existing language if they could not be conscious and self-conscious *before* obtaining language. Consequently, he repudiates the prevailing view that mind is reducible to consciousness and that consciousness is inherently discursive, and instead shows us how intelligence can move from intuition to representation and from representation to concept and word. Chapter 8, "Hegel and the Origin of Language," applies Hegel's contributions to complement and move beyond what Chomsky, Davidson, Jonas, Thompson, and Vygotsky have offered, all in order to conceive how language originates.

Ethics is the philosophy of right, insofar as right signifies the reality of freedom and normativity resides in self-determination. Hegel recognizes that only self-determination can overcome the dilemmas of foundational justification. He also understands that an agent cannot achieve self-determination individually, but must interact with other agents in order to determine the form as well as content of its own agency. Consequently, when Hegel conceives the reality of right, he develops a system of conventions consisting in the constitutive interactions of property owners, moral subjects, emancipated family members, interdependent participants in civil society, and self-governing citizens. Chapter 9, "The Logic of Right," investigates whether Hegel's division of right is valid. In so doing, the chapter shows how the reality of self-determination is a systematic whole in which political and prepolitical freedoms are necessarily interconnected.

Chapter 10, "A Dream Deferred: From the US Constitution to the Universal Declaration of Human Rights," considers the shortcomings of the US Constitution in light of how a valid constitution must secure the household and social rights without which self-government cannot operate. Laying bare how the utilitarian and social contract traditions truncate the conception of freedom and underlie the fundamental omissions in the US Constitution, the chapter considers how Roosevelt's call for a new social bill of rights introduces a more adequate framework for completing the institutionalization of freedom, which the Universal Declaration of Human Rights has incorporated.

Chapter 11, "World Spirit on the Campaign Trail in Georgia: Can the Philosophy of Right Be a Guide to Social Reform?" leads philosophical theorizing on an exploration of how we can attempt to realize right in the world we inhabit. The chapter begins with a critique of the subordination of theory to practice and of knowing in general to practical concerns. Chapter 9 then considers how the autonomy of reason and the autonomy of practice are connected and what this means for the genesis of the institutions of right. The challenges of constitution-making are examined in order to frame the predicament of individuals who find themselves in a world where the institutions of freedom are substantially but incompletely realized. The chapter concludes by considering the lessons of the author's 2018 congressional race in Georgia's 10th district. The author's candidacy advocated a social rights agenda that drew upon the Philosophy of Right in order to remedy the shortcomings of the US Constitution. The history of freedom remains, as always, a work in progress.

Finally, Chapter 12, "The Classical Nude and the Limits of Sculpture," addresses how fine art can retain significance in our day by considering whether or not the classical nude provides sculpture with an incomparably perfect realization. The essay calls into question Hegel's privileging of classical sculpture by examining how fine art in general and sculpture in particular can unite meaning and configuration in ways that retain truth for our modern world.

Chapter 1

WHY WE ARE SO WISE: HEGELIAN REFLECTIONS ON WHETHER REASON CAN BE ENHANCED

Challenge to the Improvers of Reason

I, like you, inhabit this lonely planet during the brief interlude of rational animal existence, exercising my reason with a *Homo sapiens* body, residing in a modern nation, conversing in a written alphabetic language. I have framed my thoughts using pencil and pen, manual and electric typewriters, and a parade of quickly obsolescent word processors, and now I waft upon a cloud of internet connectivity as my body begins to wear out and my memory declines. Like you, I have been barraged by the assassins of reason, declaiming how my thought is limited by my species being and historical milieu, while others dangle artificial intelligence, cyborg enhancement, future evolution, genetic engineering, or encounter with more powerful extraterrestrial minds as offering escape from the enfeeblement of my conditioned rationality.

I cannot deny that my thinking depends upon contingent astrophysical conditions that allow for the evolution of intelligent life, upon a certain level of physical and psychological health, upon due upbringing in a culture within which language has developed, and upon sufficient peace and affluence to have leisure to speculate. Nonetheless, I am certain that my reason cannot be improved upon. No life-form, whether it arises in galaxies far, far away or emerges on earth through future evolution or genetic engineering, can possibly be more capable of thinking the truth. Nor can any machine or cyborg augmentation increase my ability to reason, nor can acquisition of a different language or cultural upbringing supply me with an improved rationality. Not even any divinity could surpass the prowess of my reasoning.

Why is my reason, and yours, so powerful that no matter how much it rests upon enabling conditions, it cannot be subject to any modification that would bring us closer to the truth?

It is easy to deflect the assault on reason that points to thought's enabling conditions and claims that they block our access to truth by rendering reason relative to what grounds its exercise. Whether these conditions are identified as the contingent inorganic properties of our earthly abode, the particular biology that natural evolution has produced, or the linguistic conventions, mores, and power relations fostered by history, the problem is the same. Self-refutation cannot be avoided the moment these factors are held to be juridical conditions of reason, determining what we judge true, just, and beautiful.

The claim that those conditions are contingent foundations relativizing reason is undermined by its own diagnosis of the relativity of "rational" cognition. If its diagnosis is true, our reason cannot know that or anything else without qualification. If alternately we can maintain without restriction that reason has contingent juridical foundations, then that diagnosis is contradicted by our ability to know its truth, which would depend upon those conditions leaving cognition unconstrained.

If the foundations of reason are regarded to be not contingent and particular, but necessary and universal, the same dilemma arises. If they determine what reason holds true, their own truth depends upon their conferring validity upon themselves. In that case, they cease being foundations that validate something else and instead become the self-determining substance of normativity. Then, however, truth can no longer reside in what has validity conferred upon it by some other factor. Instead, reason will be valid by being autonomous, rather than through any foundation.

This outcome does not preclude reason having enabling conditions. It only shows how it makes no sense to insist that those enabling conditions can serve to distinguish between the valid and invalid thinking they equally make possible.

Nonetheless, the self-refutation of all attempts to render reason relative to physical, biological, or historical conditions does not itself establish the unconditioned prowess of my and your thinking. Even though it is impossible to know coherently that reason is juridically conditioned, this still leaves possible that our thinking is conditioned but can never verify that or anything else with unqualified authority.

To triumph over the undertakers of reason we cannot rest with exposing the incoherence of their lazy enterprise. As Hegel observed in the introduction to the *Phenomenology of Spirit*, any attempt to set out immediately to think without presuppositions would itself be a dogmatic enterprise.[1] To avoid making any

---

1. G. W. F. Hegel, *Phenomenology of Spirit*, trans. A. V. Miller (New York: Oxford University Press, 1977), 49.

assumptions in refuting the relativizers of reason, it is necessary to show how those who presuppose that thought always confronts the given cannot sustain their own dogmatic assumption when subject to their own self-examination. Arriving at that outcome, however, may liberate reason of the twofold dependency upon predetermined form and content, but it does not offer anything more than an indeterminate starting point, with no claims concerning subject matter or method. To establish the power of our reason we must show how its enabling physical, biological, and cultural conditions leave thought with no other limits than those it imposes upon itself.

The Natural Enabling Conditions of Reason

Let us start at the beginning, not in any temporal sense but in respect to the structural unfolding of the reality constituting and enveloping our reasoning. The task requires proceeding from the most minimal natural conditions of inorganic nature through the development of animal life, and then onto the emergence of rationality and the historical development it makes possible, including all the possible progressions that natural evolution and technology may engender elsewhere in the universe. We will not be following the course sketched out by Plato in his *Timaeus*, where a demiurge produces from chaos a universe containing human life. The realities in question do not and cannot consist in artifacts that are the product of any manufacture, where antecedently given form is imposed upon given material. Instead, what lies at stake is the constitution of living minds, whose self-informing character cannot possibly be captured by the external combination of form and matter.

Admittedly, at each stage along the line, contingency enters in, as is unavoidable in nature as well as convention. Our reason is throughout conditioned by factors that might be otherwise. Every possibility, however, rests on some actuality and the power of our reason may well have an inherent grasp of what is actual. The mere fact that we acknowledge ourselves embarked on this investigation compels us to conceive the contingencies of nature and history such as to allow for our own rational existence.

Space, time, and matter in motion provide the minimal factors of nature to which electromagnetic phenomena add physical processes to the mechanics of inertial movement and gravitational systems. We are told by the fantasizers of contemporary physics that if the various fundamental forces of nature varied only slightly in magnitude the universe would be an empty tomb in which no matter could form and energy would dissipate into nothingness. Space and time, however, can have no determinate being apart from matter in motion, and even if the relation of forces may have an element of contingency, the accident of physical nature leaves undetermined all the various processes that may supervene upon them. Physicists may concoct their mathematical fantasies of alternate universes, just as undertaker logicians spin fairy tales of possible worlds. The universe is, as such, all-inclusive and what is contingent is not any plurality of universes but what the actualities of our one and only cosmos make possible. If "possible worlds" signify not planets that could arise within the one and only actual universe but possible universes, then their possibility must depend upon some actuality outside of nature—a supernatural creator who generates the universe from nothing natural. In that case, "possible world" logicians must assume a transcendent creator of nature and confront the perplexity of how such an all-powerful creator could create anything other than the best of all possible worlds. Then, of course, the world willed into being by the supreme creator is the only possible world and not at all contingent. Contingency rather pertains to what falls within the one and only universe, whose mechanisms of matter in motion and electromagnetic processes make possible the chemical reactions where differentiated materials interact, combining and breaking down into different types of substances in function of their chemical constitution. Precisely because chemical, like mechanical and physical, processes are externally caused, depending upon catalysts and the workings of other natural objects, they can be enlisted by processes of a completely different character for purposes entirely undetermined by their conditioned operations. This external determinability is what allows the self-sustaining process of life to emerge from the contingent combination of chemical reactions. They can become integrated into an "autopoietic" whole, whose semipermeable membrane absorbs and retains the chemicals whose interaction produces the starting points of a self-renewing process that not only maintains its own enclosure but also supplies the reactants, catalysts, and mechanical impulses to constitute a totality whose self-sustaining process operates as an end in itself.[2] Such a minimal organism will have a relatively fleeting existence unless it, once more by external accident, acquires the chemical means not just to renew itself but to reproduce, generating another organism like itself, capable of reproducing anew. Moreover, the capacity to reproduce will further engender an evolution of species if variations in offspring arise that affect their ability to survive and reproduce. All this can take place through nothing but the contingent combination of material motions and chemical reactions that are externally caused. Whether the chemistry be carbon based or not, to the extent that it can be integrated into the self-renewing individual

---

2. Evan Thompson discusses the minimal chemistry of such *autopoiesis* in his *Mind in Life: Biology, Phenomenology, and the Sciences of Mind* (Cambridge, MA: Harvard University Press, 2007), 107–18.

and species being of living organisms, it contributes to life processes that have a biological identity of their own that is common to, and thereby not relative to, any particular chemical realization.

Once the mechanics of matter and chemical process give rise to life, the metabolic and reproductive activity of living organisms makes possible an evolution of species through whose own contingent development the glimmerings of reason will have to emerge for our inquiry to proceed. Our lonely planet may have been the setting for a carbon-based organic world in which RNA and DNA play signal roles, but other outposts of life may have their own evolution of species with a completely different chemistry, just as earth itself may well generate life-forms with different super molecules entering into genetic development. No matter where and how life emerges, it will exhibit the sensitivity and irritability on which metabolism and reproduction depend. Every life-form must be able to discriminate among the features of its biosphere that impact upon survival and reproduction and respond in ways that further its individual and species existence.

For mind to arise, however, the evolution of species must produce organisms whose sensitivity and responsiveness cease to be limited to the local reaction characterizing the tropisms of plant life. Instead, the contingencies of evolution must give rise to organisms whose sensitivity is centralized into a unified field of sentience, allowing the life-form to perceive its environment as a unitary world, as well as perceive its own body as a unified whole. On that basis, the organism can acquire a centralized control of its irritability and respond as a unitary subject to the world it now senses in its entirety. The need for these developments of a centralized subjectivity are connected to the emergence of a metabolism that does not occur immediately, in the way that plants continuously take in water, nutrients, and sunlight directly from the environment, aided by tropic sensitivity and response. Rather, centralized sentience and bodily self-control evolve insofar as the organism cannot metabolize in such immediate fashion but must sense at a distance the objects it needs to consume and move itself with a sufficiently enduring urge to reach and devour the nutrition it requires.[3] The same imperative applies to reproduction when it requires the organism to sense, desire, and move itself to accomplish the reproductive act, as well as provide whatever care its offspring may require. These defining functions of animal life bring mind into the universe, with

---

3. Hans Jonas discusses these particularities of animal metabolism and their significance for the emergence of mind in his essay, "To Move and to Feel: On the Animal Soul," in *The Phenomenon of Life: Toward a Philosophical Biology* (Evanston, IL: Northwestern University Press, 2001), 99–107.

the threefold aspects of sentience, emotion, and motility. Any development of reason depends upon these animal endowments, no matter what form they take. For this very reason, the differences in how sense organs perceive, how emotions are embodied, and how motility occurs leave undetermined the operations of thought that a rational animal could exercise.

What thinking requires is that the animal has sufficient sentience, emotive drive, and motility to engage in the psychological functions of semiotic imagination, with which animals can produce and communicate signs. These functions require intelligence, which itself depends upon consciousness and the preconscious psyche. Not all animal species will possess the neurophysiological resources for the psychological activities by which a preconscious psyche builds habits and expresses feelings so as to organize feelings and feeling activity into independent totalities. These self-modifications of the psyche engender the subject–object divide whereby mind becomes conscious by treating its mental determinations as determinations of an objectivity that it confronts.[4] Consciousness, however, cannot alone suffice for reason because conscious awareness always confronts its objects without at the same time being aware of the mental acts by which it does so. Linguistic intelligence, on which thought depends, must be aware at once of its own semiotic expressions and the objects to which they refer. If this cannot be done, mind can hardly engage in theorizing, which requires that reason be aware of its own conceptual constructions and the objectivity they grasp. There may be countless animal species arising around in the universe that achieve consciousness, sensing what is, perceiving things and their properties, and understanding the dynamic relations of objects, and that become self-conscious in desiring the desire of others for their own desire.[5] Not all, however, will have the genetic endowment permitting their minds to make the opposition of consciousness their object, opening the way for intelligence, whose intuitions, representations, and thoughts it takes to be both its own and determinations of objectivity.

The Psychological Prerequisites of Thinking

Although my reason, and that of any other rational animal, must have a species being with enough neurophysiological capacity to have a self-feeling psyche, consciousness, and intelligence, this capacity does not thereby figure as a juridical foundation of thinking. What precludes this is the very character of the psychological requirements of thinking.

---

4. For a detailed analysis of these developments of the preconscious psyche, see Richard Dien Winfield, *The Living Mind* (Lanham, MD: Rowman & Littlefield, 2011), 120–41.
5. For an analysis of these constitutive aspects of consciousness and self-consciousness, see Winfield, *The Living Mind*, 145–228.

First of all, semiotic imagination relates an intuited content to general representations, using the former as a sign to signify a repeatable meaning that bears no connection to the content of the sign itself. Unlike symbols, whose configuration contains something that belongs to the representation it symbolizes, signs have a purely conventional, arbitrary relation to what they signify. For this reason, semiotic imagination is able to generate meanings that are not beholden to any particular intuitive content. They thereby free mind from having to depend upon imagery and allow intelligence to arrive at the threshold of thought, where imageless concepts become the material of awareness. Moreover, because what serves as a sign is determined arbitrarily by semiotic imagination, there is no limit to the production of new signs or to the semiotic imagining of new meanings. The communicability of signs may depend upon situations where intelligent animals express their signs to one another in relation to commonly observed objects and expressions. Once, however, names have emerged, signifying animals are in a position to develop communicable relations between words that allow for propositional discourse and the determination of meanings through logical relations. Of fundamental importance is that the grammar by which words enter into propositional relations is generative in character, allowing for the formulation and communication of an unlimited array of novel statements. Not only can new words always be coined in relation to new congeries of other words, but also the propositions in which words figure are freely determinable. Neither the given vocabulary nor the given grammar of a language can condition what meanings and propositions its users can express. Because both naming and grammar are freely generative, language provides precisely the protean vehicle by which thought can operate freely.[6] Moreover, because the meanings of words and propositions can always be communicated by different verbal expressions, discourse is inherently translatable so long as rational animals have sufficient exposure to the use of any language they encounter.

So long as a rational animal is able to make signs and engage in linguistic interaction with others, nothing about its biology and psychology can restrict what it ultimately can think. Admittedly, language competency develops both ontogenetically and culturally in stages that do limit how language users engage in discourse. Children first use words in ways that confine their meaning to imagery and the individual things to which images apply (e.g., "flower" to refer to a particular rose), and only later develop the ability to use those same

---

6. For further development of these points, together with a critical consideration of Chomsky's formulation of the generative character of grammar, see Richard Dien Winfield, *The Intelligent Mind: On the Genesis and Constitution of Discursive Thought* (Houndmills, UK: Palgrave Macmillan, 2015), 78–180.

names in propositions in which they obtain a logical meaning (e.g., the genus to which "flower" generally refers), defined through conceptual relations. The same development can occur in the early history of a linguistic community, whose participants are just beginning to enact and master the grammatical relations by which propositions can be formulated and communicated. Even in linguistic communities where language has a fully developed grammar, individuals may still use words in ways that restrict their meanings to nonconceptual, pictorial representations. Luria recounts how illiterate peasants in Soviet Central Asia used language in this figurative way until they became formally educated and took part in the running of collective farms in which abstract policies had to be understood and fulfilled. Then they began to converse with much more logically determined meanings, without having to adopt a different language.[7] What this illustrates is that so long as rational animals can use language with propositional resources, they are in a position to converse with conceptually determined meanings. Then they not only may make judgments and inferences but eventually engage in autonomous philosophical thought, which overcomes the dependence upon given premises and given algorithms that hobbles those who limit thinking to demonstrative calculation.

Philosophy must be the freest of all sciences, as Aristotle long ago recognized,[8] for unless philosophical inquiry liberates itself from all given dogma and becomes fully responsible for its form and content, the quest for truth will remain confined to labors of opinion. Hegel posed this requirement in the most radical terms, pointing out in the introduction to his *Science of Logic* that so long as thinking begins with any given subject matter, it automatically remains doubly relative—first with respect to the particular content it addresses and second with respect to the method with which it accesses that content.[9] To escape this dual bondage, philosophy must begin without confronting any given and without thereby distinguishing knowing from its object. Instead, philosophy must begin logically, overcoming the opposition of subject and object by thinking thinking, which, at the outset, has yet to determine that which constitutes both its method and its subject matter. Accordingly, philosophy must start with no determinate claims about what is or about knowing and instead proceed in a completely self-determined manner, which can only occur if philosophy begins with no given content or given method, but becomes what it determines itself to be.

---

7. A. R. Luria, *Cognitive Development: Its Cultural and Social Foundations*, trans. Martin Lopez-Morillas and Lynn Solotaroff (Cambridge, MA: Harvard University Press, 1976), 161–64.
8. Aristotle, *Metaphysics*, Book I, Chapter 2, 982b27–8, in *The Complete Works of Aristotle*, ed. Jonathan Barnes (Princeton, NJ: Princeton University Press, 1984), volume II, 1555.
9. G. W. F. Hegel, *Science of Logic*, trans. A. V. Miller (New York: Humanities Press, 1976), 43.

Universality, Self-Determination, and Rational Autonomy

Philosophy can realize the autonomy that frees it from dogmatic foundations due to a logical truth that equally vindicates philosophy's reliance upon thinking as its privileged instrument. This truth is explicitly developed by Hegel in the "Logic of the Concept" where he shows how universality, that is, the concept as such, is equivalent to self-determined determinacy.[10] Contrary to the dogmas of the assassins of reason, concepts are not empty or rigid abstractions from given individuals. Instead, concepts are self-differentiating unities that particularize themselves into new determinations that remain at one with the universality that pervades them. Without particulars, the universal does not have its unity in diversity and without its particulars being differentiated, that is, individual, they collapse into one, eliminating their difference from the universal, and subverting the very nonempty bond of universality. Whereas given factors owe their determinacy to their contrast with one another, and determined factors derive their character from a determiner that determines something other than itself, the universal has its own defining identity only through the particularization by which it determines itself. The particulars, which, as plural, are individuals, are not given separately from the universal, nor does the universal appear in them as derivative phenomena. Instead, the particulars are constitutive elements of the universal's own constitution. Since particularity and individuality are ingredient in universality, it can be no surprise that individuality possesses its unique, nonderivative character through nothing but its own pregnant unity, whereby it is determined in and through itself, exhibiting the same concrete independence as the self-differentiating, self-determining universal. Consequently, conceptual determination is both synthetic and analytic at once, engendering new content that remains at one with the unity of the universal underway determining itself.

Conversely, self-determination itself involves universality, particularity, and individuality, as Hegel shows willing to illustrate in the introduction to his *Philosophy of Right*.[11] To be autonomous, the self does not determine something other than itself, but instead gives itself new determination. Since this new determination is its own, the self-determining self remains at one with itself in this, its self-differentiation. Accordingly, it determines itself as universal, remaining self-identical in a particularization that provides

---

10. Hegel, *Science of Logic*, 600–22.
11. G. W. F. Hegel, *Elements of the Philosophy of Right*, trans. H. B. Nisbet (Cambridge: Cambridge University Press, 1991), §5–7, 37–42.

the sphere of its encompassing unity. Since the self's determining process provides it with its defining selfhood in and through itself, it is equally individual. By contrast, all categories of essence involve some privileged factor determining some subsidiary term, where the determiner determines not itself but something else. This is why self-determination only arises, as Hegel documents in the transition from the Logic of Essence to the Logic of the Concept,[12] when the relation of determiner and determined reverts to a causal reciprocity where what determines is equally determined by what it determines, leaving each term playing both roles, eliminating the distinction between determiner and determined. With this elimination, the two-tiered categories of Essence[13] give way to those of self-determination, where the determiner determines itself and the universal arises in its constitutive self-differentiating autonomy.

This identification of self-determination and universality secures the autonomy of thought, as well as the ability of conceptual determination to grasp objectivity. Whereas conditioned appearance is determined by some undisclosed ground, objectivity is determined in and through itself and therefore can only be grasped by a cognition that does not determine its topic externally but engages in the conceptual self-development that allows its object to unfold in its own self-constitution. This is why the autonomy of conceptual determination allows reason to think the "*Sache selbst*," that is, objectivity in its own right, and arrive at the truth (what Hegel calls the "*Idee*") consisting in the unity of concept and objectivity.

Consequently, because thought, as real conceptual determination, is self-determining, once sufficiently endowed animals engage in the linguistic interaction empowering them to formulate and express concepts, nothing in their enabling natural or conventional conditions can prevent their thinking from determining itself. Since autonomy may have *enabling* conditions, but not external *determining* conditions, the physiological, psychological, and linguistic instruments of discourse can in no way direct and thereby relativize the thinking they make possible. Accordingly, so long as rational animals can engage in discourse, any limit upon their thought can only be what reason imposes upon itself.

---

12. Hegel, *Science of Logic*, 569–71.
13. From essence and illusory being, through ground and grounded, and cause and effect, every relation of essence involves a prior determiner that posits a determined determinacy. Whereas the categories of essence are determined by positing, those of self-determination arise through development, where a subject gives itself new determinacy.

The Effect of Terrestrial and Extraterrestrial Evolution upon the Life of the Mind

What then can terrestrial and extraterrestrial evolution, as well as genetic engineering contribute to the life of the mind? The contingent vagaries that attend the emergence of life and its speciation through natural selection can certainly give rise to organisms with very different sense organs, motility, and neurophysiology, as well as very different metabolic rates and scales of existence. Rational animals therefore may have different kinds of sensory reception, with various degrees of acuity, different natural desires reflecting different metabolism and forms of reproduction, and different types of motor control and modes of communication. In addition, rational animals may possess different types of neurotransmission and central nervous systems of varying size and structure, allowing mental processes to operate at different speeds as well as with different capacities of recall and attention. Moreover, sexual differences reflecting diverse forms of reproduction may involve natural urges and emotive responses that vary between different rational animal species, as well as among each one's own members.

All of these genetically determined variations can affect the content of feelings, sensations, and intuitions, as well as of figurative representations that memory recalls and imagination configures. Moreover, the differences in speed and capacity of neural processes among rational animal species can certainly impact upon computational prowess and informational command.

One might wonder why natural endowments far exceeding our own have yet to be confirmed in close encounters of the third kind. The failure of extraterrestrial intelligent life to make its presence unequivocally known to us may reflect the vast distance between planetary systems, the rarer scattering of inhabitable planets, the disparate timings of the existence of intelligent life on other worlds, and the limited lifetime of rational civilizations, whose capacity to self-destruct is all too easily triggered.[14] Nonetheless, there is every reason to suppose that somewhere sometime extraterrestrial rational animals will emerge with more powerful sensory and motor apparatuses, more capacious memories, and faster mental operations. Moreover, further evolution on our lonely planet might arrive at similar enhancements, especially if genetic engineering is allowed to steer our future species inheritance.

---

14. Stanislaw Lem discusses how all these factors might underlie our failure to encounter intelligent life elsewhere in the universe. See Stanislaw Lem, *Summa Technologiae*, trans. Joanna Zylinski (Minneapolis: University of Minnesota Press, 2013), 41–76, as well as Lem's novel, *Fiasco*, trans. Michael Kandel (New York: Harcourt Brace Jovanovich, 1987), 87–92.

Can Technology and Artificial Intelligence Augment Our Wisdom?

These developments might well yield improved powers of empirical observation and calculation. On the other hand, artificial means might provide equal or even more enhanced perception, computational wizardry, and information retention and access than natural evolution and bioengineering could gift some lucky rational animals. Technology already offers a plenitude of sensory extenders, computing machines, and online search instruments for compensating the limitations of my natural sensibility, memory, attention, and computational abilities. Moreover, technological implants are beginning to allow me to become a veritable cyborg, internalizing the artificial augmentations that external instruments provide.

I can hardly deny that in all these ways, evolution and technology can improve upon my sensory reception, memory, powers of attention, reckoning, and information handling. Nevertheless, neither evolutionary nor technological progress can possibly enhance the conceptual self-determination in which philosophical wisdom consists.

The assassins of reason are content to follow Hobbes in reducing thought to reckoning,[15] but thinking is something very different from the mechanical operations of "artificial intelligence." So-called thinking machines exhibit the generic character of artifacts, so distinct from living things, let alone rational animals. Machines do not reproduce themselves, grow through a metabolism with their environment, or repair themselves. They have a design that can and must be antecedently represented by the agents who fabricate them, imposing that design upon independently given materials. The resulting product not only does not make itself but depends upon external agents to provide it with energy, feed it with materials to act upon, and repair it when necessary. A computing machine applies this mechanical character to information processing, where it takes in externally supplied "information" and subjects it to an external manipulation according to some formal procedure or algorithm, all according to the external necessitations of efficient causality. Since such necessitation acts externally upon what it determines without regard to its particular nature, it involves the same formal, lawful determination that applies to the "empty" reasoning modeled by formal logic. Such calculative thinking involves operations that apply to externally given contents with indifference to their specific character, as exhibited in the variables of logical demonstration. The universals here at play are immobile abstractions that do not differentiate

---

15. Thomas Hobbes, *Leviathan*, ed. C. B. Macpherson (Harmondsworth, UK: Penguin, 1968), 110–11.

themselves and develop. As such, they are governed by the principle of non-contradiction and offer nothing but forms of consistent ordering of given contents. Accordingly, the artificial "thinking" of computing machines is a reckoning that subjects input to an external formal determination that is indifferent to their particular nature. This allows for quantitative prowess, but the "expert systems" that such information processing can provide only apply to what is subject to mechanistic determination. Anything specific to what is living, let alone intelligent, eludes the scope of artificial "intelligence."

Philosophical thought is in principle beyond the realm of artificial intelligence precisely because it involves the self-determination of universality, where the self-differentiation of the universal is hardly indifferent to the particulars it pervades but is essentially at one with them. Consequently, although computers may serve me as instruments for performing calculations and other mechanistic manipulations with unnatural speed and accuracy, it cannot augment my ability to reason. Computers may give me unheralded access to information and allow me to sort it according to formal parameters, but they can never supply the philosophical truth that consists in autonomously conceiving objectivity in its immanent self-constitution.

Although artificial intelligence may be unable to augment reason, the very autonomy of rational animals gives them a nonnatural ability to intervene upon natural evolution, both restricting natural selection by caring for the less adapted and modifying inheritance. Living organisms naturally sort themselves into species according to the biological and geographical limits that determine with what other organisms they can reproduce and share genetic materials. Rational animals, by contrast, can further modify the limits of their reproductive pool by enacting cultural norms that restrict what other members of their own species they permit themselves to reproduce with. This can give rise to subgroups sharing the same species being, as well as the same territory, but developing distinct group inheritances that may be manifest in phenotypical features. I have happily miscegenated for decades, producing three mongrel offspring with presumably more diverse genetic backgrounds than we parents, who both come from groups that culturally restricted intermarriage and were shunned in turn by adjacent communities. Can such differences in genetic heritage among members of the same rational animal species possibly affect powers of reason? Can, for that matter, any other natural distinctions, such as sex and sexual orientation, possibly impact upon our reasoning or that of any rational animal?

It is not inconceivable that inbreeding among a subgroup of a rational animal species could lead to neurophysiological deficits that undermine intelligence or that some natural differences among members of the same rational animal species could be tied to intellectual impairments. Nonetheless, the protean character of language and the autonomy of thinking that linguistic interaction makes possible offers a guarantee of its own. Namely, any language user who can competently engage in propositional discourse wields a power of reason whose only limits are those it imposes upon itself. Whatever natural differences leave this competency unimpaired are completely irrelevant to the operations of reason and the conduct that depends upon it.

The autonomy of reason is therefore what gives rational animals an infinite character that has often been ascribed to what is divine. To the degree that reason is self-determining, how it unfolds is not subject to any external limitations. Although reason has enabling conditions, its lack of determining conditions signifies that reason is not finite in the sense of having boundaries imposed by something beyond itself. Reason, as self-determining, does give itself specifications and thereby limits itself. In so doing, however, it is *self-limiting*, which is to say, self-determining. Thereby reason exhibits the character of what Hegel duly calls the true infinite, containing within its externally unlimited process the finite as well as what lies beyond it (the nonfinite).[16] Both fall within autonomous reasoning since the self-differentiation of universality contains particularizations and the further determinations that supersede them in its ongoing conceptual development. From the ancients onward, philosophers have recognized this "divine" character of reason. In so doing, they acknowledge that because reason is self-determining, it needs nothing else to be what it determines itself to be and can therefore not be enhanced by anything additional. A divine reason could not do more, although, if reason and animal life go together and thinking depends upon linguistic interaction, the very possibility of an immaterial omniscient and omnipotent supreme being is questionable, to say the least.

Those who celebrate the advancing "creolization" of humanity may be duly recognizing how the autonomy of thought and conduct transcend natural differences and cultural distinctions tied to birth. If, however, they follow Nietzsche in ascribing special wisdom and right to anything particular,[17] they join the assassins of reason in fleeing the universal,[18] as if thought were empty

---

16. Hegel, *Science of Logic*, 137, 143–50.
17. In *Ecce Homo* Nietzsche explains "Why I Am So Wise," appealing not to any dialectic of reasoning but to the "fatality" of a particular form of "healthy" life that repudiates the "decadent" embrace of universal norms characterizing the modern world. See Friedrich Nietzsche, *On the Genealogy of Morals & Ecce Homo*, trans. Walter Kaufmann (New York: Vintage Books, 1969), 222–35.
18. See Carl Rapp, *Fleeing the Universal: The Critique of Post-Rational Criticism* (Albany: State University of New York Press, 1998), for devastating critiques, inspired by Hegel, of this postmodernist ideology.

and concepts were immobile ghostly abstractions that cannot lay hold of anything individual, active, and objective.

You who deny the infinite power of my and our reason have only yourselves to blame, for autonomous thinking can only be limited by what it itself conceives to be the valid boundaries of truth.

Chapter 2

SELF-DETERMINATION IN LOGIC AND REALITY

From the beginnings of philosophical investigation, there has been widespread recognition that reason must be autonomous to think the truth and that philosophy must be the freest of all disciplines.[1] The freedom reason and philosophy must wield has two sides.

On the one hand reason must possess the negative freedom to liberate itself from all determining conditions. If reason fails to do so and lets itself be guided by any external authority, every claim reason makes will be relative to the particular grounds that rule its operation. To overcome the hold of unexamined opinion, reason must emancipate itself of all presuppositions regarding its subject matter and methodology. Otherwise, thought remains bound by dogmatic claims about its topic and procedure, unable to obtain knowledge that surmounts particular opinion and enjoys unconditioned universal validity.

By casting aside the hold of assumed foundations, such liberation indicates how the autonomy of reason and philosophy is tied to the attainment of the unconditioned universality that gives thought its special role as a vehicle of truth. Nonetheless, by itself, this emancipation leaves liberated reason utterly empty unless it can exercise an autonomy that is not just negative but positive as well.

The negative freedom that revokes acceptance of given opinion may free thought of all predetermined form and content, but this liberation leaves thought with a universality that is devoid of any particular content, rendering its unconditioned character a vacant promise. Only if reason can determine by itself what its subject matter and method should be, can reason move from its empty negative emancipation to a positive constitution of philosophical wisdom. Philosophy can proceed from repudiating dogmatism to being fully responsible for all its own claims only if it exercises the positive

---

1. In Book I, 982b28, of the *Metaphysics*, Aristotle describes philosophy as "the only free science, for it alone exists for itself." See *The Complete Works of Aristotle, The Revised Oxford Translation*, ed. Jonathan Barnes, volume Two, 1555.

self-determination where the unconditioned universality of thought shows itself to be pregnant with content.

To be the freest of all sciences, as the search for wisdom requires, philosophy must commence as logic. Any nonlogical starting point automatically leaves thought encumbered with given assumptions about both its form and its content. Whereas logic is a thinking of thinking, nonlogical investigation thinks what is different from thought. As such, nonlogical investigation cannot account for the thinking it employs, since it enquires into something distinct from the reasoning it exercises. Nonlogical investigation must presuppose not only its method but also the defining boundaries of its subject matter. Only by assuming that its topic has a given character distinct from thought does nonlogical science have anything to investigate. On both counts, nonlogical science is conditioned and relative. Whatever results it achieves are tainted by acceptance of the predetermined procedure and content with which it begins. Nonlogical science, as immediately undertaken, is doubly unfree, doubly heteronomous. It establishes neither what its subject matter should be nor what procedure it should employ. Both are simply taken for granted.

Philosophy escapes this twofold heteronomy by beginning in the element of logic. Only as logical can philosophy escape taking for granted its method and its subject matter. In logic, there is no difference between form and content, between subject and object of knowing, between procedure and topic. Neither can be given at the outset of logical investigation for the aim of logic is to validly think what valid thinking is. Only at the end of its investigation can logic determine its method and subject matter, for only when logic concludes its investigation is valid thinking fully unveiled. Hence, logic must begin without any given method or any given subject matter and yet, from this indeterminate starting point, develop valid thinking without relying upon any external givens. Logic must therefore be a self-determined development of self-thinking thought, where that autonomous development proceeds from the elimination of any difference between subject and object, between form and content.[2]

The logic with which philosophy should begin is not to be confused with formal logic. Formal logic accepts the divide between thought and its object by modeling a thinking whose form does not determine its content. Instead, the thinking represented in formal logic finds its content from outside thought and manipulates it in ways that are indifferent to its content. That is why formal

---

2. Hegel delineates the above-described distinction between logical and nonlogical investigation on the opening page of his "Introduction: General Notion of Logic" in his *Science of Logic*. See G. W. F. Hegel, *Science of Logic*, trans. A. V. Miller (New York: Humanities Press, 1976), 43.

logic can represent its externally conditioned thinking in terms of relations of variables, *P*'s and *Q*'s, whose content is unspecified. Formalizable thought is incapable of generating any content of its own, including the content of its own form determination. Both must be presupposed, which leaves the thinking governed by formal logic incapable of determining truth. Whatever truth tables it may stipulate can only distinguish between what is consistently or inconsistently thought in accord with formal provisos that are taken for granted.

Logic proper, which does not distinguish thought and the object of thought, must develop without any determinate claims about its knowing or the object of its knowing. For this reason, it will be in a position to furnish an account of determinacy. Only genuine logic can provide this service, since any inquiry that begins with determinate givens will beg the question if it pretends to be a theory of determinacy. Further, logic, as a presuppositionless theory of determinacy, will equally be a theory of self-determined determinacy. Since whatever determinacy arises in logical investigation will be determined by nothing outside that inquiry, it will comprise a content that has generated and ordered itself. Insofar as this self-determination relies on no particular conditions, it will have a direct connection to universality and therefore be ingredient in conceptual determination.

Self-determination will provide the logic of the concept, that is, the universal, in both the negative and positive aspects of freedom. By obtaining its character without being determined by external factors, what is self-determined will not be conditioned and particular. It will thereby exhibit the negative universality of being unbeholden to any given factor. On the other hand, by giving itself its own character, what is self-determined will exhibit the positive universality of having a particular content that is completely inherent in the unity of the self whose identity lies in its self-determination. The logic of the concept will thereby be that of a concrete universal, pregnant with content, enabling philosophy to generate determination through thought alone, wielding a *synthetic* a priori reason.

Overcoming the Logical Challenge to Self-Determination

All these considerations of how self-determination is central to reason and philosophy might seem vain reveries in the face of withering objections that some of the greatest philosophers have directed at the conceivability of freedom.

In Plato's *Republic*, Socrates exposes the apparent absurdity of self-determination, pointing out that any notion of self-control or self-rule requires that the same factor be both patient and agent at once! This seems so nonsensical that Socrates offers no further argument to dismiss that convergence. Instead, he declares that both the soul and the city must be divided into ruling and ruled parts, where a rational component imposes normative order upon its irrational counterpart.[3]

Aristotle accepts this same denial of self-determination in respect to mind and political association, dividing the intellect into active and passive parts,[4] while treating the equality of citizens as something empowering them to rule in rotation over one another, but never to exercise the perplexing reflexivity of self-rule.[5] Although Aristotle might seem to accept some form of self-determination in characterizing nature as self-moving, he regards self-motion to be just as unintelligible as self-rule. Animals may seem to move themselves, but that semblance, Aristotle maintains, is due to one part moving the others thanks to the impulse provided by nourishment from outside.[6] Holding that everything in motion is set in motion by something else, Aristotle must conclude that the source of all motion resides in an unmoved mover.[7] Somehow, the unmoved mover is supposed to be less mysterious than self-determined agency.

In all these denials of self-determination, the alleged incoherence of agency that acts upon itself is avoided by embracing causal determination, where one factor acts upon another, altering its state in some respect. With regard to locomotion, causation involves efficient causality, where alteration is indifferent to the form of the recipient, which only has its location changed over time. In the case of the rule of a rational factor over a subject, causation involves the formal causality of technique, where the active agent imposes new form upon the passive patient. No matter what type of causality is at stake, the distinction of determining cause and determined effect is invoked with confidence that this dynamic relationship commands a cogency that self-determination cannot possibly possess.

Yet, as ancient skeptics in both East and West long ago observed,[8] the relation of cause and effect cannot coherently sustain itself. A cause, no matter

---

3. See Plato, *Republic*, Book IV, 430e–431a, in Plato, *Complete Works*, ed. John M. Cooper (Indianapolis, IN: Hackett, 1997), 1062–63.
4. Aristotle, *De Anima*, Book III, Chapter 5, 430a10–19, *The Complete Works of Aristotle*, volume One, 684.
5. Aristotle, *Politics*, Book I, Chapter 1, 1252a16–17, *The Complete Works of Aristotle*, volume Two, 1986.
6. Aristotle, *Physics*, Book VIII, Chapter 4, 254b12–32, Chapter 6, 259b5–17, *The Complete Works of Aristotle*, volume One, 425, 433–34.
7. Aristotle, *Physics*, Book VIII, Chapter 6, 259a10–260a11, *The Complete Works of Aristotle*, volume One, 432–34.
8. For classic examples of this skeptical critique of causality in the Eastern and Western philosophical traditions see the surviving texts of the ancient Indian Carvaka school (*A Sourcebook in Indian Philosophy*, ed. Sarvepalli Radhakrishnan and Charles A. Moore

what type of causality it wields, is a cause only insofar as it has an effect. Although the cause is supposed to posit its effect, the cause's own character turns out to be posited by its supposed consequence. The cause and the effect thus both figure each as cause and effect of one another. This reciprocity, into which causality resolves itself, gives way as well. Precisely because each reciprocating term ends up playing the identical roles as its counterpart, all difference between what determines and what gets determined eliminates itself. Through the crucible of reciprocity, causality gives rise to nothing other than self-determination, which emerges when agent and patient can no longer be differentiated.

The very relationship to which the deniers of self-determination retreat ends up resurrecting the very freedom they spurn. Causality and its division of determiner and determined proves unable to maintain itself as an ultimate principle, presenting through its very own workings the intelligible emergence of self-determination as that in which determiner and determined, agent and patient are indistinguishable.

The same reversal afflicts all attempts to uphold foundational justification, which locates normative validity in the determining act of a privileged factor that confers validity upon what comes to possess validity. Foundational justification has become almost a universal dogma in epistemology, ethics, and aesthetics, mandating that truth, right, and beauty are grounded in some validating factor, making beliefs true, conduct right, and art works beautiful. In every case, however, the authority and content of the privileged foundation of justification is subject to question and the only way any such foundation can satisfy its own validation principle is if it confers validity upon itself. When, however, the foundation of validity becomes self-referentially consistent, grounding its own privileged content, the defining foundational distinction between what confers and what possesses validity is eliminated. Just as cause and effect cease to maintain their differentiation, so the distinction of foundation and what is founded gives way. With the erstwhile foundation of normativity impelling itself to become self-grounding, foundational justification transforms itself into the assertion of self-determination as the only coherent substance of normativity. No other option can be sustained, for if the exclusive normativity of self-determination is rejected, then foundational

---

[Princeton, NJ: Princeton University Press, 1957], 231–33, 239–46) and the writings of Sextus Empiricus (Sextus Empiricus, *Outlines of Pyrrhonism*, trans. R. G. Bury [Cambridge, MA: Harvard University Press Loeb Classical Library, 1933], Book III, Chapters IV–V, 13–29, 333–45; and Sextus Empiricus, *Against the Physicists*, Book I, 195–248, in Sextus Empiricus, *Against the Physicists, Against the Ethicists*, trans. R. G. Bury [Cambridge, MA: Harvard University Press Loeb Classical Library, 1936], 99–123).

justification returns, resurrecting autonomy once the foundation is called upon to satisfy its own standard of validity.

The respective self-eliminations of causality and foundational justification provide a negative "deduction" of self-determination by exhibiting how heteronomous determination, where what determines is different from what is determined, collapses on its own terms, leaving the identification of agent and patient before which Socrates stood perplexed.

How that identification can possibly proceed might still seem inscrutable in the face of the Kantian objection that any attempt to affirm self-determination sets reason in an antinomy of equally supportable contradictory claims. Kant presents the classic statement of this dilemma in the *Critique of Pure Reason*'s Third Antinomy.[9] Significantly, self-determination is here presented as a "transcendental Idea of freedom" that consists in the uncaused cause providing the unconditioned ground for the causal chain of natural events, each of which is determined by some antecedent state of affairs according to a law indifferent to the specific nature of the objects in question. Freedom is here presented not as a self-activity, where what is determined is identical with what does the determining, but as an unmoved mover, spontaneously initiating the series of happenings externally determined by efficient causality. The freedom whose problematic character Kant aims to expose is equivalent to the principle to which Aristotle must appeal owing to his rejection of self-motion and, more broadly, of self-determination. Instead of addressing the autonomy that arises from the self-elimination of causality, Kant characterizes freedom in terms of causality, identifying it as an uncaused cause. Can, however, the category of causality be employed in determining what is self-determined? Does Kant's antinomy arise from a fundamental category mistake, confusing causal determination with self-determination?

The argument Kant presents to challenge the "transcendental freedom" of uncaused causality revolves around its alleged incoherence. The pure spontaneity of this freedom is directed at determining something other than itself. Since what is caused by the uncaused cause is the occurrence of an alteration in something else, that event must be preceded by a time when the spontaneous eruption of freedom has not yet taken place. Since, however, the transition from inactivity to uncaused causal activity cannot be governed by any necessitating law, it fails to have the lawfulness on which events depend. As such, freedom cannot operate without contradicting the causal character of

---

9. Immanuel Kant, *Critique of Pure Reason*, trans. Paul Guyer and Allen W. Wood (Cambridge, UK: Cambridge University Press, 1998), A444/B472–A451/B479, 484–89.

events that it supposedly grounds as the first cause in the series of necessitated happenings.

This argument depends upon the assumptions that all events are externally necessitated and that nothing can be experienced unless it exhibits the material lawfulness of such mechanistic determination. Kant purports to have established this in his account of the possibility of experience, where the unity of self-consciousness allegedly depends upon the external lawful connection of representations by which they can convey something objective.[10] Kant's transcendental idealism leads inexorably to its mechanistic result. If knowing must first be validated before what is can be known, then the only way a prior investigation of cognition can establish knowledge to be objective is if the object of knowing is determined by the structure of knowing, rather than by any correspondence to inaccessible "things in themselves." This mandates that knowable objectivity will be determined from without, by the structure of knowing. Moreover, since the same cognitive structure determines what is knowable in every possible object, the external necessitation that applies to them all will do so irrespective of what they are. This means that the law to which objects must be subject is indifferent to their specific form and applies to them as material things in general. The law of knowable objectivity will therefore be a mechanistic material law of efficient causality.

If, however, objectivity as it can be experienced is a mechanism, in which all events are determined externally with indifference to the nature of the objects involved, the self-activity of life and mind can never be experienced. Self-consciousness becomes problematic, for such objectivity has no place for the spontaneity that Kant admits to be basic to our understanding and reason,[11] as well as to self-organized beings in general. Under such conditions consciousness can never have itself as an object, nor can persons ever experience the free activity of themselves or of any other agents. Morality, like self-consciousness and consciousness of other minds, is left devoid of any possible realization. To overcome these conundrums, objectivity must have place for the self-activity of life and mind. For self-consciousness to be actual, the fabric of events must accommodate the presence of selves that are self-determining. Instead of being at one with itself in confronting a world of blind mechanism, self-consciousness must be ratified in an objectivity in which its own spontaneity is manifest.

---

10. Kant's "Deduction of the Categories" revolves around drawing these connections. See Kant, *Critique of Pure Reason*, A84–130/B129–169, 219–66.
11. See Kant, *Critique of Pure Reason*, A51/B75, 193; A68/B93, 205; B130–132, 245–46; and Immanuel Kant, *Critique of the Pure of Judgment*, trans. Paul Guyer and Eric Matthews (Cambridge, UK: Cambridge University Press, 2000), §65, 5:372–76, 244–47.

Freedom is subject to the problem of the Third Antimony only if it be misconstrued in causal terms as an uncaused cause and if objectivity be reduced to a mechanism. Both of these commitments are common fixtures of early modern philosophy and of the contemporary schools that remain stuck in that view. These assumptions are joined together in the endorsement of the principle of sufficient reason, which asserts that everything has a ground. This dogma, which Kant embraces as a principle of experience,[12] absolutizes the categories of foundationalism, for which whatever is objective, right, and beautiful is determined as such by some privileged determiner. Since, however, foundationalism subverts its own distinction of ground and grounded whenever it seeks to validate its privileged foundation, the very notion of an uncaused cause leads back to the very different concept of self-determination.

Kant may regard reason to always fall into self-contradiction when it seeks the unconditioned determiner of what is conditioned, but reason rather uncovers the untenability of foundational determination.

Although self-determination is irreducible to causal determination, the special challenge of conceiving freedom is highlighted by the self-elimination of foundationalism and the conversion of causality to reciprocity and the collapse of the differentiation of determiner and determined. The convergence of agent and patient, enabling determination to be *self*-determination, cannot be immediately given. Self-determined determinacy may be what it determines itself to be, but the process of self-determination has enabling antecedents.

Self-determination presupposes determinacy in general as well as the two-tiered specification of a determiner and the determined determinacy it posits. Freedom may proceed upon the indistinguishability of determiner and determined, but both aspects must be present. Otherwise self-determination gives itself no determined determinacy nor thereby determines itself as a determiner of its own determinate being. Self-determination cannot begin with sheer indeterminacy, for the indeterminate is just being without further qualification, not self-determined determinacy.

The requisite provision of determinacy and of the relation of determiner and determined might appear to sabotage any conception of freedom, for how can what is self-determined be based upon anything but itself? Would not any enabling conditions turn self-determination into something heteronomous, something having a ground, a sufficient reason? That would be the case if the conditions had two features. First, they would maintain their independent existence while making self-determination possible. Second, they

---

12. Kant, *Critique of Pure Reason*, A201/B246, 311.

would not just pave the way for the emergence of self-determination, but give self-determination its distinguishing character.

The first feature would leave self-determination constitutively related to something different from itself, in the way a ground remains the sustaining condition for the grounded. The second feature would render the identity of freedom something not given by itself but imposed upon it by something else.

The logical emergence of self-determination from reciprocal causality precludes both of these scenarios. When causality or, more generally, foundational determination is driven by its own dynamic to eliminate its constitutive distinction between determiner and determined, what results does not confront the abiding presence of any given determinacy or any two-tiered process in which some factor is determined by another. Instead, the outcome of reciprocal causality arises from the elimination of the independent being of these forms of determinacy. The resultant process in which determiner and determined are the same is poised to unfold without standing in any determining relation to anything else. That process may logically follow from the emergence of determinacy from indeterminacy and the emergence of mediated determinacy from given determinacy, but it begins with no continuing connection to what precedes it. That prior logical development is only an enabling condition of self-determined determinacy that in no way determines how freedom develops. The very character of what has arisen guarantees that this is so. Freedom, after all, has resulted such that it develops itself, which it can only do if its enabling conditions leave it free to be what it determines itself to be.

Self-determination may not be logically defined by its contrast with or determination by any independent factor, but it does contain otherness and the relation of determiner and determined within its own self-differentiating unity. To be self-determined, freedom must give itself new determination that is other to what it is at the outset. In so doing, freedom determines the determinacy it gives itself, operating as a determiner of something determined. Insofar, however, as what it determines is itself as self-determined, the otherness it obtains has its externality eliminated, so that what is determined is the determiner. Unlike an uncaused cause that produces effects beyond itself, the differentiation that freedom involves is an internal differentiation, which constitutes the identity of self-determination as what remains at one with itself by giving itself specification that it does not immediately possess.

The self of self-determination is neither given nor mediated by another. Rather, it is self-mediated and must consist in the process whereby its autonomous identity is established independently of its contrast with something else or of its being determined externally. In contrast to substance, which lords over its accidents as an absolute power that is indifferent to what they are, self-determination has an identity that is essentially connected to the determinations it produces.[13] Freedom must have this intrinsic connection to its content since its generation of determinacy is a self-production, in which each emergent content is constitutive of the whole that is underway forming itself. The development is the self of self-determination and the specification it obtains is a self-ordering one.

Self-Determination and Conceptual Determination

These distinctive features of self-determination are exhibited in universality, particularity, and individuality, testifying to both the conceptualizability of freedom and the autonomy of thought.[14] The traditional dilemmas in conceiving the universal all revolve around a failure to grasp how it consists in self-determined determinacy.

Most historical thinkers have construed the universal as either a given determinacy or a determiner of something determined. Empiricists past and present regard the universal to be a content that is found in a plurality of representations of things and then is abstracted from them as a given mark they share. The so-called particulars from which the universal is abstracted are otherwise indifferent to its content, since all their distinguishing features fall outside the common content that is extracted. What the proponents of this view can never establish is how the abstracted "universal" can be both multiple and common. The shared content does not itself provide for its multiple extracted embodiments any more than do these multiple embodiments account for how they can be identical. The abstracted universal is supposedly common to the concrete individuals that all contain it in addition to the differences that individuate them from one another. Found as part of the manifold content of each individual, the abstracted universal is itself a multiplicity of extracted factors that have nothing to differentiate them in their own plurality. All are the same, but their sameness contains no resource for differentiating them as plural instances. As an inert, given content, the abstracted universal has nothing about it that provides for any self-differentiation. Its own universality is thus an enigma. Either all the identical marks collapse into one,

---

13. See Melvin Woody, *Freedom's Embrace* (University Park: Pennsylvania State University Press, 1998), 191, for further discussion of this contrast between substance and subject, that is, the self-determined self.
14. Hegel's account of the concept in his *Science of Logic* centers upon this connection between self-determination and universality, particularity, and individuality. For a more detailed discussion of this connection, see Richard Dien Winfield, *From Concept to Objectivity: Thinking through Hegel's Subjective Logic* (Aldershot: Ashgate, 2006), 51–65 and Richard Dien Winfield, *Hegel's Science of Logic: A Critical Rethinking in Thirty Lectures* (Lanham, MD: Rowman & Littlefield, 2012), 197–230.

forfeiting their commonality, or they retain their multiplicity, keeping a distinct individuality that subverts their alleged identity.

The situation is no better when universality is identified as an essence, reflected in a multiplicity of appearances. This view, which treats the universal as the determiner of its secondary instances, is often ascribed to Plato, although he himself depicts its difficulties in the *Parmenides*.[15] Instead of treating particulars as the self-differentiation of the universal, the conflation of the universal with an essence affirms an abiding gulf between the primary reality of the essential universal and the derivative domain of its particular appearances. The latter owe their deficient being to the former, which has an antecedent actuality whose eternal fixity reflects how it does not involve any process of differentiation. As a consequence, the divide in ontological level between universal and particular leaves inexplicable how the universal generates its particulars as well as how they are to retain their identity as its particularization. Since the universal exists apart, determining something other than itself, it cannot be in its so-called particulars. If the universal is not in them, how are they its instantiation? So long as the universal exists separately, any connection to its particulars would have to lie in a third factor mediating this tie, calling for an endless introduction of further factors to represent what the remaining terms could share in common.

Self-determination enables the universal to escape the dilemmas of being ascribed a given determinacy and of being identified as an essence of derivative appearances. The particular does not suffer from an uncertain "participation" in the universal if it is determined by the universal as its own self-specification. Then the universal has no prior fixed character in the face of its instances any more than they have an independently given identity apart from the universal. Instead, the universal is universal through the differentiation of its particulars, which are particulars only by being that through which the universal has its own identity. The universal and particular do not face each other across a chasm of different ontological levels. As the self-determination of the universal, particularity is the whole that is at one with itself in the universality that pervades it. The universal continues itself over into its particulars, just as their unity in diversity enables the universal to be self-identical in its process of diversification.

The tie to self-determination is made explicit in individuality. The universal cannot just involve particularity, for unless particulars are differentiated from one another as individuals, their plurality collapses and, with it, the distinction between universal and particular. To determine itself as particular, the universal must therefore incorporate individuality. Conversely, the individual

---

15. See Plato, *Parmenides*, 130b–135c, in Plato, *Complete Works*, 364–69.

cannot have its unique identity unless it is determined in and through itself, that is, unless it exhibits self-determination.

Determination through external contrast with otherness cannot provide individuation because something and other share their roles in being what their counterpart is not. Just as something is the other of its other, so the other that something confronts is something for which its counterpart is its other. Accordingly, determination by negation may distinguish something and other, but in doing so, each factor ends up with the same dual character of being something and other.[16]

Individuation is no more achieved through being determined by some determiner. Any factor that posits another can always have multiple posits. Essence can have many appearances, just as any ground can condition indefinitely many grounded entities. Hence, being posited or grounded does not individuate terms from the others that can always share that character. Even the polar opposition of positive and negative cannot provide an exclusive identification. The negative may be the positive's own exclusive other rather than just something other in general. Nevertheless, the positive plays the same role as the negative, being the negative's own exclusive other. Consequently, positive and negative are indistinguishable in their polar differentiation, making it a matter of indifference whether one pole is identified as positive or negative.[17]

Only when something is specified not by negation or by being posited, but by being determined in and through itself, can it retain a unique identity. Self-determination thus provides for individuality, enabling the individual to exhibit the universality of a self that concretely pervades its own particularization, without which its own unique unity is absent.

The connection between self-determination and the universal, that is, the concept as such, may secure the conceivability of freedom and the autonomy of thought, but does this logical truth save the cultural reality of philosophy from heteronomy? The logic of self-determination may unfold without abiding externalities, but the worldly reality of theory and practice immerses thought and action in encompassing conditions that threaten to render autonomy a vain illusion. How can individuals think freely if they inhabit a world of material causality, trapped in a mechanically, chemically, and biologically determined body, and embedded in an historical world in which preexisting linguistic conventions condition any operation of thought?

---

16. Hegel shows this in his account of something and other in the *Science of Logic*. See Hegel, *Science of Logic*, 117–19.
17. This is why, logically speaking, polar opposition reverts to contradiction, where the defining difference of the opposed terms entails their going to ground. See Hegel, *Science of Logic*, 431–35.

How can anyone act with self-determination when one's own agency cannot fail to have a given biological nature as well as a psychologically and culturally determined character?

Overcoming the Psychological Challenge to Self-Determination

Any theory that nature, psychology, or culture juridically conditions thought and action undermines the very possibility of successfully arguing its case. If nature and psychology subject all life and mind to external necessitation, the world simply has no room for any autonomous theorizing that could critique the given and raise any normative concerns of truth, right, and beauty. If history subjects all thought and action to cultural determinism, then all values are relative and this very situation can never be known with any authority. Just as any philosophy of nature and mind must conceive the world so that it can contain true knowing by and of intelligent life, so any philosophy of culture must conceive history so that convention can include the rise of autonomous theory and practice. Otherwise, these theories incoherently bar the very possibility of their own achievement.

How then can nature have room for the self-activity of life? How can life contain an autonomously thinking self? And how can the historical conditions of discursive intelligence leave thought and conduct free?

There is no need and little plausibility to denying that autonomous thought and action have enabling conditions including the mechanical, physical, and chemical processes on which life depends, the general biology on which animal life rests, the zoology on which intelligence relies, and the cultural conditions of linguistic interaction on which the freedom of persons is based in theory and practice. Just as freedom can logically presuppose determinacy and the relation of determiner and determined, without forfeiting its self-determined character, so the worldly reality of thought and conduct has multiple preconditions that might not make heteronomy insurmountable. Our challenge is to comprehend how these preconditions can function as enabling conditions without determining which of the thoughts they make possible are true or false and which of the actions they permit are right or wrong, that is, without subverting the autonomy of reason and conduct.

The most basic natural process, the mechanics of matter in motion, duly determines the mere material being of nature insofar as it subjects things to an external ordering completely indifferent to what they are. Mechanism thereby wields an efficient causality, whose material determinism continues to be absolutized by the stubborn disciples of early modern thinkers through Kant, even though universalizing mechanism bars the worldly presence of consciousness, self-consciousness, and all normative theorizing and action.

Mechanism cannot possibly be the exclusive determining principle of nature not just because that would preclude any true knowledge of nature but owing to the defining character of mechanistic necessitation. Material causation governs spatial and temporal alterations of things that are indifferent to what they are as specific individuals. Mechanism presupposes that the factors to which it applies already have a determinate individuality that is completely impervious to the mechanistic alterations they undergo. Mechanism cannot account for the specific natures that distinguish things or for their given plurality and the contrasts that involve. Therefore mechanism must be supplemented by other determining principles that individuate the things subject to material necessitation.

Moreover, mechanism is open to the further ordering of things by other principles precisely because material causes are themselves subject to determination from without. Since they act only by being impelled to do so, they can always be enlisted by processes that act upon them so as to use their material causation for other ends. Such employment of mechanism for nonmechanistic purposes is evident in the external teleology of technical production and in the internal teleology of life. An agent can impose new form upon a material thing by employing mechanical process, just as an organism can enlist the mechanics of matter in its metabolic and reproductive life activity.

There is no need to invoke any quantum indeterminacy to explain how external and internal teleology can be compatible with mechanism and incorporate material causation in their purposive activity. Since the external teleology of technical production presupposes conscious agents, who depend upon being alive, the internal teleology of organisms comes first. The road to life traverses the realization of mechanics in the inertial and gravitational motions of material bodies, the physical processes of electromagnetism, providing the polar dynamism of positive and negative force fields, whose differentiation makes possible specific elements, and the chemical reactions these allow. All of these inorganic aspects of nature remain governed by the blind necessity of external determinism, where every causal factor depends upon another to be activated.[18] Although chemical relations proceed upon the qualitative differences of molecular structure, chemical process still depends upon the external impetus of a catalyst to precipitate reactions, which always lead to something different from their starting point.

---

18. This is true of gravity and electromagnetic force since these produce alterations only in the presence of other bodies that wield forces of their own.

Nonetheless, nothing more is required for the self-renewing process of life to get underway. The externally determined relations of matter in motion, in electromagnetic interaction, and in chemical reaction can come to constitute a self-organizing entity through the blind chance occurrence that inorganic alterations interlock so as to provide the minimal self-renewing reality distinguishing the most elementary living cell. *Autopoiesis*, the self-sustaining process of life, comes to be once the appropriate chemicals happen to fall in an enclosed perimeter where they enter into a series of reactions that as a whole both brings itself back to the constituents with which it began and produces the selectively permeable boundary that allows that renewing process to exchange the material it uses and keep its necessary elements from being dispersed or drawn off into extraneous relationships.[19] Although every factor in the self-sustaining whole is engaged in mechanical, physical, and chemical processes, the way they have been integrated constitutes a self-organized entity whose distinctively self-active nature is the principle of its being. The autopoietic whole is a subject whose self-sustaining process has itself as its end. Its internal teleology, however, operates through nothing other than component chemical reactions, all of which are externally determined, depending upon some catalyst, and resulting in something different than the point of departure of their own reaction. There can thus be no incompatibility between the blind necessity of the inorganic processes contained within the living organism and its self-activity. The organism must indeed prevent itself from being subjected to external mechanical, physical, and chemical relations that interfere with its own metabolism and reproduction, letting entropy conquer its living unity. The organism does so, however, through nothing other than enlisting those same relations in the interconnection that builds the life process.

The external determinism of inorganic nature therefore provides the enabling conditions of life, without impeding or determining the specific character of organisms. Nonetheless, the self-activity of life does not constitute the self-determination of thought and action. The reciprocal functionality of the organs of the living thing, the metabolic relation of the organism with its environment, and the reproduction of living individuals all proceed upon a given species being that the life processes sustain, subject to the accidental modifications of evolution. Although all the functions of life depart from the material indifference of mechanism by upholding the specific nature of the living thing, in so doing they remain bound to a genetic identity. How can

---

19. See Evan Thompson, *Mind in Life: Biology, Phenomenology, and the Sciences of Mind* (Cambridge, MA: Harvard University Press, 2007), 91–127, for a more detailed account of *autopoiesis*, drawing from contemporary biology.

thought and action be self-determining if the living agent has this biological foundation?

In order for rational agency to gain a foothold in the world, life must give rise to a specific type of life that possesses a self that can act upon the organism to which it belongs and thereby further determine itself. All life has a sensitivity to its biosphere, minimally present in the selective permeability of the cellular membrane, and an irritability, minimally present in the self-sustaining reaction of the organism to its environment. These life functions can proceed, as in plants, in a purely localized manner, where sensitivity operates on the surface of the organism in direct contact with its environment and each part of the organism responds directly to the stimuli that affect it. What plants do not have is the centralized sensitivity and motor control that allows the organism to sense its environment as a unitary whole and respond as one active individual. Animal life provides this unified selfhood by lacking the immediate, uninterrupted metabolism with the environment that plants enjoy, having instead to perceive nonadjacent objects of satisfaction that it must make a unified effort to locate and obtain over an intervening space and time. This combination of centralized perception, motility, and motivating desire comprises the zoological foundation of a living mind that can then move from having perception at a distance, desires, and motivated behavior to develop habits, memories, and general representations with which intelligence can develop.[20]

The physiological realization of these defining animal functions involves nothing more than the same mechanical, physical, and chemical processes that comprise the self-activity of life in general. A central nervous system, musculature, and sufficiently cohesive supportive structure together permit the animal to perceive its biosphere, move itself as a whole, and sustain its urge to satisfy desire during the effort its mediated metabolism and reproduction require. These zoological features consist in nothing but material factors, each of which is externally determined, but which together in their total integration enable the animal to possess a mind. That mind is located not in any one organ of the animal but rather in the centrally controlling unity that pervades its body in its entirety.

Although animal intelligence can learn and improvise in manifold ways, so long as the animal mind remains dumb, it has no resources for entertaining anything universal, with which it could enter the normative domain of knowing

---

20. These contrasts between plant and animal life have been drawn by Hegel and Hans Jonas. See G. W. F. Hegel, *Philosophy of Nature: Part Two of the Encyclopaedia of the Philosophical Sciences (1830)*, trans. A. V. Miller (Oxford: Oxford University Press, 1970), 303–445, and Hans Jonas, *The Phenomenon of Life: Toward a Philosophical Biology* (Evanston, IL: Northwestern University Press, 2001), 99–107.

and acting on principle. Animals may recognize the family resemblances that distinguish species members from natural enemies, but conceptualization remains impossible without language.

How then can animal psychology provide the basis for the emergence of linguistic intelligence and how can language leave thought and conduct free? Given that thought and language go together, any transition from dumb to discursive intelligence requires that the animal mind can be aware of its own sensations and representations, be able to give bodily expression to those it seeks to communicate, and be able to recognize other animals and their expressions without already being able to think and converse. Only then can embodied individuals perceive how their expressions could convey shared meanings that apply to objects they perceive in common. For this to be possible, three dogmas of much contemporary philosophy of mind must be countermanded: the dogmas of mind/body dualism, of the discursive character of all consciousness, and of the reduction of mind to consciousness. The dualist gulf between mind and body precludes individuals recognizing their own bodily expressions to be communications of their mental contents or recognizing the presence of other minds and their communications. The dogma that consciousness necessarily involves conceptual awareness, without which representations cannot convey anything objective and fit within self-consciousness, prevents individuals from having any consciousness or self-consciousness prior to their participation in linguistic interaction. The reduction of mind to consciousness imposes its own psychological dualism by treating all mental contents as determinations of an objectivity from which consciousness is extricated. Absolutizing this opposition of consciousness bars the preconscious psyche, without which the unconscious habitual aspects of language and thought could not operate, and intelligence, whose awareness of both objects and mental activity is crucial for any grasp of signs and meaning.

The dumb animal is the living refutation of all these dogmas, exhibiting unconscious habits and memory, consciousness of objects, other conscious animals, and itself, and an intelligence that can associate its representations, learning family resemblances and dynamic relationships. The road to thought and language enlists these psychological capabilities, first in a semiotic imagination that connects an intuitable expression with a recalled general representation, itself culled from the association of similar images. This connection renders that intuitable expression a sign insofar as its content has no other connection to the general representation it signifies. Imagination's ability to make this connection enables mind to take a crucial step toward liberating mental content from any direct dependence upon imagery. The same process of internalization that allows images to be recollected allows for this semiotic connection to itself be remembered and repeated. That semiotic memory makes it possible for imagination to associate signs freely with one another, without mediating their connection through imagery.[21]

These psychological developments put mind at the threshold of thought and language, but they must be supplemented by an interaction of individuals with semiotic imagination in order for communicable meanings to be established. Individuals who can produce and recollect signs must use them in a mutually observable way in relation to mutually observable objects and activities in order for words and relations of words to obtain an intersubjectively recognized significance. Only then can any individual have any objective, nonarbitrary standard for the correct use of signs and be in a position to distinguish erroneous meanings and apprehend the difference between true and false propositions.[22]

Once individuals have engaged in recognizably communicable use of words to designate common experiences, they can then enhance the range of linguistic meaning by introducing mutually acknowledged syntax, where the ordering and modifications of words provide the means for expressing judgments and inferences. Although these developments frame discourse in a determinate grammar, which makes propositional communication possible, it cannot limit either what words are produced or what thoughts are conceived.

To begin with, each individual wields a semiotic imagination that is free to associate any intuitable expression it can produce with any general representation it imagines. Moreover, semiotic recollection enables each individual to associate signs with one another in any way intelligence may choose. The communicative interaction of sign producing individuals may establish standards for what these signs mean, but those standards impose no limits on what those signs are or on how they are connected with others. Not only may individuals employ signs in ways that deviate from recognized meanings, but they can always establish new signs and new propositions.

Although language may be an enabling condition for thought, it cannot be coherently advanced as determining what thought must think to be true or false, right or wrong, and beautiful or devoid of aesthetic worth. The moment language is held to condition thinking in any normative way, what one thinks is rendered relative to the language one uses, leaving one unable to know this

---

21. For a concise account of these psychological developments, see G. W. F. Hegel, *Philosophy of Mind: Part Three of the Encyclopaedia of the Philosophical Sciences (1830)*, trans. William Wallace and A. V. Miller (Oxford: Oxford University Press, 1971), §457–464, 210–23.
22. This point is the crux of Wittgenstein's argument against private language. See Ludwig Wittgenstein, *Philosophical Investigations*, trans. G. E. M. Anscombe (New York: Macmillan, 1958), §259–274, 92e–95e.

or anything else with authority unless that language in no way limits knowing. If it does limit cognition, that truth can never be known without qualification. If it does not limit knowing, however, then it ceases to play the foundational role it has been ascribed.

What allows language to leave thought free is the infinitely generative character of grammar, which allows for the establishment of an indefinite repertoire of words and an even more unlimited production of propositions and the thoughts they express.[23] Combined with how the association of signs frees meaning of bondage to imagery, the plasticity of language provides precisely the protean vehicle for the untrammeled autonomy of thought.

The self-determination of reason therefore cannot be undermined by the natural and psychological enabling conditions of linguistic intelligence. Can the same be said of the self-determination of action, which must move beyond the theoretical endeavors of discourse to the practical strivings of conduct?

Even if animal life provides the motivated motility of a perceiving agent and linguistic intelligence enables the rational animal to conceive goals that are universal in character, it remains far from evident how a choosing individual can overcome the Socratic challenge to being patient and agent at once and achieve self-determination.

Overcoming the Practical Challenge to Self-Determination

Socrates is quite right to expose the impossibility of any agent singly being both determiner and determined, and so long as the isolated individual remains the locus of freedom, action cannot be self-determined. By itself, the individual choosing will is doubly conditioned. Although the faculty of choice endows the agent with the negative freedom to set aside any goal and pursue another instead, this liberty has a formality that reflects the given character of its own form of willing and the independently given content of the options from which it can choose. On both accounts, the choosing will is a natural will, endowed with a capacity to choose that is not a product of willing but the precondition for any choice. This natural will is accordingly a faculty rather than an actuality, for it retains the same character given prior to any individual act of will that puts it in play. The form of the choosing will is common to every act of choice and therefore has a universality with no intrinsic connection to

---

23. This point is central to Chomsky's affirmation of generative grammar as the distinguishing feature of language. His most recent presentation of this claim can be found in his 2013 Dewey Lectures. See Noam Chomsky, "The Dewey Lectures 2013: What Kind of Creatures Are We?," *Journal of Philosophy*, volume 110, no. 12 (December 2013): 647, 651, 672.

what is chosen. The options from which the choosing will can select are given independently of its otherwise empty form of willing. In respect to both form and content the faculty of choice wields a universality that lacks individuality. Consequently, the choosing will is doubly heteronomous. On the one hand, its own form of agency is a natural capacity that it never determines, since every act of will presupposes, rather than produces that endowment. On the other hand, the choosing will never originates the content of its ends, which must be furnished by something else, either the external possibilities of objective circumstances or the inner subjective factors of psychological desire and intellectual ideas. Determining neither who the agent is nor what the agent wills, the natural faculty of choice fails to be self-determined. For willing to overcome heteronomy and achieve self-determination, it must determine both the form and content of the willing it comprises.

Just as life can achieve its self-activity by properly integrating the blind mechanisms of physical and chemical processes, so conduct can achieve self-determination by properly coordinating the doubly conditioned natural wills of a plurality of agents. Whereas *autopoiesis* combines inorganic relationships into a living whole, the reciprocal recognition process of rights amalgamates the choices of naturally individuated agents so as to afford them a new artificial, self-determined agency. The intersubjective exercise of rights cannot operate without its participants having the natural capacity to make choices, as well as the unique spatiotemporal embodiment, biological inheritance, and psychological-linguistic development through which agents can confront one another as different thinking individuals, already individuated independently of their willing. On this basis, individuals have all they need to interact so as to accomplish something that they can never achieve alone—will into being both the form and content of their agency.

The self-determined will cannot have just a natural capacity of choice but must give itself an artificial, conventional agency, determined through its own willing in conjunction with willing ends whose own content cannot derive from outer objective or inner subjective factors. Those ends and the artificial agency to which they are intrinsically connected must owe their defining character to the willing that thereby achieves self-determination. The individual will cannot provide itself with an artificial, conventional form of agency or with ends originating in its own volition. So long as an agent merely acts upon other things or its own embodiment, it can only employ its faculty of choice to impose antecedently given ends upon some factor distinct from its own volition. If, however, one agent chooses in relation to the act of choice of another agent, such that the choices in question cannot be made apart from that coordination, they will exercise a type of agency whose form and content do not exist prior to or apart from their interaction. Instead, they will exercise a form of choosing that can only be realized in and through others exercising a correlative willing, where the actuality of the agency of one depends upon that of its counterpart. They will be individuated from one another in this interaction, gaining a character they have imposed upon themselves by willing ends that are themselves only available within that interrelationship. Since each participant in this convention wills in the same way who they are therein and what they will, they each exercise an inherently lawful, universal form of willing that gives each an artificial agency whose self-determination is tied to that of one another. They mutually determine themselves by exercising a right, a universal lawful prerogative that can only be exercised by respecting the same prerogative exercised by the other participants in that interaction. Because their right and correlative duty to respect that of others is something universal, it can only be exercised by individuals who have the linguistic competence enabling them to recognize the universal prerogatives in which self-determination is realized. Although each right bearer can determine him- or herself only by enabling others to do the same, that requirement is not a restriction upon their autonomy but rather ingredient in its actualization. Due to the reciprocity of right, each right bearer exercises an equal opportunity, an equal prerogative, which can never involve the subordination of one agent to the will of another. Rather, each right bearer affirms its own autonomy in honoring that of its counterpart.

The most basic form of right in which self-determined conduct has its minimal reality is property right. Although an agent can take physical possession of a thing without reference to other agents, one can determine oneself as an owner only by laying one's will in some factor in a way others acknowledge by laying their respective wills in some other factors in a recognized way. In this interaction, the participants will themselves to be owners by willing correlative factors to be their property. Both the form of their agency and the end they will are only specified in and through the relation of property right that they enact. Although the participants are already individuated by nature, they give themselves the artificial identity of an individual owner by appropriating distinct factors that they mutually recognize as exclusive embodiments of their respective wills. Although these factors have natural features of their own, what makes them an object of property is solely that they are recognized to embody the wills of the owners to whom they belong. The end of property ownership can only be willed in the interaction of property right, just as one's identity as an owner can only be established through the mutual takings of ownership. These correlative acts each involve choices by the prospective owners, but those choices are circumscribed by the reciprocal prerogatives of right that enable them to codetermine the agency and ends specific to property relations.[24]

Property right is the primary, most rudimentary right because unless individuals have determined themselves as recognized owners of their bodies, nothing they do can count as their own responsibility rather than that of some master to whom they belong. Nonetheless, property right cannot figure as a determining principle or foundation of other ethical institutions, as social contract theory and procedural ethics in general wrongly assume. If property right is treated as a principle of ethical construction, the derivative institutions upon which it allegedly confers legitimacy cannot possibly exhibit the self-determined conduct in which practical normativity resides. Instead of being institutions of freedom, what issues from the procedure of social contract are heteronomous conventions, determined by a prior principle of property right. Such institutions, as a means to secure an antecedently given end, cannot be counted on to achieve their goal, since, unlike an end in itself, the mere presence of a means is never equivalent to the actuality of the end it serves. This leaves the classic pioneers of social contract theory in the dilemma of either allowing every individual to judge when civil government accords with the charge of social contract (Locke), putting civil legality in jeopardy, or to accepting whatever civil government does as right (Hobbes and Rousseau), despite the possibility of malfeasance by the sovereign.

All these difficulties are overcome when property right figures as not the principle but the enabling normative condition of the other forms of self-determination, composing moral interaction, the emancipated household, a free civil society, and self-government.[25] Moral agents must recognize one another to be owners in order to count as responsible, but they hold one another morally accountable by allowing the scope of their responsibility to be determined by the purposes and intentions with which they act, rather than just by ownership. Similarly, spouses may treat one another as codeterminers of a

---

24. The pioneering account of the reciprocal recognition process of property right is to be found in the section "Abstract Right" in Hegel's *Philosophy of Right*. See G. W. F. Hegel, *Elements of the Philosophy of Right*, trans. H. B. Nisbett (Cambridge, UK: Cambridge University Press, 1991), 65–132.
25. For systematic accounts of how and why these are the other forms of self-determination, see Richard Dien Winfield, "The Limits of Morality," in *Overcoming Foundations: Studies in Systematic Philosophy* (New York: Columbia University Press, 1989), 135–70; Richard Dien Winfield, *The Just Family* (Albany: State University of New York Press, 1998); Richard Dien Winfield, *The Just Economy* (New York: Routledge, 1988); Richard Dien Winfield, *Law in Civil Society* (Lawrence: University Press of Kansas, 1995); and Richard Dien Winfield, *The Just State: Rethinking Self-Government* (Amherst, NY: Humanity Books, 2005).

joint household only insofar as they recognize themselves to be conscientious-free persons, but they thereby exercise the ethical autonomy of shared family rights and duties, which apply not to owners and moral subjects in general but only to partners in the same household. Likewise, individuals cannot enjoy their freedoms as members of civil society unless oppression in the household has been overturned by recognition of spousal and parental rights and duties. Still, the equal opportunity of conjugal freedom is not determinative of social equal opportunity, whose civil self-determination is actualized outside the household in markets, civil legality, social interest group activity, and a public administration of welfare. Finally, individuals cannot enjoy equal political opportunity, unless deficits in property, moral, family, and social rights have been overcome, since such deficits will prevent disadvantaged individuals from engaging in politics on par with others. Nonetheless, political autonomy will not be determined by the prepolitical freedoms that make possible equal opportunity to engage in self-government. Rather, political freedom will consist in the exercise of the right to self-rule, which prepolitical associations do not provide.

Whereas the civil government of social contract theory can always fail to uphold the property right that determines its legitimacy, self-government cannot fail to uphold the other forms of self-determination. This is not because these prepolitical freedoms are the determining principles of political autonomy but rather because self-government cannot operate unless citizens enjoy their rights as owners, moral subjects, and members of emancipated households and a civil society. The systematic integration that political freedom affords all the other rights is precisely what allows the totality of practical self-determination to retain its self-governing autonomy. The relation between political and nonpolitical rights does not depend upon any authority external to self-government, for the very autonomy of self-rule necessarily involves the maintenance of nonpolitical rights in conformity with the political autonomy of citizens. That autonomy cannot issue from any prepolitical factor, such as racial, ethnic, or religious identity, which would leave political institutions heteronomously grounded by a factor extraneous to political self-determination. Instead, a free citizenry is defined by the constitution that guarantees its members all their rights, irrespective of the natural and cultural differences that are indifferent to the exercise of self-determination.

Therefore the way to the autonomy of reason and the self-determination of conduct lies open. It can least of all be barred by our contemporary gravediggers of philosophy, who resign themselves to the heteronomy of thought and action. Their own diagnosis of the relative, foundational character of "rationality" undermines the authority of their own claims. More importantly, the hegemony of heteronomy has been vanquished in thought and reality. On the one hand, the autonomous logic of self-thinking thought provides the positive deed of how juridical foundations can be overcome. On the other hand, the self-activity of life, the freedom of linguistic intelligence, and the institutions of rights exhibit how the enabling conditions of self-determination in reality leave our thinking and conduct free to conceive truth and enact justice.

Chapter 3

HEGEL'S OVERCOMING OF THE OVERCOMING OF METAPHYSICS

What is metaphysics? Is it the study of being *qua* being, that foundational ontology with which philosophy must begin to obtain the universal wisdom grounding knowledge of all particular domains? Or is metaphysics the entirety of synthetic a priori knowledge, where reason obtains new knowledge relying on thought alone? Or is metaphysics simply the enterprise of knowing things in themselves, searching for conceptual determinations in the given cognition confronts, certain of the correspondence of thought and being?

Each of these projects of metaphysics has come under withering attack so as to leave us in a post-metaphysical predicament. The alleged outcomes of those attacks have, however, all been called into question by arguments developed by Hegel. Has Hegel thereby rehabilitated metaphysics? Or has Hegel left us a systematic philosophy without metaphysics?

The Repudiation of Foundational Ontology and Its Hegelian Critique

The critique of foundational ontology has its great pioneer in Kant, whose transcendental turn proceeds from the seemingly irrefutable insight that beginning philosophy by conceiving being takes for granted the authority of philosophical knowing. Insupportable dogmatism cannot be avoided if one begins by making claims about what is without first examining knowing and establishing cognition's ability to know objects. Foundational ontology must accordingly cede first philosophy to epistemology. The knowing of knowing should be the preliminary undertaking of philosophical investigation and only if and when foundational epistemology secures some authority for cognition can philosophy turn to investigate what is.

This might seem to reprieve metaphysics by allowing ontology to operate after epistemology. Kant's own transcendental philosophy, however, shows that making epistemology primary can only make sense if the object of knowing is determined by the structure of knowing. Unless this is the case, knowing has no way of determining the objectivity of its claims, for immediate access to being is precisely what is called into question by the transcendental turn away from foundational ontology. Yet, if knowing can know its objects only insofar as they are at least in part determined by the structure of knowing, objectivity becomes something posited by knowing. Instead of being determined in and through itself, objectivity is subject to an external necessity of efficient causality, for all objects are conditioned by the same structure of cognition, no matter what they are. This means that knowable objectivity is governed by a mechanistic law that is indifferent to the specific natures of individual objects. Moreover, since knowable objectivity is relative to knowing, it is a domain of appearance, restricting knowledge to phenomena rather than things in themselves. Since the universal and necessary character of objects is determined by the structure of cognition, the preliminary examination of knowing turns out to contain the principles of possible objects of experience, which is all that philosophy can know about nature. As Kant himself admits, his subsequent *Metaphysical Foundations of Natural Science* merely extrapolates upon what is already established in the *Critique of Pure Reason*.[1] Hence, the metaphysics that epistemology is supposed to secure turns out to be doubly undermined. On the one hand, it consists in knowledge about what necessarily applies to objects of experience, that is, mere phenomena. On the other hand, it has nothing fundamentally new to offer beyond what epistemology reveals in its knowing of knowing. Metaphysics in any wider speculative sense is dead.

Hegel, however, shows that foundational epistemology's enfeeblement of metaphysics succumbs to the same dogmatism of which it rightfully accuses foundational ontology. Just as foundational ontology made direct reference to what is without critiquing the knowing it employs, so foundational epistemology's knowing of knowing makes claims about the structure of knowing and its constructive determining of the object of knowledge without ever establishing the authority of the knowing of foundational epistemology. By turning to investigate the knowing of objects, foundational epistemology puts under scrutiny a type of cognition necessarily different from that it employs. Whereas the knowing it investigates is a knowing of phenomena, the knowing the epistemologist wields is a knowing of knowing. Consequently, the foundational epistemologist's own cognition is not put under scrutiny and its authority remains dogmatically presupposed. Moreover, as Hegel never tires of pointing out, the only "objective" cognition that Kant legitimates is a "knowing" of appearance, which can hardly qualify as genuine

---

1. Immanuel Kant, *Metaphysical Foundations of Natural Science*, trans. and ed. Michael Friedman (Cambridge: Cambridge University Press, 1984), 5, 10, 13.

knowledge.[2] Not only does the cognition of phenomena remain subjectively conditioned, restricted as it is to what knowing puts into its "object," but the conditioned character of posited objectivity precludes the spontaneity of knowing from being known "objectively." The determining structures of cognition must remain a noumenal domain, just as inaccessible to objective knowledge as things in themselves.

In the face of these Hegelian criticisms, the reduction of metaphysics to knowledge of what holds true universally and necessarily of empirical phenomena is both incoherent and unjustifiable.

The Repudiation of Synthetic a priori Knowledge and Its Hegelian Critique

Kant's critical philosophy seeks to redeem a diminished domain for metaphysics by allowing for synthetic a priori knowledge in which different concepts stand in nonanalytic necessary connection thanks to their relationship to the nonconceptual content of sensible intuition. Kant must rely upon this relation to nonconceptual content, which limits metaphysics to knowledge of what is necessary in experience, because of a fundamental assumption about concepts that precludes any synthetic a priori knowledge by means of thought alone. This assumption is none other than the principle of noncontradiction, which holds that each and every concept has a fixed given content and can become nothing other than that. All conceptual content is what it is and not what it is not. Accordingly, thought cannot connect different concepts through thought alone. In thinking any concept, thought only grasps that concept and what is contained within it. No concept, that is, no thought, can connect itself to what it is not, that is, to any concept different from itself, let alone to anything other than thought. Nor can any concept develop into something else. Governed by the principle of noncontradiction, concepts are rigid terms, incapable of any development and self-transformation. Consequently, the only way Kant can uncover any necessary connections between different concepts is within the framework of experience. There the alleged tie between understanding and sensibility within self-consciousness enables forms of sensible intuition to secure the necessary synthesis of distinct thoughts.

If, however, the Kantian transcendental account of experience is itself suspect and metaphysics consists in a body of pure synthetic a priori knowledge, then the submission of thought to the principle of noncontradiction leaves metaphysics entirely in question. So long as concepts are just what they are and

---

2. See, for example, Hegel, G. W. F., *Science of Logic*, trans. A. V. Miller (New York: Humanities Press, 1967), 46.

not what they are not, concepts cannot think relationships between concepts that are not contained within one another nor think relationships between concepts and what is not a concept. All thought can then do is think conceptual contents it finds given and analyze what determinations they contain. Thought can no more generate new conceptual content than obtain knowledge by thought alone of anything other than the given conceptual contents it happens to come across. On either account, philosophy, understood as a discipline attempting to obtain knowledge by thought alone, becomes reduced to analysis, examining the consistency of conceptual contents given by experience or linguistic usage. Truth lies outside such pure thought, precluding any metaphysics that would obtain new knowledge by thought alone, relating different concepts necessarily.

The elimination of metaphysics through the reduction of thought to analysis and submission to the principle of noncontradiction has become the shared dogma of both contemporary analytic philosophy and its postmodern counterpart. By leaving particular content outside the bounds of reason, each of these schools gives new life to the Kantian dictum that thought without intuition is empty. Analytic philosophy does so by taking formal logic to be determinative of all thinking, leaving philosophy having to turn to linguistic usage, the practice of empirical science, and given aesthetic and moral intuitions to have anything to which to apply its formal, otherwise empty reason. Postmodernism takes a similar route by turning to a "difference" outside of thought as the source of all content, while unmasking how reason is devoid of autonomy and instead conditioned by extraphilosophical factors.

The critical moves that underlie these repudiations of metaphysics are crystallized in *The Twilight of the Idols*, where Nietzsche castigates philosophy's constitutive privileging of reason as a vehicle of truth. On the one hand, Nietzsche maintains, simply by relying on reason in all its efforts, philosophy assumes that truth lies in what is thinkable. No matter what philosophy may argue, the mere fact that philosophy uses thought as its privileged instrument means that philosophy always presupposes that conceptual determination is exhaustive of what truly is. On the other hand, thought, Nietzsche observes, is a domain of fixed, abstract universals, which contain nothing individual or changing. All the becoming and individuality of reality is thereby banished from philosophical investigation, whose metaphysical labors can only substitute a ghostly scaffold of dead abstractions for real actuality.[3]

Nietzsche's critique is devastating for metaphysics so long as the thought of philosophy consists of universals lacking individuality and dynamic process

---

3. Friedrich Nietzsche, *The Twilight of the Idols*, in Nietzsche, *Twilight of the Idols / The Anti-Christ*, trans. R. J. Hollingdale (Harmondsworth: Penguin Books, 1990), 45–51.

and so long as philosophy begins by making determinate conceptual claims about either being or knowing. Certainly the debilitating presuppositions that Nietzsche exposes afflict all those philosophers who submit thinking to the principle of noncontradiction and who commence philosophizing with foundational ontology or foundational epistemology. Yet must all philosophical thought fall prey to these limitations?

Nietzsche and his later day followers seek to escape the limitations they expose by appealing to the primacy of what they identify as lying beyond the grasp of the fixed, formal thinking of past philosophy. Nietzsche embraces the allegedly authentic dynamic reality of sensuous immediacy as if it could serve as the bedrock of a self-assertion that affirms particularity devoid of any pretense of universality. Instead of laying claim to any illusory universality for rational autonomy, with its democratic, socialist, and Christian "hypocrisies," Nietzsche extends the primacy of sensuous becoming to a will to power that imposes particular, arbitrary values without concealing their lack of universality. His more recent disciples, most notably Giles Deleuze in *Difference and Repetition*, affirm the primacy of "difference," which comprises an individuality unmediated by thought that challenges our thinking to engage in philosophical reflections that neither accept the adequacy of abstract conception nor presuppose the identity of true being and what is conceivable.[4]

These Nietzschean alternatives are undermined by Hegel on two parallel fronts, one refuting the starting points that Nietzsche and his followers oppose to traditional metaphysics, the other freeing philosophical thought from the "dead phantoms" of abstract universality and any *presupposition* of the identity of thought and being.

First of all, as Hegel observes in the opening chapter of his *Phenomenology of Spirit*, any attempt to uphold the primacy of sensuous immediacy cannot help but fail.[5] Nietzsche may want to supplant the abstractions of formal thinking with the concrete givenness of sensuous becoming, but the moment he attempts to refer to that "real world" he cannot say what he means. Any descriptive account substitutes universal terms for what is supposed to be individual, whereas any mere indicative reference to what is here, now, or for me ends up conjuring a field of substitutable factors, all of which are equally here, now, or confronting an I. Moreover, even if one could refer to sensuous being without canceling its singular immediacy, affirming it as what ultimately is would be a dogmatic metaphysical claim that can no more be justified

---

4. Giles Deleuze, *Difference and Repetition*, trans. Paul Patton (New York: Columbia University Press, 1994), 26, 129–32.
5. G. W. F. Hegel, *Phenomenology of Spirit*, trans. A. V. Miller (Oxford: Oxford University Press, 1977), 58–66.

than any other first principle of being. No given determinacy can escape that pitfall, for at the beginning of philosophical investigation, any definite claim about what is or about knowing is arbitrary.

This arbitrariness applies equally to Deleuze's substitution of "difference" for Nietzsche's sensuous immediacy. Although Deleuze, like his forerunner, presents his privileged surd in reaction to the failure of abstract thought to grasp the individual, the latter's failure cannot alone justify the alternative of "difference," unless one surreptitiously accepts a principle of excluded middle. Of course, both Nietzsche and Deleuze tend in this direction since their reduction of reason to a warehouse of immobile fixed abstractions results from submitting thought to the principle of noncontradiction, whose corollary is the principle of excluded middle. Can "difference" possibly be primary?

Hegel's account of determinacy shows that determinacy itself issues from the unity of being and nothing, which arises from the elimination of all immediate claims about being or knowing.[6] Indeterminacy, or being, is nothing and insofar as nothing is being, we have becoming, whose parallel aspects of coming and ceasing to be end up paralyzing themselves into an immediate unity of being and nothing. They do so simply because the "movements" from being to nothing and nothing to being cancel themselves since the nothing to which being reverts is immediately being and the being to which nothing reverts is immediately nothing. The two sides of becoming thus turn into being *and* nothing in the form of being, for they are now immediately given together, without any other mediating factors. Determinacy can consist of nothing more than this, since anything else would beg the question by basing determinacy on something determinate. Nonetheless, determinacy can have not just being but a *determinate* being only in contrast to an other. The otherness of that other cannot be immediately given but depends upon its contrast with something else to be determinately what it is not. Something and other, however, cannot provide for their own individuations since both end up having the same specification. Something turns out to be both something and other since something is the other of its other, just as the other turns out to be something and other since the other is something in contrast to what it is not.[7] Hence, "difference" can neither just be immediate nor provide individuality as otherness.

The primacy of "difference" fares no better if "difference" is treated as a category of essence. Instead of being immediately given, "difference" then resides in the reflection of inner distinction in which identity consists. "Difference" then not only presupposes the entire development of the categories of the

---

6. Hegel, *Science of Logic*, 106–11.
7. Hegel, *Science of Logic*, 114–19.

Logic of Being but cannot be separated from identity. Moreover, neither difference nor identity can provide individuality any more than can something and other. Every self-reflected factor has both difference and identity no matter what it is.[8]

Can "difference" then signify an individuality devoid of universality, as every nominalism takes for granted? "Difference" should be determined in and through itself, without depending upon terms of reflection, like identity and essence, or upon "concepts," that is, universals. To avoid any qualitative characterization, Deleuze invokes intensity or degree as the distinguishing rubric for "difference," as if this could establish an individuality without universality.[9] Intensity, however, is a form of quantitative determination. As Hegel shows in the Logic of Being, intensity or degree emerges from the determination of the relations of quanta, which take extensive and intensive forms, each convertible into the other since every degree (e.g., the ninety-ninth) can be an extensive amount (e.g., ninety-nine degrees) and vice versa.[10] Not only does intensity presuppose the determination of quantity in general, but it presupposes the logical development of quality. Without quality, the relation of something and other, and the development of the infinite by which relation to other is overcome, there can be no self-relation. Self-relation provides the one, whose contrast to the void turns into relations of attraction and repulsion, whose reversion into one another provides the unification of continuity and discreteness constitutive of quantity. All of these logical developments are presupposed by intensive quantity, rendering any determination of "difference" through degree anything but primary.[11]

Nonetheless, can individuality otherwise retain its unique character without involving universality? Hegel's *Science of Logic* exhaustively illustrates how individuation cannot be achieved through either the contrastive determinations of the Logic of Being or the determined determining of the Logic of Essence. Qualitative difference never attains individuation because determination by negation always leaves each determinacy equally defined by what it is not.[12] Quantitative difference lacks individuality since every quantum is qualitatively indistinguishable, allowing for multiple substitutions in every extensive or intensive magnitude.[13] The same lack of individuation applies to determinations of measure, since qualitative quantities are always prey to nodal series,

---

8. Hegel, *Science of Logic*, 411–12, 417–18.
9. Deleuze, *Difference and Repetition*, 26, 117–18, 223, 230–32, 232–34.
10. Hegel, *Science of Logic*, 217–21.
11. See Hegel, *Science of Logic*, 109–87.
12. See Hegel, *Science of Logic*, 117–22.
13. See Hegel, *Science of Logic*, 202–20.

where each measure entails something measureless that is no less a determinate measure. At each juncture, the new measure relation is determined in contrast to what it is not as well as being in continuity with other examples that have not yet reached the next nodal break.[14] Either way, measure cannot be unique.

Categories of essence can never supply individuality because determiners of determined determinacies, such as ground or cause, can always determine multiple derivative factors. Since what categories of essence posit is always different from essence itself, what is posited need not be unique, but may be one of many posits of the same prior factor. A ground may condition many phenomena, just as a cause may have multiple effects.

By contrast, the logic of the concept comprises a logic of individuality due to how the universal, the concept as such, entails both the particular and the individual. The intrinsic connection between universality, particularity, and individuality holds for even the least concrete forms of universality, the abstract universal and class, with which both analytic philosophy and the postmodern deconstruction of reason tend to identify conceptual determination. The abstract universal, as abstracted from given individuals, seems to contain only what is common to them all, without specifying the features that differentiate its particulars from one another. Even though this abstraction leaves such generalization incapable of providing a priori knowledge about anything else regarding its instances, the abstract universal cannot retain its constitutive commonality unless it relates to a *plurality* of particulars. These particulars all relate to the universal in an identical fashion, all being instances of its commonality, which applies to them with indifference to their other features. Hence, the particularity of the instances does not distinguish them. If, however, the instances were just particular, standing in the same relation to their common universal, they would have nothing to distinguish them and maintain their plurality. They would collapse into one, undermining the constitutive commonality on which abstract universality itself depends. Consequently, the particulars of the abstract universal must also be differentiated particulars, that is, distinct individuals.

The same necessary tie between universal and individual holds true for class. Just like the instances of an abstraction, so the members of a class are members in the same way—each belonging to their grouping with indifference to their other features. Nonetheless, these members cannot have their plurality unless they are not just members but differentiated members. They must be individuals as well. If not, there can be no plurality of membership and the distinction between class and member becomes undermined. Here,

---

14. See Hegel, *Science of Logic*, 366–68.

too, the universality of class depends upon the individuality as well as the particularity of its members.

Although the universality of genus and species is more concrete than either abstract universal or class, it also seems to leave the individuality of its members undetermined. The members of a genus may have a particularity inherent in the genus, whose unity necessarily determines the specific differences of its species. Nonetheless, the members of the infima species, which cannot have any further species under it, are no more distinguished from one another by their species being than are the instances of a generalization or the members of a class. Still, in order for the species to have members, they must be differentiated members, requiring the genus and species to involve not just particulars but individuals as well.

Hegel may distinguish the different forms of universality in the specification of the different forms of judgment, but in the concept of the concept, which precedes the concept of judgment, the necessary connection of universal, particular, and individual is made patently clear from the side of individuality itself.[15] Not only must the universal entail individuality to have particularity, but individuality cannot have its unique character without combining universality and particularity. The individual is the unity of universality and particularity because what is individual is uniquely determined in and through itself. As individual, its differentiation is wholly bound up with its own unity or selfhood. To be unique, what distinguishes it must be its own self, whose relation to itself must pervade the entirety of its determination, uniting its universality with its particularization. The individual's determination is thus none other than *self*-determination.

The introduction to the *Philosophy of Right* makes this explicit, illustrating how individuality's unity of universality and particularity is intrinsic to self-determination.[16] The example of the will exhibits this insofar as the will cannot be free just by having a universality whereby it is not restricted to any given particular choice. This purely negative freedom is not enough, for the will must equally give itself particular determination. Otherwise it has no determination and its freedom is devoid of actuality. This particular determination will escape being determination by something else, or heteronomy, only insofar as the will remains at one with itself in its determination. That determination is *its* determination, its *self*-determination, only insofar as its particular character equally comprises the universality of the will. That is, the particular determinacy the will obtains is one it has given itself without being compelled by

---

15. See Hegel, *Science of Logic*, 600–12.
16. See G. W. F. Hegel, *Elements of the Philosophy of Right*, trans. H. B. Nisbet (Cambridge: Cambridge University Press, 1991), §5–7, 37–41.

anything else to have that determination. The will retains its universality in its particularization and thereby has individuality, where what distinguishes it is bound up with its own unity or self. That self is not something given or posited but rather constituted in and through its own free development.

The logic of the concept, or of universality, is thus not just the logic of individuality but equally the logic of self-determination. This connection between universality and freedom secures the autonomy of conceptual determination. It also secures the exclusive ability of autonomous thought to grasp objectivity, which is determined in and through itself, rather than being determined by some external ground, like mere phenomena. This self-determined character of the concept gives the lie to the postmodern claim that reason is heteronomous, always determined by some foundation or other.

It also gives the lie to the postmodern claim that there can be individuality outside of universality, opaque to thought. The unique character of individuality depends upon the unity of universality and particularity. Without that unity, all one can have is determinacy through negation or determinacy through positing, neither of which provides individuation. Deleuze may be right to acknowledge that difference cannot be individual if it is determined through contrast with an other or by being subject to determining conditions. He is wrong, however, to propose that difference can provide individuality without universality and conceptual determination.

The freedom of thought further signifies that the conceptualization of objectivity cannot rest upon any assumption of the identity of reason and actuality. Precisely because conceptual determination is self-determining, the objectivity of thought cannot be given, as something underlying reason. Rather, it must be the result of conceptual determination, which has no given character but must produce through its own activity all known content that counts as rational.

Admittedly, if thought were governed by the principle of noncontradiction it could no more determine what is other than thought than generate any new thought determinations. Such thinking could never establish its own objectivity any more than it could rise above the labors of analysis and address truth rather than consistency. If, as Hegel has argued, universality involves individuality and the concept is self-determining, thought cannot help but generate new conceptual content and be in a position to relate thought to what it is not.

Hegel and the Future of Metaphysics

If metaphysics is identified with ontology, where reason thinks what is given under the assumption of the identity of thought and being, then Hegel's *Phenomenology of Spirit* and *Science of Logic* provide, respectively, the internal

HEGEL'S OVERCOMING OF THE OVERCOMING OF METAPHYSICS 57

refutation and overcoming of metaphysics. The *Phenomenology* offers the self-undermining of metaphysics by observing how thinking that confronts the given cannot validate its knowledge claims nor uphold the opposition of subject and object on which its "metaphysical" confrontation rests. The *Science of Logic* overcomes the metaphysics of ontology by showing how conceptual determination can autonomously develop without any determinate presuppositions, including any presupposition of the unity of thought and objectivity.

In the introduction to the *Science of Logic*, Hegel noted that Kant had transformed metaphysics into logic.[17] Kant did so by supplanting ontology as first philosophy with foundational epistemology, where knowing takes knowing as its object. The knowing of knowing is the recipe of logic, which thinks thinking. The Kantian transcendental turn, cannot, however, consummate this transformation because the knowing employed by the foundational epistemologist cannot be the same as the knowing it puts under scrutiny. The knowing under investigation in foundational epistemology is not a knowing of knowing but a knowing of objects distinct from knowing. For just this reason, the transcendental critique of knowing cannot critique the knowing it employs in investigating the knowledge of objects. In order for the knowing of knowing to be properly logical, the difference between knowing and its object must be overcome, for this overcoming of the constitutive opposition of consciousness is what delivers the element of logic. That element consists in a thinking that cannot be distinguished from what it thinks. Since such logical thought does not have any object prior to the engagement of its thinking, logic proper must begin without any presuppositions regarding method and content or any differentiation of subject and object. This systematic logic, not transcendental logic, is what genuinely overcomes the metaphysics of foundational ontology.

Systematic logic could be said to comprise a body of synthetic a priori knowledge insofar as the self-development of self-thinking thought is both synthetic and analytic at once.[18] It is synthetic, since autonomous thought generates and encompasses new content, but it is equally analytic since the differentiation of categories is contained within the totality of logic that is underway constituting itself. Nonetheless, synthetic a priori knowledge is not restricted to

---

17. Hegel, *Science of Logic*, 51. There Hegel writes,

> The critical philosophy had, it is true, already turned metaphysics into logic, but it, like the later idealism, as previously remarked, was overawed by the object, and so the logical determinations were given an essentially subjective significance with the result that these philosophies remained burdened with the object they had avoided and were left with the residue of a thing-in-itself, an infinite obstacle, as a beyond.

18. Hegel, *Science of Logic*, 830–31.

logic. Precisely because the autonomy of conceptualization enables thought to grasp both what is other than itself and what is determined in and through itself, reason can advance beyond the thinking of thinking to the autonomous conceptualization of what is other than thought. In this way, Hegel's philosophical system offers a body of synthetic a priori knowledge that contains both logic and what is "real" or nonlogical.

The Hegelian project therefore supplants both the metaphysics of ontology and the metaphysics of foundational epistemology, which restricts synthetic a priori knowledge to knowledge of phenomena of experience. In so doing, Hegelian philosophy equally overturns the antimetaphysical dogmas of Nietzsche and his postmodern followers.

Death to metaphysics! Long live metaphysics!

Chapter 4

ON CONTRADICTION: HEGEL VERSUS ARISTOTLE, SEXTUS EMPIRICUS, AND KANT

No principle has enjoyed more abject fealty in the annals of Western philosophy than the principle of contradiction. From Aristotle onward, almost all philosophers have invoked this hallowed principle to support their philosophical systems or to embolden skepticism of them all. Whether identified in Aristotle's formulation[1] or in Kant's revision,[2] the principle of contradiction has yielded the same outcome: reason's search for truth has been banished from the territory in which contradiction is encountered.

For Aristotle, there are no regrets. The principle of contradiction is the fundamental first principle of reason and only on its basis can philosophy achieve any positive results. For Sextus Empiricus, our refuge from dogmatic philosophy depends upon it. The principle of contradiction is the implicit foundation of his ancient skepticism, which can thereupon confidently suspend judgment whenever argument can be shown to fall into contradiction. For Kant, the principle of contradiction is the guarantor of both logical coherence and metaphysical restraint. Although the principle provides certainty of consistency, rather than truth, it saves us from following our natural inclinations to think the unconditioned and pretend that we could attain truth through reason.

Only Hegel calls into question acceptance of the allegedly irrefutable principle of contradiction. He suspects that any skepticism that depends upon it is

---

1. "It is, that the same attribute cannot at the same time belong and not belong to the same subject in the same respect." Aristotle, *Metaphysics*, Book IV, Ch. 3, 1005b19–20, in *The Complete Works of Aristotle—Volume Two*, ed. Jonathan Barnes (Princeton, NJ: Princeton University Press, 1984), 1588.
2. "Now the proposition that no predicate pertains to a thing that contradicts it is called the principle of contradiction." Immanuel Kant, *Critique of Pure Reason*, trans. Paul Guyer and Allen W. Wood (Cambridge, UK: Cambridge University Press, 1998), A151, B190, 279.

not skeptical enough, whereas any philosophical system that pays it homage cannot possibly be valid.

Aristotle on Contradiction

The fateful embrace of the principle of contradiction finds its classic expression in Aristotle, who turns to it tellingly in pursuit of a first principle of reason. To know truth without qualification, Aristotle acknowledges, philosophy must be the freest, most sovereign discipline.[3] Instead of being captive to any particular condition or perspective, philosophy must uncover what is most universal and fundamental, for nothing can be comprehended in truth unless that without which nothing can be or be known is grasped. To overcome bondage to given phenomenon and given standpoints, philosophy must uncover that which is presuppositionless, that which is by nature rather than by convention, that which is immediate rather than mediated by some contingent condition. What is immediate can serve as an ultimate foundation for being and knowing provided it not only rests on nothing else but is that from which all else emerges and can be intelligible. The pursuit of presuppositionlessness to overcome all contingent mediation entails for Aristotle what he accordingly presumes to be the defining philosophical imperative of finding a first principle, a privileged immediacy that is foundational. This can only be the case on the fateful assumption that immediacy can be something determinate and determining, rather than indeterminate.

Aristotle acknowledges the difficulty of uncovering a first principle, recognizing that it cannot be derived from any other factor without forfeiting its privileged foundational immediacy. Precisely because a putative first principle is not determined by anything else but is rather that immediacy mediating all else, there can be no deduction of it from any premises. The only avenue left for validating a first principle is the indirect path of somehow showing that it cannot possibly be disputed.[4] Aristotle advances the principle

---

3. Aristotle, *Metaphysics*, Book I, Chapter 2, 982a16–19, 982b5, 982b27–28, in *The Complete Works of Aristotle—Volume Two*, 1554–55.
4. Aristotle writes,

> The most certain principle of all is that regarding which it is impossible to be mistaken; for such a principle must be both the best known (for all men may be mistaken about things which they do not know), and non-hypothetical. For a principle which everyone must have who knows anything, he must already have when he comes to a special study. Evidently then such a principle is the most certain of all.

See *Metaphysics*, Book IV, Chapter 3, 1005b12–18, in *The Complete Works of Aristotle—Volume Two*, 1587–88.

of contradiction as the first principle of reason because it alone supposedly exhibits this irrefutability.

Aristotle presents in Book Gamma of the *Metaphysics* his indirect proof of the principle of contradiction, "that the same attribute cannot at the same time belong and not belong to the same subject in the same respect." He there offers a two-pronged validation, addressing both being and discourse. The principle of contradiction cannot be repudiated because, Aristotle seeks to show, nothing can be determinate nor can anything determinate be meant without this principle holding sway.

Beings relinquish all determinate character without it, Aristotle suggests, for if something can have and not have at the same time and in the same respect certain qualities, magnitudes, or relations, all things become indistinguishable. Instead of something possessing a nature and features that other things do not enjoy, everything is and is not what everything else is and is not. All becomes one and that one has no determinable character of its own since it is both what it is and is not attributed to be.[5] Admittedly, Aristotle's principle refers to attributes as if they themselves were determinate, independently of whether the same subject can both possess and not possess them at the same time and in the same way. Nonetheless, attributes would similarly lose their own determinacy if the principle of contradiction were not applicable to their own specification, for unless each attribute is what it is to the exclusion of what it is not, all attributes become one and undifferentiated.

The principle of contradiction, however, is not just an indispensable foundation of determinate ontology but the basis of meaningful speech of any sort, including any denial of its own validity. Nothing can be determinately meant if the principle of contradiction is foresworn. Without it, any claim would signify both its assertion and its denial, just as every term within any claim would mean both what it is and what it is not.[6] To repudiate the principle of contradiction would be a hopeless enterprise, for without the principle being valid, its denial would equally signify its affirmation.[7] It thus appears that not only can nothing be meant determinately without subscribing to the principle of contradiction, but any argument against it must presume the principle's validity in order to deny it without not denying it.

---

5. Aristotle, *Metaphysics*, Book IV, Chapter 4, 1007b19–30, in *The Complete Works of Aristotle—Volume Two*, 1591.
6. See Aristotle, *Metaphysics*, Book IV, Chapter 4, 1006a29–1006b31, in *The Complete Works of Aristotle—Volume Two*, 1589.
7. Aristotle, *Metaphysics*, Book IV, Chapter 4, 1007b29–1008a1, in *The Complete Works of Aristotle—Volume Two*, 1592.

In sum, the principle of contradiction is impossible to escape or deny because, allegedly, nothing determinate can be nor be meant without it being true. Aristotle seems to have sealed his indirect proof and validated his first principle of reason in the only way possible. Its undeniability appears to prevail without depending upon deductive demonstration, whereas all further knowledge seems to rest upon it since any other claims can retain their identity only on its basis.

Nonetheless, the principle of contradiction does not offer any resources for determining what are the specific subjects and attributes that hold true. Since all the principle of contradiction does is certify that a subject can only be what it is and not be what it is not, it provides no means for ascertaining how being and meaning become determined and what determinations they acquire. Even if determinate being and determinate meaning depend upon the principle of contradiction, it suffers from an empty formality that leaves it unable to deliver any positive determination of anything else.

Ontologically speaking, the principle of contradiction requires supplement by some other principles to provide being with any further determination. Although determinacy may be thought to depend upon it, the principle of contradiction itself appears to depend upon the presence of determinate beings with determinate attributes to which it can apply.[8] If, however, what is can be determinate only by being what it is and not what it is not, how can being develop beyond a self-identity indifferently applicable to each and every attribute and obtain any specific differentiated content?

Epistemologically speaking, the principle of contradiction empowers reason to do no more than think the formal identity of independently given contents by certifying them to be what they are rather than what they are not. If this principle is the sovereign rule of reason, reason can only attest to the consistency of externally supplied contents, but never validate their truth, nor engender new contents through reason alone. Reason is then condemned to be merely analytic, incapable of providing any wisdom of its own, nor capable of connecting different contents to one another. It must hand over material "cognition" to the experience of phenomena and restrict itself to exercises in formal logic and reflections on the consistency of empirical science, given ethical and aesthetic conventions, and linguistic usage.[9] Epistemologically, as

---

8. As we shall see, this dependency is reflected in how Hegel will address the principle of contradiction within the doctrine of Essence, which presupposes the Logic of Being and its development of determinacy.

9. As we shall see below, this leaves us with very much what Sextus Empiricus offers as the skeptical outcome of his application of the principle of contradiction.

well as ontologically, the principle of contradiction appears to be a dead end for philosophical investigation.

Aristotle does not fully acknowledge these ramifications and instead ties the principle of contradiction to specific ontological claims. He suggests that attributing to substances only contingent attributes is tantamount to rejecting the principle of contradiction and that this is done by those who reduce being to the becoming of sensible appearances, whose perspectively relative flux has no abiding intelligibility.[10] Accordingly, it might appear that both with respect to being and meaning, subjects must have a necessary essence and that what occurs is never unqualified becoming but only change in the contingent attributes of substances.[11] In drawing these ontological corollaries, however, Aristotle invokes understandings of becoming, appearance, essence, substance, and intelligibility, without accounting for their provenance.

Presumably a first principle of reason should be something that can and must be known before anything else can be held true. Can Aristotle indirectly validate the principle of contradiction by appealing to the conditions of determinate being and of determinate discourse without presuming knowledge of something more than the principle itself? Must he already have in hand a theory of ontological determinacy and a theory of meaning? Moreover, whenever Aristotle points to the looming indeterminacies of being and meaning as indirect proof of the principle of contradiction, does he not depend upon the corollary principle of excluded middle, according to which something does or does not possess an attribute, with no other alternative? That any denial of the principle of contradiction undermines itself can only validate the principle of contradiction if either its denial or its affirmation must be true. Does the whole indirect proof thereby beg the question, presupposing the corollary of what it aims to establish?

Sextus Empiricus and the Principle of Contradiction

Aristotle may purport to anchor being and knowing on the principle of contradiction, but ancient skepticism of philosophical wisdom depends upon that same principle to suspend judgment of truth in deference to unquestioned acknowledgment of appearance and custom. Sextus Empiricus gives classic expression to this dependence upon the principle of contradiction by rooting the entire practice of skepticism in uncovering how claims about what

---

10. Aristotle, *Metaphysics*, Book IV, Chapter 5, 1009a16–1010a14, in *The Complete Works of Aristotle—Volume Two*, 1594–95.
11. Aristotle, *Metaphysics*, Book IV, Chapter 4, 1007a21–1007b1, in *The Complete Works of Aristotle—Volume Two*, 1590.

is and what ought to be can be countered by equally strong arguments to the contrary. This unceasing unveiling of contradiction could testify to how both being and meaning irrevocably involve the unity of determinacies with their negations. Instead, Sextus Empiricus regards the recurring encounter with contradiction as sufficient reason to refrain from making any assertions pro or con. Although this suspension of judgment may serve the practical aim of producing the serenity of abandoned inquiry,[12] apprehension of equal opposing determinations fosters theoretical retraction only if contradiction is recognized to stymy any determinate knowledge. What Sextus Empiricus, as well as subsequent skeptics, presume is that Aristotle is correct in maintaining that allowance of contradiction destroys determinate being and meaning, undermining any normative assertions. On this basis uncovering opposing determinations can suffice to paralyze judgment.

To bring every judgment about what is and what ought to be into opposition with its denial, Sextus employs two broad tactics. One consists in showing how normative claims are relative to some particular factor, enabling contrary claims to arise relative to a different factor. Such factors include the type and condition of knower, the situation and state of the object, and the relation between knower and object.[13] On the other hand, Sextus examines the content of normative assertions and uncovers how that content can be seen to contain its own negation.[14] Instead of regarding this unveiling as verifying the unity of opposing determinations, Sextus regards it as preventing the opposing determinations from having any validity. Kant does the same when he considers how reason, in its quest to know the unconditioned, runs into antinomies. Rather than regard the opposing determinations to be united in the nature of the unconditioned, Kant joins Sextus Empiricus in disqualifying their joint validity, leaving reason allegedly powerless to know anything that is not relative.[15]

Is Sextus, as well as Kant, dogmatically accepting the principle of contradiction? Without paying it unquestioned fealty, can either happily resign

---

12. Sextus identifies this as the "end of Scepticism," in Chapter XII ("What Is the End of Scepticism?"), of his *Outlines of Pyrrhonism*, trans. R. G. Bury (Cambridge, MA: Harvard University Press, 1933), 19–21.
13. These are addressed under the heading of the "general modes leading to suspension of judgement" in *Outlines of Pyrrhonism*, Book I, Chapter XIII, 21–25.
14. Sextus proceeds to do this in Book II of the *Outlines of Pyrrhonism* by investigating "the statements of the dogmatists." See Sextus Empiricus, *Outlines of Pyrrhonism*, 151–59.
15. See Immanuel Kant, *Critique of Pure Reason*, trans. Paul Guyer and Allen W. Wood (Cambridge, UK: Cambridge University Press, 1998), "The Transcendental Dialectic, Second Book, Second Chapter, The antinomy of pure reason," A405/B432–A567/B595, 459–550.

himself to opining conditioned appearances, suspending all attempts to get at the unqualified truth?

Sextus Empiricus' own critique of any appeal to a criterion calls into question his own reliance upon the principle of contradiction as the ultimate foundation of skepticism.[16] Although Sextus claims to leave nothing unquestioned other than appearances, his skeptical practice employs the principle of contradiction as the final criterion for suspending judgment. If Sextus justifies that reliance upon anything else, he would be invoking some other principle whose affirmation has not been suspended. On the other hand, if he endorses the principle of contradiction immediately, that endorsement has no further basis than the sheer being that its affirmation shares with any competing affirmation. Whereas this dilemma leads Sextus to repudiate any reliance upon first principles and upon criteria in general, he uniquely ignores it in surreptitiously depending upon the principle of contradiction.

In effect, Sextus, like Aristotle and all his epigones, is unwilling to confront indeterminacy and instead presumes that immediacy can somehow be determinate. The principle of contradiction is accepted by skeptics and dogmatists alike to escape the looming indeterminacy of being and meaning, whereas their acceptance of it as the bedrock of their reasoning involves the fundamental blunder of any appeal to first principles or ultimate foundations—the blunder of ascribing some determinate being to immediacy.

This blunder undermines the whole enterprise of foundational ontology, which seeks to give being qua being some determinacy. The moment ontology attempts to attribute any determinate character to being, the would-be science of being falls into the confusion of conflating being with some determinate being.[17] Since being cannot be conditioned by any particular being, without ceasing to be being as such, being is unmediated. As immediate, being, however, cannot have any determinate character, for the moment something is identified with being, everything else is deprived of being. Being is and can be nothing but indeterminate, which is to say that being is nothing and nothing is being.

Although, since Aristotle, thinkers have clutched on to the principle of contradiction so as not to forfeit determinate being and meaning, Sextus Empiricus' critique of the criterion exposes how any commencement of thought or being with a determinate principle cannot help but be capricious. If philosophy begins with any determinate first principle of being or reason,

---

16. See "Concerning the Criterion," in Sextus Empiricus, *Against the Logicians*, trans. R. G. Bury (Cambridge, MA: Harvard University Press, 1935), Book I, 29–37, 17–19.
17. Collingwood points out this problem in R. G. Collingwood, *An Essay on Metaphysics* (Oxford: Oxford University Press, 1998), 13–14.

everything that follows is tainted with the curse of arbitrariness. The fear of lapsing into indeterminacy by forsaking the principle of contradiction thus reveals itself to be a fear of truth.

Hegel's Account of Determinacy as the Thoroughgoing Refutation of the Principle of Contradiction

Hegel is the first philosopher to recognize that philosophy must begin with nothing other than what the abandonment of the principle of contradiction is feared to leave us with: indeterminacy. Indeterminacy as that with which philosophy must begin represents the overcoming of all appeal to first principles as well as to any determinate givens, be they determinations of knowing or of the object of knowing. Only starting with indeterminacy allows philosophy to make an absolute beginning, freed of the dual relativity of addressing some given content with some given form of cognition. Freeing philosophy from all determinate foundations, beginning with indeterminacy is equivalent to overcoming the opposition of consciousness, whose confrontation with the given would imprison knowing in relativity were consciousness the ultimate framework of cognition. Further, insofar as philosophy's beginning with indeterminacy signifies liberation from bondage to the principle of contradiction, it promises to emancipate reason from the empty formality to which that principle condemns thought.

Although beginning with indeterminacy might seem to confirm Aristotle's fear that only adherence to the principle of contradiction can make determinate being and meaning possible, what follows from indeterminacy is none other than the thoroughgoing refutation of that completely incoherent view.

Any attempt to ground determinate being and meaning upon a determinate principle, such as the principle of contradiction, patently begs the question of accounting for determinacy by presupposing a determinacy for its account. As Hegel recognizes, it is totally absurd to attempt to derive determinacy from any determinate factor. Determinacy can only be accounted for by generating determinacy without reliance upon anything determinate. In other words, determinacy can only arise from indeterminacy.

Hegel shows just how this occurs in thinking through the logical development from being to nothing to becoming to determinate being. This development not only provides determinacy without taking any determinacy for granted, but thereby refutes the absurd claim that determinate being depends upon the principle of contradiction.

The initial moves from being to nothing to becoming offer no possible opportunity for any application of the principle of contradiction. Being has no determinate attributes to affirm or deny any more than does nothing. Being is indeterminate precisely because it lacks all such specification. As immediacy, being provides no determinate cause or principle for the emergence of any other term. Since any determinate content or determinate procedure for arriving at something else would be an utterly extraneous, arbitrary stipulation, what follows from being can only follow immediately, without any ground or intervening basis, and consist of nothing but the same absence of determinacy. Being is immediately nothing, just as nothing is immediately being. Neither being nor nothing has anything about it that could be susceptible to contradiction, let alone safeguarded from indeterminacy. Nonetheless, being that is nothing and nothing that is being together constitute becoming and do so through nothing but their own indeterminacy. Once more, what follows does not depend upon any principle, let alone the principle of contradiction. Rather, becoming arises as just what being and nothing are in virtue of their own most impoverished immediacy. Whereas being and nothing immediately comprise being-nothing as well as nothing-being, they together constitute a two-sided result that is irreducible to either being or nothing. This third term, becoming, accordingly consists in coming to be (nothing-being) and ceasing to be (being-nothing). Its emergence cannot depend upon the support of the principle of contradiction, let alone any other foundation, for it immediately emerges from what is itself devoid of determinacy.[18]

Although becoming is not a determinate being, but just coming and ceasing to be (nothing that is being and being that is nothing), becoming provides all that is required for determinacy. Once more, there is no need or any possibility of appealing to the principle of contradiction for securing the advance. The very absence of any attributes in ceasing and coming to be leads to their paralysis, for insofar as being is immediately nothing and nothing is immediately being, coming to be is immediately ceasing to be and ceasing to be is immediately coming to be. That is, the nothing into which being ceases immediately cancels that cessation by converting into being, just as the being that comes to be immediately cancels its emergence by converting to nothing. What results is a dual cancellation of the two sides of becoming, leaving being and nothing in an immediate unity. Being that is nothing reverts to being, together with nothing that is being reverting to nothing. They stand together in the form of immediacy, or being, since nothing else mediates their presence. They are both at hand, being with nothing, immediately, because nothing but their own indeterminacy makes the process of becoming come to a standstill.

---

18. Although the linguistic expression of how being is nothing and nothing is being and how becoming consists in both may avail itself of propositions in which subjects and predicates appear, the thought determinations themselves do not consist of judgments.

Determinacy cannot be characterized by using any determinate specification, since that would beg the question. Determinacy can only consist of indeterminate components and that is why the being and nothing into whose immediate unity becoming develops are the necessary and sufficient constituents of determinacy. Contrary to the principle of contradiction, determinacy is none other than what both is and is not, being and nothing! Far from securing determinacy, the principle of contradiction blocks the constitution and intelligibility of determinacy.

As Hegel's *Science of Logic* shows in following out how determinacy gives rise to a determinate being, the immediate being of the unity of being and nothing itself undergoes the same becoming that leads to determinacy, rendering determinacy a determinate determinacy or something.[19] Since being is nothing, the being of determinacy is equally the non-being of determinacy. Accordingly, determinacy involves both reality (the being of determinacy) and negation (the non-being of determinacy). The immediate unity of reality and negation, or of the being and non-being of determinacy, is determinacy that is *determinately*. It is not just quality but *a* quality, that is, not just determinacy but *a* determinacy or *something*. Again, the principle of contradiction cannot possibly play any role in accounting for a determinate being. Something has no attributes to affirm or deny, since they would be something themselves. Instead, something is nothing but what something other is not. That other, the *determinate* negation of something, is, however, itself a something that is not what is other to it. Hence, something and other are each something and the negation of something (their other). Thus, not only does determinacy challenge the principle of contradiction but so does each and every determinate being, every something or other.

Why Hegel Addresses Contradiction and Its Principle in the Logic of Essence

Although Hegel may be our great emancipator from the principle of contradiction, he does allow it place in the Logic of Essence, where it arises in connection with the essentialities of identity and difference and where contradiction itself

---

19. As Hegel writes,

> Determinate being, however, in which nothing no less than being is contained, is itself the criterion for the one-sidedness of quality as determinateness which is only *immediate* or only in the form of *being*. It is equally to be posited in the determination of nothing, when it will be posited as a differentiated, reflected determinateness, no longer as immediate or in the form of being.

See Hegel, *Science of Logic*, 111. See also Hegel, *Science of Logic*, 109, 114–15.

emerges as that into which the polarity of positive and negative develops.[20] It is of crucial significance that contradiction and its principle comes up in the Logic of Essence and not in the Logic of the Concept. The Logic of Essence develops all the categories in which some determinacy is posited by another, where determinacy is mediated by or relative to some prior determiner. The Logic of Essence presents the categorial domain of foundationalism, of conditioned being, and it should be no surprise that its categories are those that Kant privileges in restricting knowledge to an "objectivity" of appearances that is conditioned by the transcendental structures of knowing.

The essentialities of identity and difference involve relations where an essence, that is, a determiner of determined determinacy, is at one with itself through contents whose independent existence it nullifies and incorporates. Self-identity here enters in as a relation wherein an essence is reflected in a differentiation that remains wholly internal to itself. As Hegel notes, self-identity can be turned into the principle of contradiction insofar as it involves a formal unity in which the specific content of self-identity's internal differentiation is left unspecified by how it reflects itself therein.[21] Just as the principle of contradiction applies to any content whose formal consistency can be affirmed, so self-identity never goes beyond itself in whatever content it is manifest. For this reason, self-identity involves *internal* difference, but a difference to which its unity is indifferent, even though it contains it. As a result self-identical factors are diverse, owing their determinate being not to their contrast with one another but through their reflection into themselves. That reflection, as formal self-identity, possesses a content that is itself fixed, lifeless, and devoid of subjectivity. Only then can it belong to formal identity, which contains its content insofar as the latter has a consistency involving no immanent principle of differentiation.

Whereas self-identity excludes any extraneous difference, contradiction arises when factors oppose one another but undermine their opposing identities through their very opposition. Contradiction does subvert the terms it opposes, but it does not result in indeterminacy, as Aristotle and Sextus Empiricus suggest.[22] In order for contradiction to arise, determinacies must develop that are what they are through their very opposition and at the same

---

20. See Hegel, *Science of Logic*, Book Two: The Doctrine of Essence, Chapter 2: the Essentialities or Determinations of Reflection, 408–43.
21. See Remark 2: First Original Law of Thought, Hegel, *Science of Logic*, 413–16, and Remark 3: The Law of Contradiction, Hegel, *Science of Logic*, 439–43.
22. One might wonder whether the opposition of consciousness exhibits a contradiction that results in indeterminacy. Certainly the self-examination of consciousness that is observed in Hegel's *Phenomenology of Spirit* ends up rendering subject and object indistinguishable, eliminating the opposition of consciousness and ushering in the indeterminacy with which philosophy proper can begin. This development, however, is

time cancel their opposition. The polar determinations of positive and negative provide just this relationship. Positive and negative fall into contradiction since their distinctive identities depend upon their opposition, yet in that opposition, they play indistinguishable roles. Whereas something may have indifferently many others, the positive has *its* essential other in the negative, just as the negative has *its* essential other in the positive. Neither can be without opposing its counterpart, yet in and through their opposition, each relates to the other in precisely the same way. As a consequence, positive and negative eliminate their essential difference through their opposition, which collapses. Their contradictory polarity itself "goes to ground" insofar as their self-annulling opposition results in a relation in which two factors have the same content, once as positing its other and again as being posited, as ground relates to what is grounded.[23]

Both self-identity and contradiction exhibit the two-tiered character of foundational determination, where determinacy is determined or posited by a determiner or positor. Self-identity does so by rendering difference something internal to its underlying unity, whereas the polarity that generates contradiction does so by superseding the equipollence of something and other with an opposition where one pole reflects itself in what is distinguished from it. What the entire development of the Logic of Essence shows is that none of these relations can sustain themselves as independent, immediate factors that could serve as ultimate principles. Instead, the relation of positor and posited continually undermines itself insofar as the positor can only play its determining role by being in relation to what is posited. What is posited, as posited, effectively posits the determining character of its positor, such that the positor is posited and the posited operates as a positor. This outcome comes to a head in the final relationship of the Logic of Essence, reciprocity, which issues from causality.[24] Since a cause is a cause only by having an effect, the effect is the cause of the cause's efficacy. Cause and effect thus end up both being cause and effect of one another. Although this reciprocal relation has each factor be both cause and effect of its counterpart rather than of itself, their mutuality removes all difference between them, eliminating the distinction

---

not a logical development, nor does the systematic determination of consciousness, which Hegel provides in the *Encyclopedia Philosophy of Mind*, lead to the annulment of conscious awareness, but rather proceeds to theoretical intelligence, which makes the opposition of consciousness its object, treating mental determinations as both subjective and objective.

23. As Hegel writes, "opposition is not only *destroyed* [*zugrunde gegangen*] but has withdrawn *into its ground*." See G. W. F. Hegel, *Science of Logic*, trans. A. V. Miller (New York: Humanities Press, 1976), 434.
24. Hegel, *Science of Logic*, 569–71.

between determiner and determined. With this development, the logic of foundationalism eliminates itself, giving way to the logic of self-determination, where determiner and determined are one and the same.[25]

If universality and conceptual determination fell within the orbit of foundational logic, formal self-identity and the principle of contradiction might retain a stranglehold on reason. Hegel, however, recognizes that the logic of self-determination is the Logic of the Concept, which signals that universality can be pregnant with content, that concepts need not be empty, and that reason need not confine itself to analytic labors of certifying the consistency of given terms under the governance of formal logic.

The Logic of the Concept and Emancipation from the Principle of Contradiction

The logic of self-determination is the logic of the concept because the universal, the concept as such, is a self-differentiating unity that is what it determines itself to be. Even the most formal universals, the abstract universal and class, have their constitutive identity only in and through their particulars, their instances and members, respectively. Without these particularizations, the abstract universal and class would forfeit their differentiated unities and become a self-identical one. Moreover, their particulars must themselves be individuated to sustain the plurality preventing their collapse into the universal. If the universal had just one particular, they would be indistinguishable and the universal would revert to an immobile unity, losing its constitutive encompassing, self-differentiating identity. The universal must instead involve both particularity and individuality, even though it is not reducible to any one particular. Particularity and individuality are both immanent to the universal, which is at one with itself only through these determinations of itself. By contrast, formal self-identity is indifferent to the content of its inner differentiation, which is why it can be governed by the principle of contradiction. Universality cannot insofar as it carries itself over into the distinguishing character of its particulars, each of which it both is and is not since it pervades them all.

---

25. Although Sextus Empiricus similarly exposes how causality turns into reciprocity, he fails to see how reciprocity ushers in self-determination because of his adherence to the principle of contradiction. See Sextus Empiricus, *Outlines of Pyrrhonism*, Book III, Chapter IV–V, 13–29, 333–45, and Sextus Empiricus, *Against Physicists*, Book I, 195–257, in Sextus Empiricus, *Against Physicists, Against Ethicists*, trans. R. G. Bury (Cambridge, MA: Harvard University Press, 1936), 99–127.

Moreover, even though the universal's particulars must be differentiated from one another and thereby be individual, their opposition cannot involve contradiction, which would cancel their self-subsistence. The universal does not undercut their independent being and reduce them to posits of some ground. Rather, the particularization of the universal is its very own self, that is, its *self*-determination. Contra Platonism,[26] which treats the universal as an essence reflected in derivative deficient phenomena, the universal has no being apart from its particularization, which is why that particularization is not inessential and why the universal determines itself and not something else.

The self-determination inherent in universality is what enables conceptualization to be both synthetic and analytic at once. Because the universal is self-differentiating, concepts are not empty but develop themselves, generating new determinations whose synthetic connections constitute the very analytic identity of the concept underway determining itself. Reason can therefore provide synthetic a priori knowledge without having to rely upon something other than concepts. Although Kant recognized that philosophy depends upon the possibility of synthetic a priori knowledge, his adherence to the principle of contradiction left Kant only able to retrieve a synthetic a priori knowledge of conditioned appearance by appealing to how sensible intuition and understanding connect in the constitution of experience. Hegel's logic of the concept demonstrates how reason can escape Kant's appeal to the given, overcome heteronomy, and determine itself. The universal's self-determining self-differentiation is what allows concepts to lay hold of objectivity, which unlike conditioned appearance is determined in and through itself. Precisely because objectivity is what is in its own right, it can be the proper object of truth and transparent to a reason whose autonomous development can think through the self-development of an unconditioned subject matter. Whereas a thinking governed by the principle of contradiction can never grasp what is unconditioned, a self-determining reason can think what is self-constituted.

Our emancipation from the principle of contradiction is crucial not just to thinking truth but to doing right. Hegel makes this manifest in the *Philosophy of Right*, where he underscores how universality involves self-determination by showing how the will is autonomous only by giving itself new determination that remains at one with its self-constituting agency. To determine itself, the will cannot just be what it is and remain caught in the immobile fixity ordained by the principle of contradiction. Instead, the will must negate its given determinacy and become what it is not, thereby achieving its dynamic

---

26. In Plato's *Parmenides*, this "Platonic" view of the universal is itself mercilessly critiqued. See Plato, *Parmenides*, 131a–135c, in Plato, *Complete Works*, ed. John M. Cooper (Indianapolis, IN: Hackett, 1997), 364–69.

identity as self-determining. In so doing, the will overcomes the empty universality of being unrestricted to any given content and resolves to act, taking on a new aim that is its own self-determination, giving the will a character it imposes upon itself, enabling the will to individuate itself. The will thus achieves self-determination insofar as it exhibits universality, particularity, and individuality.[27]

Only by having the same self-determining, self-differentiating character as the concept can the will escape the formal self-identity that plagues Kant's application of the categorical imperative, the enslavement of which to the principle of contradiction deprives volition of the immanent individuation on which freedom depends. As Hegel never fails to point out, the empty consistency that satisfies the principle of contradiction can apply indifferently to any course of action, provided no further limitations are surreptitiously introduced.[28] Willing achieves self-determination not in obedience to the formal self-identity of non-contradiction but through the contrastive individuation of the exercise of rights, where individuals interact with one another, determining their own identities as property owners, moral subjects, family members, civilians, and citizens through particular entitled actions by which they differentiate themselves as autonomous agents.

In theory and practice, only liberation from the reign of the principle of contradiction can secure the self-determination on which truth and right depend.

---

27. See G. W. F. Hegel, *Elements of the Philosophy of Right*, trans. H. B. Nisbet (Cambridge, UK: Cambridge University Press, 1991), §5–7, 37–42.
28. See, for example, the Remark to §135 of Hegel, *Elements of the Philosophy of Right*, 162–63.

Chapter 5

OVERCOMING ACTUALITY: HOW HEGEL FREES US FROM THE PRISON OF MODALITY

The Prison of Actuality

Since the rise of early modern Western philosophy, the modal categories of actuality have reigned supreme over almost all the philosophical academy. Possibility, actuality, and necessity have become the encompassing framework of the world most thinkers purport to be able to know. Imprisoned in these three modalities, our universe has become inhospitable to life, right, beauty, and reason, for none of these can fit the chains of necessity that actuality imposes.

Only one thinker has put actuality in its proper place. He has shown how its modal categories subvert themselves and usher in a different order of objectivity in which freedom, not necessity, has its place. This thinker is Hegel and if we follow him in thinking through the categories of actuality, we discover how reason can liberate itself from their chains.

Putting Actuality in Its Proper Place

It is crucial to avoid indiscriminately applying the category of actuality and thereby accepting it as an ultimate scaffold of thought and being. Hegel, like many other thinkers, carefully distinguishes between reality, existence, actuality, and objectivity.

So differentiated, reality signifies no more than the being of determinacy. In this sense, Descartes describes ideas having reality simply by being determinate, whether or not they have any mind-independent being.[1] Reality, as merely the being of determinacy, is not an appearance, in which some essence reflects itself. Appearance itself incorporates reality in two respects: in the determinacy of its mediated show and in the determinacy of the essence

---

1. See René Descartes' *Meditations on First Philosophy*, trans. Donald A. Cress (Indianapolis: Hackett Publishing, 1993), pp. 27–28.

it discloses. Reality falls within the categorial realm of what Hegel calls the Logic of Being, whose terms stand in contrast to other coeval factors, rather than being determined by some prior level of determinacy.

Existence, in contrast to reality, comprises a domain containing factors that stand in dependent interrelation with one another. Unlike reality, which simply *is* determinate, existence is a field of relativity, in which each entity conditions and is conditioned by its counterparts.

Actuality, unlike reality and existence, contains the condition of its own existence. Actuality operates, however, in a manner fundamentally different from how objectivity stands determined in its own right. Whereas actuality retains the conditioned contents of existence, objectivity is thoroughly determined in and through itself. This is what allows objectivity, rather than what depends on anything else, to be the proper object of knowledge. If apprehension restricts itself instead to appearances that rest on some foundation, apprehending appearances leaves out of account what grounds their truth as appearances. On Hegel's account, objectivity has the independence worthy of the object of knowledge by possessing individuality, to which universality and particularity are intrinsically connected. Individuality enables objectivity to comprise a realm in which the external relations of objects do not impinge upon what they are in themselves, as well as to provide for teleology, where ends bring into being their own specific determination.

With objectivity in hand, Hegel can then develop the categorial domain of the Idea, in which the relations of concept and objectivity work themselves out. These include the self-sustaining internal teleological process of life, the striving of theoretical and practical cognition to overcome the initial opposition of concept and objectivity, and finally the unification of theory and practice in the self-constituting self-cognition of logic itself.

If we ignore these further developments and instead regard actuality as the final category of thought and being, we forfeit all access to teleology, life, cognition, and logic itself.

Why Actuality Falls in the Logic of Determined Determinacy

Hegel treats actuality in the Logic of Essence, which develops all of the categories in which a determiner determines a determined determinacy. The two-tiered Logic of Essence both presupposes and follows from the Logic of Being. The Logic of Being proceeds from indeterminacy to develop all the categories of determinacy, in which coeval terms have their character through their contrast with one another. The Logic of Essence presupposes contrastive determinacy insofar as both a determiner and determined determinacy incorporate determinacy. Although, for example, essence mediates appearance, appearance still has a given determinacy. This is why the ancient skeptics, who rendered relative what dogmatic philosophers considered true in itself, did not doubt the determinacy of appearances. Moreover, the Logic of Being engenders the two-tiered domain of the Logic of Essence. This occurs when measure relations, which incorporate both quality and quantity, give way to an infinite series in which the quantitative range of each measure passes beyond itself into a new measure relation. Since the ensuing measureless procession contains all qualitative and quantitative determinacies, they end up mediated by its underlying determining, rendering them posits of its positing.

The resulting two-tiered domain of determined determinacy is privileged by transcendental philosophy, which must conceive knowable objectivity to be governed by an external necessity, indifferent to the specific nature of its objects. The transcendental turn renders all possible objects of knowledge determined by one and the same foundation: the conditions of knowing. Accordingly, all objects are mediated by a common determiner, which subjects them all to a rule that applies no matter what they are. This renders knowable objectivity a nature governed by material law, indifferent to specific form and import, rather than by a hierarchy of species and genus. The concepts determinative of knowable objects thereby consist of categories of determined determinacy, the categories that Hegel addresses in the Logic of Essence.

Kant's *Critique of Pure Reason* exhibits this privileging of determined determinacy in his table of categories, which appropriates the metaphysical concepts of early modern philosophy as pure concepts determinative of all possible objects of experience. Among these pure concepts, the modal categories of possibility, actuality, and necessity figure prominently, presiding over an "objectivity"[2] in whose conditioned process life, freedom, and beauty have no place.

Whereas Kant introduces the categories of possibility, actuality, and necessity with little more than a "metaphysical deduction," invoking the authority of Aristotelian logic, Hegel generates them in systematic succession. The third section of the Logic of Essence, entitled "Actuality," develops these modal categories in the second of its three chapters, falling between the thinking through of "the Absolute" in the first chapter and "the Absolute Relation" in the third chapter, which brings the Logic of Essence to its conclusion. Under the heading of "the Absolute," Hegel addresses the categories of substance, attribute, and mode fundamental to Spinoza, whereas the development of

---

2. "Objectivity" here amounts to what the knowing subject confronts as the opposing domain of appearance, of what can be experienced. Hegel terminologically distinguishes between this "objectivity" and that which is the self-standing domain worthy of knowledge with the terms "*Gegenständlichkeit*" and "*Objectivität*," respectively.

"the Absolute Relation" thinks through the categories of substance and accident, cause and effect, and reciprocity, which figure so centrally in all early modern philosophy up through Kant. Unlike the early moderns and Kant, Hegel seeks to provide a systematic generation of all these categories. That genesis consists in a development in which they progressively transform themselves, leading to a final transformation in which the entire two-tiered framework of the Logic of Essence collapses. At that point, ushered in by the logic of reciprocity, the differentiation of determiner and determined subverts itself. What results is the Logic of the Concept, in which the indistinguishability of determiner and determined unfolds in a logic of self-determination, securing the autonomy of thought. Hegel's account of "Actuality" amounts to the systematic refutation of all early modern philosophy up through Kant to the extent that Hegel successfully determines these categories and shows how they undermine themselves as the ultimate categories to which our thinking must capitulate.

Hegel's point of departure is the outcome of the determining of appearance, which itself arises from the logic of ground and grounded. The ground relation emerges when the contradictory relation of positive and negative subverts its own defining polar opposition. Since positive and negative oppose one another as each one's respective reflected other, it is a matter of indifference whether a factor figures as positive or negative. The positive opposes the negative in exactly the same way as the negative opposes the positive. As a consequence, the opposition on which polarity depends forfeits its own defining difference, leading positive and negative to "go to ground," where the same content figures as both posited and positing. This is the characteristic relation of ground and grounded, where the ground posits in the grounded nothing but what it contains.

Since, however, the ground plays its grounding role only in virtue of the grounded, the grounded grounds the ground. Since ground and grounded thereby end up each being both ground and grounded, the ground relation reverts to a domain of existence, in which every factor both conditions and is conditioned by its counterparts. These factors contain this dual relation in themselves, as things that have properties, through which they interact.

Existence thereby subjects its elements to the same law of interdependence. Since their interaction immediately reflects that law, existence becomes a world of appearance. Although initially the occupants of existence condition and are conditioned by one another, the common law applying to them all determines their entire interaction as *its* appearance. In so doing, the lawful mediation of the world of appearance yields a differentiation of form and content. Appearance exhibits two sides, the form of lawful interdependence and the content it regulates. Although the form and content stand in relation, they are not coeval factors that differ qualitatively, like something and other. They differ not in qualitative content but in form, between that which forms and that which is formed. Nonetheless, since content cannot be formless and form cannot lack content, form cannot be indifferent to content. Form immediately is its content and this identity yields the relation of whole and parts, where the whole directly encompasses the parts, whose independent determinations are just as directly absorbed into the form of the whole. Since, however, the parts have a given content that provides the whole its exhaustive filling, they are nothing but the expression of the whole, which, for its part, does nothing but posit them as its constituents. The erstwhile whole expressly does this in the relation of force and expression. Whatever expression force may have, that expression's distinction from force does not rest on any difference of content. The content of the force is exhibited entirely and nowhere else than in its expression. Consequently, the relation of force and expression turns into the purely formal distinction of inner and outer, whose contents are indistinguishable.

With no qualitative difference in content, what is outer, in appearance, is just as much what is inner, in essence. Here, appearance manifests nothing that is not in essence, just as essence has no content that appearance does not exhibit.[3] The existence by which essence appears consists in the very same content as essence itself. Since both have the same given determinacy, to which the form difference of positor and posit adds nothing but formal self-identity, existence and essence have become united.[4] What appears just is because it is. This is the formula for the relationship of substance, which inaugurates the categories of actuality.

They remain within the logic of essence, of determined determinacy, due to the formality that distinguishes necessity from freedom. In all the relationships constituting actuality, mediated being rests upon a given determiner that does not gain any essential further determination through its mediating service.

Since this relationship starts with a unity of essence and existence that encompasses all appearance, it debuts as the one and only substance, an absolute that manifests itself in attributes and modes showing nothing not already contained in itself. The manifestation of this one and only substance

---

3. As Hegel writes, "What is inwardly is also found outwardly, and vice versa. The appearance shows nothing that is not in the essence, and in the essence there is nothing but what is manifested." See G. W. F. Hegel's *Logic: Being Part One of the Encyclopaedia of the Philosophical Sciences,(1830)*, trans. William Wallace (Oxford: Oxford University Press, 1975), §139, 196.
4. As Hegel puts it, "Actuality is the unity, become immediate, of essence with existence, or of inward with outward." See Hegel, *Logic*, §142, p. 200. See also, G. W. F. Hegel, *Science of Logic*, trans. A. V. Miller (New York: Humanities Press, 1969), 529.

cannot help but consist in determinations attributable to substance yet indifferent to its identity. The attributes and modes exhibit nothing but the substance to which they belong, which has no limits and therefore is infinite. Spinoza displays the empty formality of this self-identity by acknowledging that substance has infinite attributes, while stipulating without explanation just two—thought and extension. Because substance has both a given essence that contains its existence, there is no development by which any determinations can be shown to arise from the infinite unity of substance.[5] Whatever transient appearance emerges in and through substance amounts to an accident, which adds nothing to the prior identity of substance.

The modal relations of actuality, possibility, and necessity display an analogous contingency of appearance. Whatever is possible ends up having to have its condition present in actuality, rendering it no less necessary. Whatever is necessitated, however, cannot be a change *in* the necessitating substance, for that substance's given character is not altered by its necessitation. Instead, necessitation must be the condition for contingencies applying to another substance, whose identity remains indifferent to what change it undergoes among its accidents.

As Melvin Woody points out, because the category of substance renders every entity's identity something given by its essence, any self-determination is precluded on several key accounts.[6] First, since self-identity governs substance, any alteration must be accidental to it and have its ground outside the entity in question. Secondly, cause and effect relations cannot apply to consecutive states of the same substance. Since the identity of any substance is indifferent to any change, whatever change it undergoes or precipitates must involve a relation between it and other substances. The identity of substances is always prior to and indifferent to the causal relations among them.

By contrast, what is self-determined does not have a given, prior identity, residing in an essence to which its existence is united. Instead, freedom applies to a self that is what it determines itself to be. Accordingly, the changes it gives itself are not accidental or indifferent to its identity. Rather, new determinations that are self-determinations are constitutive of the autonomous identity of what gives itself its own character. Unlike substances, free entities undergo alterations that are not contingent upon relations to other entities.

---

5. For this reason, as Hegel observes, Spinoza inevitably fails to derive the attributes and modes of substance from its given identity. Spinoza can only point to them, just as Kant can only point to the categories of substance and actuality as gifts of Aristotelian logic. See Hegel, *Science of Logic*, 537–38.
6. See J. Melvin Woody, *Freedom's Embrace* (University Park: Pennsylvania State Press, 1998), 191–92.

The alterations pertaining to what is free are grounded in the self rather than in something external. They are not accidents but elements of the self-engendered character in which self-determination consists. The modal categories of possibility, actuality, and necessity here lose applicability, for they all depend upon the assumption of substance, where given essence retains its rule and actualization depends upon necessity, where change is contingent, that is, externally conditioned. Equally falling by the wayside are the relations of causality, in which external relations between substances cause all alteration.[7] We can characterize freedom no more by the categories of causality than by the modal categories of possibility, actuality, and necessity. Self-determination is not self-actualization nor, contra Kant, an uncaused causality. Moreover, once we recognize the subject to be a self-determined entity, we can no longer treat it as a substance, immaterial or otherwise, blindly governed by the modal categories of actuality.

Although the inability of the categories of actuality to accommodate freedom is evident, the fundamental difference between them and those of self-determination does not itself refute early modern philosophy's privileging of relations of substance, modality, and causality. What does is the self-elimination of the categories of actuality. It brings the entire Logic of Essence to internal collapse, ushering in the Logic of Self-Determined Determinacy, that is, the Logic of the Concept. Let us explore the itinerary, first laid out by Hegel, through which the categorial development of actuality frees us from the rule of necessity.

From Substance to Modality

How does substance, the immediate unity of essence and existence or of inner and outer, revert to the modal nexus of possibility, actuality, and necessity? Because substance is ultimately that which is because it is, its externality or manifestation is at one with its own power. Although substance is nothing but the manifestation of itself, it still has a manifestation, distinguishable but

---

7. As Hegel writes,

> We must note the *inadmissible application* of the relation of causality to relations of *physico-organic* and *spiritual life* [...] that which acts on a living being is independently determined, changed and transmuted by it, because the living thing does not let the cause come to its effect, that is, it sublates it as cause. [...] it is rather the nature of spirit, in a much higher sense than it is the character of the living thing in general, not to receive into itself another original entity, or not to let a cause continue itself into it but to break it off and to transmute it.

See Hegel, *Science of Logic*, 562.

relative to substance's being. Substance itself is absolute since, to begin with, it neither confronts anything other nor has any conditions of its own, but it has modes and attributes, that is, forms of manifestation and manifest determinations. They cannot owe their character to anything other than substance, but they can still be qualitatively different from one another as well as immersed in a network of mutual interdependence, all of which manifests nothing but the one and only absolute.

Unlike a mere whole, form, force, or what is inner, substance has a concrete given being with the power or conatus to posit its entire manifestation. The whole is immediately its parts, but as whole, in distinction from its parts, it is an empty inert shell. Form may order content, but without content of its own, form cannot appear. Force has nothing in itself apart from its expression. Inner has no determinate content different from what is outer. None of these forms of essence can account for the determinacies they mediate, which by default have an immediate subsistence of their own.[8] By contrast, substance, in virtue of its own essence, makes manifest what it is through an existence that amounts to none other than its own attributes (the absolute in its determinacies),[9] which comprise its mere manner or mode of being.[10] By running through its attributes and modes, substance proves itself to be the power to generate existence, which remains nothing but substance's own display.[11] That power renders existence immanent to substance, without, however, adding any new determination to the essence of substance.[12] The relation of substance to its self-manifestation thereby opens the terrain of actuality, which is the field of manifestation.[13] Here existence is no longer just the appearance of underlying conditions but rather the movement of its own actualization, whose conditions belong to itself.[14]

The self-manifesting movement of actuality is, at its start, none other than possibility.[15] The possible is what can be brought into existence by what not

---

8. See Hegel, *Science of Logic*, 533.
9. See Hegel, *Science of Logic*, 533.
10. See Hegel, *Science of Logic*, 534.
11. This power to generate existence is what allows Hegel to describe the absolute as both "absolute form," which generates what is only a "display of what it is," and "absolute content," whose "indifferent manifoldness" is "only *one* substantial identity." See Hegel, *Science of Logic*, 529–30.
12. As Hegel emphasizes, "the absolute does not *determine* itself," for it is an "absolute identity," which does not itself undergo any becoming. See Hegel, *Science of Logic*, 531.
13. "The actual is therefore manifestation." See Hegel, *Science of Logic*, 542.
14. See Hegel, *Science of Logic*, 541.
15. As Hegel notes, "Possibility is what is essential to reality, but in such a way that it is at the same time only a possibility." The manifestation of substance will entail the process in which possibility, actuality, and necessity unfold. See Hegel, *Logic*, §143, 202.

only is but has the power to make the possible exist, without acquiring any new determinacy of its own.[16] On the terrain of actuality, anything that exists is possible, for here existence is the manifestation of what has the power to exhibit itself.[17] The possible, *as* possible, however, does not yet have the existence that that power can confer. The possible is a *mere* possibility and, as such, its passage from possibility to actuality is contingent upon something existent that can bring it into being. Possibility thus brings with it contingency, for possibility depends upon the furnishing of the condition by which it can come into existence.[18] In order for possibility to be, but not yet be realized, what the possible is contingent upon must not exist and already wield its power to make the possible actual. Possibility and impossibility thus go together, since what is merely possible is no less impossible if its facilitating condition is absent.[19] This condition must itself be contingent, for if it were necessarily at hand and operative, possibility would have become actualized.[20] Possibility would then have given way to actuality, where what exists contains the condition for its own existence. Chance, or the accidentality of contingency, thus goes hand in hand with possibility.

Nonetheless, possibility as well as impossibility stand in relation to actuality, to that which exists without being merely hypothetical. What is actual determines what is possible or impossible. Still, possibility, as it first emerges through substance, is *formal* possibility insofar as it may or may not be actualized, depending upon what exists. Similarly, what is actual exercises a *formal* necessity, since its necessitation is contingent upon what happens to be actual.[21]

Nevertheless, for something to be *actually* possible, the conditions that enable it to become actual must be at hand. Otherwise, the possible has merely formal but no *real* possibility. Real possibility thus depends upon the presence of what brings the possible into existence. This enabling condition must be actual, rather than contingent. If it remains contingent, so too does

---

16. Insofar as actuality is the unity of inner and outer, possibility can be characterized as the "external inward." It lies within the existence of actuality but only as a posited still inward mode of manifestation. See Hegel, *Logic*, §143, 202.
17. See Hegel, *Science of Logic*, 542.
18. As Hegel puts it, "Possibility and Contingency are the two factors of Actuality." See Hegel, *Logic*, §145, 205. Contingency is the "unity of possibility and actuality," insofar as what is possible depends upon actuality for its possibility. See Hegel, *Science of Logic*, 545.
19. See Hegel, *Science of Logic*, 543–44.
20. As Hegel puts it, "the contingent has no ground because it is contingent and equally, it has a ground because it is contingent." See Hegel, *Science of Logic*, 545.
21. See Hegel, *Science of Logic*, 546.

the possibility whose actualization depends upon its presence. Real possibility thus rests upon a *real* actuality sufficient to bring it into existence.[22]

Then, however, possibility loses its defining distinction from actuality. The presence of real possibility's condition cannot fail to make it actual. What really is possible turns out really to be necessary. Possibility, provided with the actuality on which its real possibility rests, becomes the process of real necessity.[23]

Necessity is the relation whereby actuality, the basis of real possibility, converts possibility into necessitated existence. Nonetheless, the actuality by which possibility is real is, as such, the condition of that possibility, rather than of its own. Its own possibility is therefore contingent upon something else.[24] Consequently, real necessity itself involves contingency. Although real necessity makes actual what given actuality brings into existence, what is actual in the first place and what thereby is necessitated are both themselves contingent. Real necessity is therefore *relative*.[25]

It should be no surprise that Kant treats the modal categories of possibility, actuality, and necessity as adding nothing to the concept of an object. Rather, the modal categories merely indicate the purely subjective relation of the object to the faculties of empirical cognition. This subjective formality of Kantian modality reflects how the manifestation of substance in no way adds to its antecedent essence.[26] The manifestation is contingent and the nexus of modality exhibits how whatever arises is conditioned by what is given. Although given actuality necessitates all alteration, no given phenomena can have a necessary existence of its own. The existence of everything given is equally contingent upon antecedent conditions.

The appeal to logics of possible worlds exhibits a similar subjection to contingent necessity. As an all-encompassing modality representation, "possible worlds" logics should properly refer to possible universes, not just to worlds within an encompassing universe. Since possible universes can have within themselves nothing sufficient to make them actual, they must depend upon a condition outside of nature to make them possible in their entirety. The logic of "possible worlds" thus requires invoking something like a divine creator, lying beyond time and space. Of course, if such an all-powerful Creator is perfect, the one and only possible universe that the Creator can will into being

---

22. See Hegel, *Science of Logic*, 546.
23. See Hegel, *Science of Logic*, 549.
24. See Hegel, *Science of Logic*, 547.
25. See Hegel, *Science of Logic*, 549.
26. Hegel notes this in the *Encyclopedia Logic* in the Remark to §143, 202–3, referring to Kant's *Critique of Pure Reason*, B266.

is the best of all possible universes. Then, its possibility becomes a real possibility, whereby the "best" universe is no longer merely possible but necessary, forfeiting all comparative ranking.[27] Nonetheless, the one and only universe will still contain contingency in conjunction with its necessity.

From Modality to Causality

The contingency tied to necessity entails that the actuality necessitating the coming into existence of what is possible is itself conditioned by another actuality. This cannot be otherwise, since given substance remains the underlying foundation of whatever alterations pass from possibility to actuality. As Woody points out, the framework of substance mandates that successive states of the same substance cannot be in a relation of cause and effect, for what happens to substance must be indifferent to its identity, which its own prior essence mandates. Although substance is itself *"being* that is *because* it is,"[28] whatever alterations a substance undergoes must be accidents that, as such, leave its identity intact. Alterations, as accidents, must have their source in something external that acts upon a substance, generating alterations indifferent to its identity. The identity of the cause in no way determines its specific efficacy or the character of the accident it conditions. Causality, like the necessity of actuality, is therefore blind.

The resulting necessitation, arising from substance and the flux of accidents,[29] consists in the relation of cause and effect. This causal relation is formal insofar as whatever necessity is manifest in the effect is already present in the cause. Since the effect manifests nothing than the manifestation of the power of the cause, what content figures as cause is simply repeated in the effect.[30]

Nonetheless, since neither the efficacy of the cause nor the alteration in which the effect consists are rooted in the essence of substance, the causal

---

27. Michael B. Foster points this out in highlighting the incoherence of Leibniz' theodicy. See Michael B. Foster, "Christian Theology and Modern Science of Nature," Part II, *Mind*, vol. 45, no. 177 (January 1936), footnote 1, 20.
28. Hegel, *Science of Logic*, 555.
29. Hegel introduces the relation of substance and accident through the development of "Absolute Necessity," in which the unity of necessity and contingency, arising from the process of real possibility, real actuality, and real necessity, renders necessity such that "that which is simply necessary only *is* because it *is.*" Because the flux of accidents has no independent being but reflects the absolute necessity of substance, substance relates to itself in that flux and, as therein existing for itself, becomes the causal relation of substances to one another. See Hegel, *Science of Logic*, 552, 556–57.
30. Hegel, *Science of Logic*, 560.

relation involves an interaction of substances through their contingent accidents, whose occasion is external.

Thus arises the determinate causal relation of one substance to another, in which, to begin with, one substance figures as active and the other as passive.[31] The active substance causes alterations in the passive substance, which count as the contingent effects of the cause.

Since alterations are accidents, the causal efficacy of an active substance cannot lie in its essence any more than the effects can be intrinsic to the essence of the passive substance. Unlike an end, whose content carries over into its realization, the cause has no essential connection to its effect. The causality of the active substance is not a feature of its own conatus, whereby it upholds its own identity as a unity of essence and existence. Instead, the substance's active role is itself contingent upon the efficacy of another substance, whose causal power has the same blind contingent character. Similarly, whatever alteration the passive substance incurs can serve as a contingent efficacy by which it operates as an active substance upon some other substance. In this way, the relation of substances becomes an infinite network of disseminating cause and effect relations, where every substance functions both as active to some other substance and passive to yet another.[32] In these relations, each substance figures as both cause and effect, but not to one and the same other substance. Substance's relation as active produces an effect in another substance that is different from the substance to which it relates as passive.[33]

The causal network of substances concretely develops the necessity intertwining possibility and actuality. The dual passive and active roles of each substance, however, become operative with respect to the same substance, transforming the disseminating causal nexus into a relationship of reciprocity, with decisive ramifications for the entire fate of substance and necessity.

From Causality to Freedom

What leads from the nexus of causality to reciprocity is how the active role of each substance depends upon the passive role of its counterparts. To be a cause, the active substance must posit an effect in the passive substance. By undergoing an effect, the passive substance is the enabling condition of the efficacy of its active counterpart. With respect to its counterpart, the passive

---

31. The causal relation is no longer formal but determinate insofar as the relation of active and passive substance renders each a cause, contrasted with its counterpart in a relation of action and reaction. See Hegel, *Science of Logic*, 568.
32. See Hegel, *Science of Logic*, 564.
33. See Hegel, *Science of Logic*, 565.

substance thus acts as an active substance, making the erstwhile active substance take on its causal role. The efficacy of the active substance is thereby the effect of the reaction of the passive substance, which exhibits causal efficacy to the same substance to which it serves as an effect. Unlike the infinitely disseminating causal nexus, where each substance figures as cause and effect to different substances, each substance now is both active and passive to the same substance. As a result, causal interaction turns into a relation of reciprocity, where one substance is both cause and effect of another, which plays the same dual roles of active and passive to it in return.[34]

Reciprocity is a relation of two substances in which, when one is active, it is efficacious to its counterpart in the latter's role as passive, while equally being passive to its counterpart in its role as active. Both substances simultaneously figure in both capacities, where the passivity and activity of each tie themselves respectively to the complementary roles of its counterpart.

This relationship cannot sustain itself, however. The opposition of positive and negative foreshadows on a simpler plane what happens to reciprocity. Positive and negative went to ground because although they are opposites of one another, they relate to one another in exactly the same way. Each is the essential counterpart of its opposite, attracting its opposite and repelling what is like itself. Which factor is negative and which is positive is a matter of utter indifference. Consequently, their relationship undermines its constitutive opposition and collapses into a ground/grounded relation, where the same content operates as positor and posited. In reciprocity, the more complicated relation of mutually causal substances exhibits an analogous collapse. Since each substance is both cause and effect in precisely the same way, there is no way to differentiate them from one another. In being both cause and effect of its counterpart, each substance ends up being cause and effect of itself. The entire distinction between determiner and determined is thereby undermined, for what determines and what is determined can no longer be differentiated. Their equalization extinguishes the externality of necessitation, since what is determined is now determined by itself. The resulting self-determination also supersedes the given determinacy of substance, which serves as the absolute basis of the modal categories and the causal relations they yield. Once determination is self-determination, what determines has no essential given identity. It now first obtains its identity through what it determines itself to be. Instead of being a substance, it has become a subject.

Through the self-elimination of reciprocity, whereby what determines *is* what is determined, the two-tiered domain of essence, of determined determinacy, gives way to the logic of freedom, of self-determination. Hegel can

---

34. See Hegel, *Science of Logic*, 566–69.

call this categorial domain the logic of the concept because the concept, or the universal as such, is neither a quality nor an essence but a self-determining subject.

Self-Determination and the Concept

The universal does not have its determination in contrast to something other, like the qualitative categories of the Logic of Being. The particular and the individual do not confront the universal as alien factors, given independently of its unity, as nominalists and "Platonists"[35] both contend. The universal cannot be what it is unless it participates in the particular and equally involves individuality. This is because particulars will collapse into one and forfeit their differentiation from the universal unless they are distinguished from one another as individuals. Further, individuality cannot be unique unless it has a unity encompassing its particularity, as universality provides. Only then does individuality owe its determinate content to itself. The contrast of something and other can never achieve individuation, since something and other are each something as well as the other of their counterpart, rendering them indistinguishable. Although something ends up relating to itself, making it one, it is not thereby an individual. The self-related being of the one has no particular determinacy by which it could be distinguished from any other one. By contrast, the universal's immanent development exhibits how individuation and self-determination go hand in hand. By being both particular and individual, the universal has the dynamic identity by which it is what it determines itself to be: a self-determined determinacy, without further qualification.

Accordingly, we must also refrain from treating the universal as an essence, reflected in secondary appearances, which the ancient theory of forms tends to do.[36] Unlike any type of two-tiered determination, from the positor of illusory being through substance, the universal does not have any given identity prior to its own particularization. It does not actualize what is antecedently determined to be possible and thereby exhibit necessity. By participating in its own particularization, the universal makes itself what it is, while equally constituting individuality, which is in and through itself. No form of essence can provide for individuation because what determines a determined determinacy can just as well posit another without altering its own prior identity. Just as a ground can ground indefinitely many factors, so a whole can have multiple parts, just as a cause can have indefinitely manifold effects.

---

35. Although some of Plato's dialogues contain expressions of this view, Plato also presents its refutation in the *Parmenides*.
36. The theory of forms, attributed to Plato, tends to construe the universal as an essence.

If actuality and modal logic reigned supreme, thought could not have the autonomy of the concept. Necessity would instead rule thinking, canceling any possible normativity for reason. Thought could neither liberate itself from the hold of the given, nor exhibit the self-responsibility of accounting for its determinations through its own activity. Whatever thinking might actualize would be a possibility mandated by the necessity of given substance, whose rule could never be questioned nor legitimated. Under the sway of blind necessity, actuality would leave no place for teleology, the self-activity of life, the independence of beauty, or the free achievement of right and truth.

Insofar as substance yields the modal relations of possibility, actuality, and necessity, these give rise to causality, and causality develops into reciprocity, which renders determiner and determined indistinguishable, neither reason nor being can remain entrapped by the limits of actuality. The path that Hegel has trailblazed by thinking through the Logic of Essence and its transition to the Logic of the Concept systematically refutes the dogmas of early modern philosophers and their contemporary epigones.

Free at last!

Chapter 6

TIME AND REASON

The Inscrutable Ubiquity of Time

Time is inescapable, whether we turn within or without. Nothing in the material universe can evade the hold of temporality, nor can anything in the inner sanctum of our mental life fall beyond its reach. Whatever endures in nature or mind must do so through time, just as whatever comes and goes must find its place in temporality. Whether real or imagined, no factor we consider can avoid possessing a temporal determination of its own or a temporal site in our consideration.

Just as ubiquitous are all the phases and modes that time is always recognized to have. Past, present, and future continually present themselves in everything outer and inner, just as do simultaneity, duration, and succession. Every experience incessantly confronts us with every phase and all the basic modes of time. It matters not whether we observe our environment, our bodies, or psychological phenomena—nowhere and never are the full coterie of temporal determinations absent.

Nonetheless, as ubiquitous and familiar as they are, every one of time's phases and modes seems to lack any confirmable reality and to defy any rational account. The being of past, present, and future disappears as soon as it is considered. What is past is no longer, what is future is not yet, and the being of the present instantaneously slips into the nonexistence of the past, while an equally ephemeral moment enters from the future only to follow the immediate demise of its predecessor. No interval can be found between past and present and future, for each has nothing to hold off the supplanting of the future by the present and the present by the past.

The same lack of being seems to plague the modes of time, which might otherwise appear to surmount the ephemeral phasing of past, present, and future. Simultaneity offers the relation of distinguishable factors at the same time, be they spatially or mentally distinct. Yet if the present has no more being than nothingness due to its immediate slippage into the past, how can any simultaneous factors have any reality of their own, let alone a real relation? If their coeval being is at an instant of no temporal breadth, how can their presence be distinguished from their absence? Since the moment they are, they vanish, their simultaneity has no more reality than that of any now, everyone of which instantly gives way to another no more separable from its own disappearance.

The succession of time might seem to range over the rise and fall of all instants, yet how can their series retain any reality if the moments in which it consists themselves have no determinate extent? Every present is indistinguishable from every other, immediately coming from the future and just as immediately falling into the past. If simultaneity and the succession of time cannot contain anything that ever has an enduring being, how can duration itself retain reality? Whatever is from one moment to the next seems condemned by time to never have a presence that does not immediately disappear.

In every phase and every mode the same paradox arises: the being of time and the being of everything in time cannot be kept apart from its own non-being. This seems to leave all aspects of time beyond any rational account, since they all equally are and are not,[1] contradicting the supposedly irrefutable first principle of reason that, to quote Aristotle's original formulation, "the same attribute cannot at the same time belong and not belong to the same subject in the same respect."[2] Compounding the problem is that if the phases and modes of time both are and are not, how can any attribute belong to a subject at some time in some respect without equally not belonging to it? Time seems to leave reason's allegedly most certain principle teetering on the edge of collapse.

These difficulties have led many thinkers to locate the reality and comprehensibility of the phases and modes of time in something else. On the one hand, those who retain faith in the external reality of time explain temporality in terms of motion. On the other hand, those who seek the reality of time in the inwardness of mind explain temporality in psychological process.

The Attempt to Root Time in Motion

The external motion invoked to explain time need not be limited to locomotion, where bodies change their position in space over time. More generally,

---

1. Sextus Empiricus exposes all these difficulties in Chapter XIX, "Concerning Time" of Book III, 136–50, of his *Outlines of Pyrrhonism*. See Sextus Empiricus, *Outlines of Pyrrhonism*, trans. R. G. Bury (Cambridge, MA: Harvard University Press, 1933), 419–27.
2. Aristotle, *Metaphysics*, Book IV, Chapter 3, 1005b19–20 in Aristotle, *The Complete Works Volume Two*, ed. Jonathan Barnes (Princeton, NJ: Princeton University Press, 1984), 1588.

the motion enlisted can involve any physical process that occurs with some commensurate succession, such as the oscillations of electromagnetic radiation, the decay of atomic particles, the dissipation of order in entropy, or biological cycles. If there is to be one absolute time, then the privileged change by which time is determined must count as the "standard motion" by which all others are measured. The heavenly orbit of the stars around earth could serve this role to the ancient Greeks, since everyone could view that same allegedly constant "standard motion" and find there a common reality for time. For Einstein, the alleged constancy of the speed of light precludes any such common "standard motion" insofar as observers in different inertial systems encounter dilations of time as their relative motion approaches the speed of light. Nonetheless, time still is determined for each such observer by the privileged motion of something serving as a clock, whether the clock in question exhibits the analogue continuity of locomotion or the digital succession of quantum leaps.[3]

For physicists from Ptolemy to Einstein, some motion has had to be invoked to explain time, for otherwise no reality or account of time seemed possible. Nonetheless, all their ploys have the obvious pitfall of explaining time by something whose own account includes time. Motion, after all, is a change of some physical process over time. No standard motion or any constant speed of light can constitute the reality of time for time is itself a prerequisite component of their very being. Whether any motion is standard or constant presupposes that its change be uniform, which can only be established by comparing it to some independently given realization of time. Motion may be used to measure time, but only insofar as time is an independent factor with an antecedent being of its own.

Moreover, any motion involving material substance presupposes some enduring matter that fills space. Extension cannot be identified with matter without falling into Descartes' befuddlement of eliminating empty space, rendering differences in density inexplicable and turning all motion into groundless vortexes.[4] The material occupation of space must instead be a dynamic capacity to exert moving forces of repulsion and attraction, enabling a body to fill space to the exclusion of other entities. Both repulsion and

---

3. Eva Brann describes Einstein as replacing the cosmic clock of Plato's *Timaeus*, where the cosmos in its motion *is* the clock, with the local artificial clocks of observers in different inertial coordinate systems. See Eva Brann, *What, Then, Is Time?* (Lanham, MD: Rowman & Littlefield, 1999), 7.
4. See Sections 1–25 of Part Two of Descartes' *Principles of Philosophy*, in Rene Descartes, *The Philosophical Writings of Descartes, Volume I*, trans. John Cottingham, Robert Stoothoff, and Dugald Murdoch (Cambridge, UK: Cambridge University Press, 1985), 223–33.

attraction must be combined, for repulsion alone will instantaneously disperse all matter to infinity, whereas attraction by itself will instantaneously reduce all matter to a point. By exerting moving force, however, matter cannot ground time, for matter cannot involve attraction and repulsion without including time as its determinant, leaving real motion once more predicated upon, rather than constituting time.

The Attempt to Root Time in Mind

In the face of perplexity of time's own phases and modes, the obvious circularity of using motion and matter to account for time leaves no apparent option other than removing time from the external universe and placing it in the nonspatial inwardness of mind. Augustine paves the way by locating the being of past, present, and future in the psychological processes of memory, intuition, and expectation.[5] Newton similarly anchors the absolute reality of time in the sensorium of the divine creator of nature, on the basis of which motion can occur.[6] Kant, who transfers the governance of nature from God to self-consciousness, grounds time as a form of pure intuition by which all our sensible intuitions are ordered.[7] In all these maneuvers, the phases and modes of time are rooted in mental processes, be they Divine or mortal.

Although mind may temporally order its mental contents, this does not itself locate the being of time exclusively in those mental processes. If mind produced temporality without qualification, its constituting process could not itself be temporal, for mind's operation would generate time and thereby be the source rather than an object of time determination. Further, if mind's time-generating process were rooted in individual finite consciousness, any unified intersubjective reality becomes problematic. Only if all other minds were themselves constituted by individual consciousness could their time orderings be jointly governed. Then, however, those other minds would really only be constituted objects, rather than constituting subjects, leaving the finitude of the sole time-constituting consciousness in question.

Undermining any attempt to make mind constitutive of time is how the mental process by which time becomes an object of apprehension involves

---

5. Saint Augustine, *Confessions* (Harmondsworth: Penguin Books, 1979), Book XI, §27–28, 275–78.
6. See Isaac Newton, *Opticks* (Amherst, NY: Prometheus Books, 2003), Book Three, Part I, 403.
7. Immanuel Kant, *Critique of Pure Reason*, trans. Paul Guyer and Allen W. Wood (Cambridge, UK: Cambridge University Press, 1998), A30–32/B46–48, 162–63, 178–79.

a successive ordering that itself proceeds in time. When Augustine invokes the operations of memory, intuition, and expectation, these mental functions proceed in temporal sequences, without which their very distinction collapses. Memory must follow intuition, just as expectation must follow certain memories and intuitions, be simultaneous with others, and precede still more that will arise later.[8] Newton's divine sensorium can hardly constitute time without providing an enduring support. Similarly, Kant's pure intuition of time can hardly generate time's phases and modes without an ensuing mental activity that takes its own time.

Compounding the untenability of any mental constitution of time is the problem of upholding a purely immaterial conception of mind. Without being embodied *in* space and time, how can any mind individuate itself and be the exclusive subject of all its mental contents and modifications? A mere thought of an "I" that accompanies all its representations is no different than any other "I," leaving the individual ownership of mental contents in question. Kant himself can hardly exclude the spatiotemporal embodiment of self-consciousness from creeping into his account of the constitution of temporal awareness. In his famous "Refutation of Idealism" in the *Critique of Pure Reason* he argues that there can be no awareness of the temporal flow of representations unless consciousness can be aware of some enduring spatial objectivity to provide for their temporal continuity.[9] Yet, to confront any determinate spatial objectivity, consciousness must do so from a spatially situated vantage point. That self-consciousness has its own embodied place equally underlies Kant's accounts of the modes of time in the "Analogies of Experience." Kant there maintains that consciousness cannot be aware of any objective temporal sequence unless it can observe necessary motion. As his example of a boat flowing downstream indicates, no motion can be observed without the observer having a determinate location.[10] Similarly, when Kant shows how consciousness of simultaneity rests upon the order indifference with which objects are observed, this depends upon the observer not only being at a determinate location but altering its spatial orientation in time, so as to observe what is present whether first turning left to right or right to left.[11] Consciousness of objective duration equally presupposes the spatiotemporal embodiment of consciousness, for awareness of any conservation of matter through time depends upon observing how mass and force are exhibited in the motions

---

8. Saint Augustine, *Confessions*, Book XI, §27–28, 275–78.
9. See Kant, *Critique of Pure Reason*, B274–279, 326–29.
10. Kant, *Critique of Pure Reason*, A192/B237, 307.
11. Kant, *Critique of Pure Reason*, A211/B257–258, 316–17.

of objects, which once more presupposes a spatiotemporal location of the observer.[12]

From Space to Time

That mind as well as material motion presuppose rather than constitute both space and time does not leave time an utterly groundless being. As every account of physical and mental activity suggests, time goes hand in hand with space. This does not render space and time equally primordial immaterial natural abstractions. Neither space nor time can rest upon any material factor, since matter itself presupposes them both. Space, however, has rudimentary being without time, whereas time cannot be without space.

Space comprises the most elementary factor of nature because of this asymmetrical relation to time. Nothing in nature can be prior to space because every further natural entity, time included, involves spatial determination. By itself, space is that self-external totality whose every part has others outside itself.[13] This ubiquitous self-externality renders space completely continuous and uniform in its self-dispersion. Every part of space stands in the same relation to every other. All are in the same position of having other parts of space beyond themselves. Containing no further differentiation that can surmount the immediate difference and identity of every part of space, space by itself is absolute in its unbounded, unrelieved, continuous diffusion. Only with the further concretion of nature into a material universe of matter in motion can and do relative spaces emerge.

What makes time the first feature of nature to supervene upon space is the very self-externality of extension. Space is other to itself within itself. Space cannot help but contain its own negation in the point. The point, however, inescapably has itself outside itself, just like every part of space. The point has another where it begins and ends, and this point gives way to another, forming a line. The line, like the point, cannot fail to have itself outside itself,

---

12. Kant, *Critique of Pure Reason*, A204–206/B250–251, 313.
13. Hegel accordingly regards the self-externality of space to constitute the most minimal nonlogical determination. He regards it to result from nothing other than the completed self-development of logic, which begins with indeterminacy and concludes with the Absolute Idea, which unites concept and objectivity in a process whose conceptualization of itself is its own complete constitution. Once this occurs, the concluded logical development takes on the form of being, wherein it can be said to be external to its own concluded determination. Hegel regards this as the systematic, nonarbitrary move from logical determinacy to nonlogical determinacy, where space provides the point of departure included in all subsequent developments of the total reality of nature and spirit.

with another line alongside it no different from itself. That line, however, has another alongside it as well, such that just as the point gives way to an infinity of points comprising a line, so the line gives way to an infinity of lines comprising a plane. The self-externality of the point and the line applies just as much to the plane, for the plane has another where it ends, which just as much has beyond itself a plane no different from itself. In these extending continuities of points, lines, and now planes, space disperses into its infinite volume of three dimensions, each of which is indistinguishable from its counterparts.

Whereas the self-externality of point, line, and plane falls within space, the self-externality of the infinite volume of space has nowhere else to go. In order for the infinity of extension to retain its constitutive character of being self-external, the totality of space must be other to itself and the only way this can occur is for that totality to be at one time and then at another. Time is this succession consisting in nothing but the process by which the totality of space retains its self-externality, being present and then being immediately displaced by itself. Each moment of time is a determination of spatial totality external to every other determination of spatial totality. Since space has no further spatial distinction by which its totalities can be distinguished, the moments of time are just as different as identical. Each now is the totality of space, with nothing separating it from the next presence of the totality of space. Due to this indistinguishability of each self-externality of spatial totality, time presents a becoming, where the being of space is just as much its nonbeing, just as its nonbeing is just as much its being. The ceasing to be of the spatial totality is the immediate passage of the present into the past, whereas the coming to be of the spatial totality is the immediate passage of the future into the present.[14]

The Concrete Material Determination of Space–Time

In the absence of any more concrete natural factors, such as matter in motion or electromagnetic energy and electrically charged matter, space and time have nothing by which points in space and moments of time can be distinguished. Nothing is at hand by which any absolute space or time can be differentiated from any relative space and time. Just as every point, line, and plane has others outside no different from itself, so every moment in time is no different than any other in its relation to past, present, and future. Nonetheless, without

---

14. Hegel develops all of the preceding arguments concerning the primacy and character of space and how time emerges from space in §254–59 of his *Philosophy of Nature*. See G. W. F. Hegel, *Part Two of the Encyclopaedia of the Philosophical Sciences (1830)*, trans. A. V. Miller (Oxford: Oxford University Press, 1970), 28–40.

space and time having this abstract being, neither matter nor motion nor electromagnetic physical processes can be or be conceived.

The primacy of space over time and of space and time over motion, matter, and physical electromagnetic process cannot consist in any determinate temporal sequence, as if there were a beginning stage in time in which matter in motion was absent. Space and time may be without motion and matter, but that immaterial being has no determinate temporal location, since every empty now, as well as every empty past, present, and future, is just as indistinguishable as every empty here and there. Only with moving bodies does nature possess sufficiently concrete factors with which to exhibit any determinate measures of space and time, let alone any determinate spatiotemporal frameworks that could be relative to one another.

Space and time may be equally continuous in the externalities of their respective parts, with moments in time falling beyond one another in as uninterrupted a becoming as the dispersion of points in space. Nonetheless, their joint presence in the flow of time comprises the space–time differentiation of places. These are each a distinct here *and* now, distinguished from others by both its spatial and temporal determination. Since, however, every here and every now has nothing to distinguish it from any other, each here and now is in continuity with its counterparts. This engenders the formal determination of motion insofar as every here can just as well be at another moment in time, allowing the self-externality of space to present itself as a passage of time, whereas every now can equally be at a different here, allowing the self-externality of time to present itself as a passage through space. The becoming of time thereby proceeds as motion, with past, present, and future unfolding as a spatiotemporal arrow of time.

This motion is completely formal for it involves nothing material that could count as an abiding individual subject of motion. The passage of one here to another here over time and of one now to another now through space is completely indistinguishable from any other motion since here's and now's are all in the same relation to empty space and to the past, present, and future. The only way any motion can be distinguished from any other is if its trajectory has an occupant that excludes other occupants from its here's and now's.[15]

---

15. Hegel develops all the preceding aspects of place and formal motion in §260–61 of his *Philosophy of Nature*. In §260 he explains,

> Space is within itself the contradiction of indifferent asunderness and differenceless continuity, the pure negativity of itself, and the *transition, first of all into time*. Similarly, time is the immediate collapse into indifference, into undifferentiated asunderness of space, because its opposed moments which are held together in unity, immediately sublate themselves. In this way, the *negative* determination

The constitution of matter is an insoluble mystery so long as one commits the obvious question-begging of seeking to generate matter from out of material factors. Instead, matter must be constituted from immaterial natural factors and the only such factors available are space, time, the place of space–time, and the formal motion through empty space–time.

The dynamic constitution of matter from the moving forces of repulsion and attraction accomplishes just such a nonmaterial derivation of matter. What minimally distinguishes matter from empty space is that it excludes other matter from a determinate extended place over a determinate period of time. Unless matter extends beyond a point to occupy some bounded extension, it can have no spatial reality. On the other hand, this determinate spatial reality must subsist beyond a mere moment, for a now is just as much present as vanishing. Nothing can determinably *be* material unless it occupies a determinate extension, be it stationary or mobile, over a determinate period of time. Otherwise, a matter's presence is indistinguishable from its absence. What makes such occupation more than an empty receptacle is that it be comprised of the complementary attractive and repelling moving forces that enable an exclusive natural entity to fill some location over time and maintain that occupation over the trajectory of a determinate motion. To constitute matter, attraction and repulsion cannot be thought of, as Kant tends to do in his *Metaphysical Foundations of Nature*, in the terms of mechanics, where what are attracted and repelled are already constituted bodies.[16] To avoid this question-begging, the matter-constituting attraction and repulsion must be thought of

---

> in space, the exclusive point, no longer only implicitly [or in itself] conforms to the Notion, but is posited and concrete within itself, through the total negativity which is time; the point, as thus concrete is *Place*. (Hegel, *Philosophy of Nature*, 40)

In §261 he writes,

> Place, as this posited identity of space and time is equally, at first, the posited contradiction which space and time are each in themselves. Place is spatial, and therefore indifferent, *singularity*; and it is this only as a *spatial Now*, as time, so that place is immediately indifferent towards itself as *this* place, is external to itself, the negation of itself, and is *another place*. This vanishing and self-regeneration of space in time and of time in space, a process in which time posits itself spatially as *place*, but in which place, too, as indifferent spatiality, is immediately posited as *temporal*: this is *Motion*. (Hegel, *Philosophy of Nature*, 41)

16. Kant commits this blunder in Explication 2 of his *Metaphysical Foundations of Natural Science*, writing,

> *Attractive force* is that moving force by which a matter can be the cause of the approach of others to it (or, what is the same, by which it resists the removal of others from it). *Repulsive force* is that by which a matter can be the cause of others removing themselves from it (or what is the same, by which it resists the approach of others to it).

as a force field that fills a determinate space over time, with the correlation of its own moving forces keeping each from separately collapsing into a point or dispersing to infinity. Only on the basis of that dynamic filling of space can there be distinct bodies to interact through gravitational attraction and the inertial motions of mechanics.[17]

The origination of matter obviously cannot be due to any material cause, nor can the number and position of bodies be derived from the continuous dispersions of space and time. Where matter is located and how many bodies there may be is inherently contingent and only upon the basis of that natural contingency do the workings of gravitational force have an opportunity to further order what is left undetermined by the elementary being of matter. These contingencies bring with them the emergence of relative inertial frameworks, but without yet providing the material resources for relativity theory. This occurs only once matter involves not just dynamic occupancy of space but the physical differentiations of polar electrical charges. On this basis, electromagnetic and nuclear processes can bring further physical dynamics into play, which determine not only the number, size, mass, and movements of bodies but also their atomic and molecular structures. Then light can become a factor in the concrete determination of space and time.

The Psychological and Historical Determinations of Time

The psychological determination of time operates with all of these physical processes at hand, complemented by the generation of organic from inorganic process and the emergence of animal from plant life. Just as it is folly to conceive mind as immaterial, it is folly to restrict the psychological reality of time to rational animals. The very nature of animal metabolism involves an apprehension of temporality. Unlike the continuous photosynthesis and osmotic absorptions of plants, the satisfaction of animal need transpires over an interval of space and time, where the objects of sustenance must be located from afar and the animal must motivate itself to move to them and break them down into a form that can be metabolized. All this requires an intervening effort of self-motion, where perception at a distance, desire-driven urge, and

---

See Immanuel Kant, *Metaphysical Foundations of Natural Science*, ed. Michael Friedman (Cambridge: Cambridge University Press, 2004), 35 [498]. Kant's misconception is explicitly criticized by Hegel in the Remark to §262 of the *Philosophy of Nature* (Hegel, *Philosophy of Nature*, 45).

17. Hegel sketches out an argument of this sort in the Remark to §261 in his *Philosophy of Nature* (Hegel, *Philosophy of Nature*, 41–42).

motility all operate together in function of spatiotemporal awareness and orientation.[18]

What rational intelligence adds to time awareness is the second nature of historical process, where time's arrow supplements its physical and biological clocks with cultural becoming. Insofar as all conventions have a contingent and particular scope, the periodization of history can never be genuinely universal. Even on our lonely planet, it is only when a culture has made itself global that history can become a unified process with a unified calendar. This can occur when institutions have arisen that have no parochial roots but are instead conventions of self-determination that, as such, are universal in character, rather than conditioned by any particular foundations. These institutions achieve the global reach to which their universal freedoms are fit through colonialism, imperialism, revolution, and postcolonial emancipation.[19] Thereby all the isolated formations of civilization become absorbed into a single all-encompassing development, building a world-historical time. We earthlings may then share our historical temporality, but that framework is itself but a fleeting interval among innumerable other equally transient planetary histories occurring somewhere far, far away amidst the cycles of solar births and deaths.

To comprehend any of this requires freeing our reason from the all too rampant dogma that thought is empty and analytic, bound by the principle of non-contradiction, and thereby incapable of generating any new content of its own. Time challenges us to repudiate such irrationality, which degrades reason into a formal tool for confirming the consistency of given terms. Time never ceases upending such analytic identity, for every moment of temporal becoming both is and is not. Once we grasp this, we know that philosophy is not a vain enterprise, for our thinking can be pregnant with content. If we can think time, we can conceive universals that particularize themselves, remaining self-identical in their differentiation. Every type of universal exhibits this identity of identity and difference, for the encompassing unity of any universal requires a particularization to be at one with itself. No abstract universal can be a common mark without inhering in particulars, any more than a class can retain any extension without particular members to incorporate. In every case, these particulars must be distinguished from one another as individuals

---

18. Hans Jonas gives a detailed account of these distinguishing aspects of animal metabolism in the essay, "To Move and to Feel: On the Animal Soul," in Hans Jonas, *The Phenomenon of Life: Toward a Philosophical Biology* (Evanston, IL: Northwestern University Press, 1966), 99–107.
19. For a more detailed account of the nature of this globalization, see Richard Dien Winfield, *Modernity, Religion, and the War on Terror* (Aldershot, UK: Ashgate, 2007), 69–92.

in order to retain the plurality on which their difference from the universal depends. The universal is thus inherently tied to both particularity and individuality. This is what allows thought to be autonomous, for self-determination combines universality, particularity, and individuality. To be determined without losing itself in otherness, the self must exhibit universality, pervading all its determinations, which must thus both particularize and individuate it. Precisely because the logic of universality is at one with the logic of self-determination, the conceptual determination of reason can wield a freedom by which thought is synthetic and analytic at once. Unlike the formal thinking of deductive calculation, which depends upon external content to manipulate according to given algorithms, pure reason is synthetic by generating new determinations and analytic by remaining within the unity of the concrete universality of autonomous thought. This may be a conceptual self-development, completely atemporal given the absence of spatial externality. Nonetheless, we have its natural analogue in the self-differentiation of time, which we cannot evade. The call of autonomous reason is ever ticking away.

Chapter 7

HEGEL AND THE PROBLEM OF CONSCIOUSNESS

Philosophy and the Opposition of Consciousness

Hegel announces in the introduction to his *Science of Logic* that the opposition of consciousness bars the way to philosophy and must be overcome.[1] This is because consciousness treats its mental content as an opposing objectivity from whose given material mind must fill itself in order to arrive at knowledge. If knowing is such as to always confront the given as the underlying standard of truth, it remains doubly conditioned. Such oppositional cognition is relative to the predetermined content that provides it with a determinate subject matter and it is relative to the method or thinking with which it addresses its topic. Since the subject matter is something given confronting knowing, it is different from the cognition employed in its investigation. Such investigation can never account for the knowing it uses, since it always addresses something distinct from how it knows. Accordingly, such investigation must presuppose both the given content of its subject matter and the method by which it is addressed. Philosophy can do neither without forsaking truth for opinion. Therefore, Hegel recognizes, philosophy must abandon confronting a given opposing its cognition and begin without any determinate claims about knowing and the object of knowing.

To do so, philosophy must commence in the element of logic, which overcomes the opposition of consciousness by thinking thinking, where the difference between knowing and its object is eliminated. Logical investigation may seem to start with the preconception of self-thinking thought, but this cannot have any predetermined form or content. Logical investigation must begin without any given procedure or topic, since the logical thinking that is both the method and topic of logical science must be established through the completion of logical inquiry, not taken for granted. At the outset, logical investigation, as well as philosophy itself, is, Hegel notes, but an empty word.[2]

---

1. G. W. F. Hegel, *Science of Logic*, trans. A. V. Miller (New York: Humanities Press, 1976), 45.
2. Hegel, *Science of Logic*, 78.

Freeing knowing from confrontation with the given, logic's overcoming of the opposition of consciousness inaugurates presuppositionless philosophy.

Any failure to begin inquiry without eliminating the difference between knowing and its object falls into the dilemma of foundational justification, which grounds normative validity in a privileged factor that confers truth, right, or beauty on something different from itself. That privileged foundation cannot meet its own validation standard unless it grounds itself and eliminates the difference between what confers and what possesses validity, the difference defining foundational justification. Philosophy, which can genuinely commence only by overcoming of the opposition of consciousness, operates without foundations precisely by making an absolute beginning where neither knowing nor its object has any given determinacy, let alone any that would distinguish them from one another.

Insofar as the oppositional cognition of consciousness involves confrontation with the given, if consciousness is identified with knowing in general and thereby rendered the universal mode of awareness, philosophy is precluded. The dual identification of consciousness with cognition and mind has been the fatal dogma crippling modern epistemology and modern philosophical psychology and Hegel provides its largely ignored remedy.

Hegel recognizes that overcoming the opposition of consciousness and the dogma that absolutizes it is precisely what allows for a systematic account of consciousness. Doing philosophy without foundations establishes that neither consciousness nor any other given factor can ground knowing and have any epistemological significance for philosophical investigation. The philosophy of mind therefore cannot play any juridical role with regard to knowledge. Nevertheless, the philosophy of mind does and must provide the psychological enabling conditions for philosophical cognition, including the valid conception of consciousness. To the extent that consciousness is the psychological configuration that treats its mental content as an opposing objectivity confronting awareness, consciousness cannot be the exclusive form of mind. Rather, the philosophy of mind must show how there is a theoretical intelligence that can be aware of its own mental content as being not just objective but subjective as well. Only then can mind be aware of language and theorize, forming mental determinations that mind recognizes to be its own product, yet no less objective.

From the Modern Philosophy of Mind to Hegel's Systematic Account of Consciousness

Most modern philosophy of mind has not only reduced awareness to consciousness but regarded all consciousness as discursive, following Kant's dogma that consciousness of objectivity depends upon necessary conceptual orderings of representations. Hegel recognizes that this makes it impossible for language or thought to be acquired. Subjects can hardly come to recognize their own expressions as well as those of others and learn to communicate if they cannot be consciousness or self-consciousness without already having concepts and the linguistic competence thought involves.

Hegel provides the outline of a systematic account of consciousness that escapes all these difficulties. First, he recognizes that philosophy must establish the legitimate categories of determinacy in a logical investigation that takes nothing for granted, presenting the autonomous self-development of reason. Having accomplished this task in his *Science of Logic*,[3] Hegel proceeds to think through the constitution of nature, whereby space, time, and matter in motion provide the minimal material conditions for electromagnetic physical processes, which themselves make possible the chemical reactions whose contingent ordering into a self-renewing whole brings life into being. As Hegel's *Philosophy of Nature* argues,[4] the minimal form of life involves a self-moving organism that metabolically sustains itself in relating to its biosphere and gives itself a species being through reproduction. These fundamental life processes involve a sensitivity and self-affirming responsiveness that is exhibited in dispersed localized form in the tropisms of plants. Only with animal life do sensitivity and responsiveness achieve a centralized subjective form, establishing sentience and self-controlled motility, motivated by an equally centralized emotive drive.[5] With this development, mind comes to be as essentially embodied in animal life.

Accordingly, when Hegel proceeds to develop how mind constitutes itself from its most minimal to its most complete determination, he is operating with a mental reality that never succumbs to mind–body dualism but also involves the embodied processes of an animal organism. Moreover, animated mental reality does not consist exclusively of consciousness but involves two other mental processes, one of which provides the psychological enabling conditions of conscious awareness, and another which incorporates consciousness but constitutes the intelligent awareness of mental content as both subjective and objective, allowing for language, thought, and the philosophy of mind.

---

3. For a critical examination of Hegel's *Science of Logic* that shows how he has provided a compelling fulfillment of systematic logic, see Richard Dien Winfield, *Hegel's Science of Logic: A Critical Rethinking in Thirty Lectures* (Lanham, MD: Rowman & Littlefield, 2012).
4. G. W. F. Hegel, *Philosophy of Nature*, being *Part Two of the Encyclopaedia of the Philosophical Sciences (1830)*, trans. A. V. Miller (Oxford: Oxford University Press, 1977), §343–44, 303–5.
5. Hegel, *Philosophy of Nature*, §350–51, 351–53.

On Hegel's account all stages of mind involve embodied subjectivity, which is what it is in function of how it apprehends its own mental content. The minimal configuration of mind that is both incorporated by and presupposed by consciousness is what Hegel calls the *Seele* or the preconsciousness psyche.[6] It relates to mental content as nothing but its own determination. Not yet distinguishing subject and object, the psyche communes solely with itself, feeling its own feelings, rather than sensing objects or having intuitions by which mind is aware of immediately accessing objectivity as well as its own mental activity. In order for the psyche to pave the way for consciousness, the activity of feeling must come to organize the content of feeling and the activity of feeling into self-standing, distinguishable totalities. Hegel argues that the psyche's repeated feeling generates habits, whereby feeling becomes mediated by its own past activity, allowing the psyche to develop universal dispositions as well as detached habituations.[7] This produces a separation between the content and activity of the psyche that gets further enhanced through the expression of feeling by the psyche, where mind makes its feelings into phenomena to which it stands in relation.[8] Hegel maintains that these two preconscious developments enable mind to become conscious by relating to its own mental content as a self-standing totality that confronts the equally unified activity of mind.[9] The opposition of consciousness thereby arises without having to rely upon any introduction of discursive conceptual organization, which would preclude any pre-linguistic, pre-conceptual consciousness, and with it any *emergence* of language and thought.

Mind becomes conscious once the same mental content that figured as the feeling of the psyche's own feelings is now treated by mind as the sensation of what immediately confronts it. This is the most basic opposition of consciousness, the sense-certainty where conscious awareness is immediately aware of what is, without in any way discriminating or mediating the content it opposes.[10] Starting with this most elementary shape, Hegel presents three successive stages in the unfolding of consciousness, which lead up to self-consciousness: sense-certainty, perception, and understanding.

Sense-certainty gives way to perception once consciousness uses the attentive activity already present in the psyche to focus upon a group of

---

6. G. W. F. Hegel, *Philosophy of Mind*, being *Part Three of the Encyclopaedia of the Philosophical Sciences (1830)*, trans. William Wallace together with the *Zusätze in Boumann's Text (1845)*, trans. A. V. Miller (Oxford: Oxford University Press, 1977), §388–412, 29–152.
7. Hegel, *Philosophy of Mind*, §409–10, 139–47.
8. Hegel, *Philosophy of Mind*, §411, 147–51.
9. Hegel, *Philosophy of Mind*, §412, 151–52.
10. Hegel, *Philosophy of Mind*, §418–19, 158–61.

sensuous contents, gathering them together as the sensuous properties of a thing. Since consciousness is not conscious of its own activity but only of what it confronts, the thing has a problematic unity, which cannot be unequivocally located in the sensuous contents or in the otherwise empty receptacle the thing provides. Since the sensuous manifold is immediately given, none of its contents are mediated by one another, whereas the grouping that contains them has no additional content of its own that could secure their combination.[11] Since consciousness finds itself moving back and forth from the indifferent immediacy of the sensuous manifold to its combination into things, the only basis for things is an activity that produces their mediated unity.

This leads consciousness to understand what it perceives to have a dynamic unity where sensuous properties are treated by consciousness as the expression of forces that posit them. Since all forces exhibit the same activity of positing, the dynamic domain of posited sensuous entities presents a phenomenal realm of law, which is the unchanging essence of the continual flux of appearances.[12] The law of forces may regulate that flux, but it cannot provide the determination of all the content that is subject to it. Since, however, understanding is aware of both, it is in a position to advance to an awareness of the concrete dynamic unity of life, whose self-sustaining organic process reproduces its content in its totality. Hegel maintains that understanding life confronts consciousness with the same concretely unifying process that consciousness itself engages in understanding.[13] Consciousness thereby comes to the threshold of confronting in its object something equivalent to itself.

None of the above shapes of consciousness involve concepts, language, or thought. Instead, they comprise prediscursive modes of awareness that can be shared by pre-linguistic dumb animals and children, as well as conversing intelligent animals.

Hegel's Account of Prediscursive Self-Consciousness

Hegel has here set the stage for the emergence of self-consciousness, where consciousness confronts itself as an object. To do so, consciousness cannot lapse into sense-certainty, perception, or understanding, where it faces something different from its own awareness. To oppose an object that manifests consciousness, consciousness must instead engage in practical relations to what it confronts. Hegel offers three successive stages in this practical development of

---

11. Hegel, *Philosophy of Mind*, §420–21, 161–62.
12. Hegel, *Philosophy of Mind*, §422–23, 162–64.
13. Hegel, *Philosophy of Mind*, §423, 164–65.

self-consciousness, all of which are prediscursive and need not involve speech or thought.[14]

The first, most minimal self-consciousness consists in appetitive desire, where consciousness, as a living embodied organism, consumes its object of desire, thereby becoming aware of its obliteration of the independent objectivity of what it confronts. Although this practical living engagement momentarily provides an experience of conscious' own presence, that presence is entirely negative and devoid of any persisting objectivity.[15]

An abiding awareness of consciousness as an object confronting consciousness can instead be achieved in interacting with another consciousness. Although the confrontation with another consciousness enables consciousness to be an object opposing conscious awareness, that opposing consciousness is distinctly other in virtue of its own living embodiment and consciousness cannot be *self*-conscious in the face of that difference. If consciousness attempts to eliminate that difference by destroying the living being of the other, mind reverts to a consciousness sensing, perceiving, or understanding nonconscious phenomena.[16] The only way of obtaining an abiding self-consciousness is if the other consciousness confronting consciousness does so such as to reflect consciousness' own subjectivity. This can occur in a relation of unequal domination, where the other consciousness serves the appetite of its subordinating counterpart.[17] Then, however, the two parties play different roles and consciousness does not find itself in its subservient partner. To eliminate the difference and secure self-consciousness, the interaction must be reciprocal, so that each party relates to its counterpart as that counterpart relates to it. Individuals can achieve this by expressing their desire for the desire of one another. Then, each confronts itself reflected in another who has the same type of consciousness as its own. This enables consciousness to have a universal self-consciousness where it confronts an object that it knows to be a self-conscious individual like itself.[18] Thereby consciousness knows its own self-consciousness to be common in structure with that of its object.

As a result, Hegel argues, consciousness takes on the form of reason, obtaining certainty that the object it confronts is at one with its own self-consciousness.[19] Hegel invokes reason because reason operates with a knowing whose own determinations are presumed to be at one with true objectivity.

---

14. Hegel, *Philosophy of Mind*, §424–37, 165–78.
15. Hegel, *Philosophy of Mind*, §426–28, 167–69.
16. Hegel, *Philosophy of Mind*, §431–32, 171–73.
17. Hegel, *Philosophy of Mind*, §433–35, 173–76.
18. Hegel, *Philosophy of Mind*, §436–37, 176–78.
19. Hegel, *Philosophy of Mind*, §438, 178.

The interaction of universal self-consciousness provides consciousness with a certainty that has the form of reason, but it does not constitute a theoretical reason that conceives the correspondence of its concepts with objectivity. Instead, consciousness as reason is aware of the identity between its self-consciousness and consciousness, where its confrontation with consciousness as an object is at one with its confrontation with an opposing object. Here the phenomena consciousness experiences correspond to its consciousness of self, such that mind is certain of finding in its awareness of the given its own subjective activity. This certainty is of *correctness* in the fit of mental content with experienced phenomena, not certainty of theoretical *truth*, which matches concept and objectivity.

From Consciousness to Intelligence

Hegel regards this result of universal self-consciousness to lead mind from the opposition of consciousness to spirit (*Geist*), where mind becomes aware of its mental content being not only what is objective but also mind's own subjective determining. Spirit, which immediately comprises theoretical intelligence, has both poles of consciousness as its object. Whereas consciousness is never aware of its own relating to its mental content but only confronts what is given to it, intelligence knows that its mental content is both objective and the product of mind. This dual comprehension transforms sensation into intuition, which intelligence knows to be its own mental content as well as the immediate determinacy of something objective.

Those who absolutize the opposition of consciousness and make it the ultimate presupposition of knowing are compelled to acknowledge that the act of consciousness can never be available to consciousness itself. Even when consciousness makes its psychological activity an object of conscious awareness, the act of reflection by which this is done is only an object for a different, further reflection, whose own act is only available to awareness in an additional reflection presenting the same limitation. Husserl acknowledges this situation, admitting that phenomenology can never complete its account of knowing, since it is left facing an endless progress where every act of consciousness can only become an object of awareness by means of a different act that reflects upon the former.[20] Because Husserl sees no way of overcoming the opposition of consciousness, but considers conscious intentionality to be the "presuppositionless" foundation of all cognition, he simply ignores the problem, as if it might go away.

---

20. Edmund Husserl, *Cartesian Meditations: An Introduction to Phenomenology*, trans. Dorion Cairns (The Hague: Martinus Nijhoff, 1960), 152.

Hegel escapes this impasse by providing psychological closure to consciousness by moving beyond it to the activity of spirit, whose theoretical intelligence can at one and the same time be aware of its object and of the subjective act by which it is apprehended. This allows for theorizing as well as language, for both require that mind be aware of mental constructs (theory and linguistic expressions) together with the objects to which they refer.

Hegel's account of consciousness makes possible both the emergence and comprehension of language and thought by providing for a pre-linguistic and pre-conceptual consciousness and self-consciousness. To begin with, the activity of the psyche provides the psychological resources for the emergence of the subject–object opposition of conscious awareness without need of invoking any conceptual ordering of representations. Second, sense-certainty, perception, and understanding all operate without language or thinking. The same is true of the different forms of self-consciousness. Appetitive desire and appetitive recognition allow consciousness to confront negatively and positively the presence of consciousness in terms of coordinated expressions of desire without need of any speech or conceptualization. All of these psychological developments enable individuals to make expressions to one another in reference to commonly observed objects without already having to possess words and thoughts.

Hegel's account of consciousness thereby makes psychologically intelligible how philosophy can know in truth the reality of consciousness. Mind is not restricted to the opposition of consciousness, which would bar the path to philosophical cognition. Moreover, mind is not caught in mind–body dualism but always involves the activity of an animal organism, endowed with feelings as well as sensations and intuitions. Finally, our very engagement in conceiving consciousness confirms that there are minds whose theoretical intelligence can generate signs, words, and propositions and inaugurate the career of thinking animals.

Unfortunately, Hegel's own publication of his systematic treatment of mind is limited to the schematic outline presentation of his *Encyclopedia of the Philosophical Sciences*, which served as a chapbook companion to his university lectures. The *Encyclopedia Philosophy of Mind* has subsequently been supplemented by publication of some of the surviving student transcriptions of the lectures that Hegel delivered on mind from year to year. These texts have been largely ignored by Hegel scholars and philosophers of mind in general.

Instead, most attention has been paid to the sections in Hegel's *Phenomenology of Spirit* that observe the self-examination of shapes of consciousness and self-consciousness.[21] Hegel's *Phenomenology of Spirit* is expressly not a work of

---

21. G. W. F. Hegel, *Phenomenology of Spirit*, trans. A. V. Miller (Oxford: Oxford University Press, 1977), Parts A and B, 58–138.

systematic philosophy but rather an immanent critique of the epistemological dogma that restricts knowing to the opposition of consciousness. All the knowledge claims made in the *Phenomenology* are claims affirmed by the shapes of consciousness under observation and all those claims are subjected to examination by the shapes of consciousness in question, which ends up undermining their validity. Far from providing a doctrine about the nature of consciousness, the procession of shapes of consciousness offers a demonstration of how knowing, bound to a confrontation with the given, is incapable of verifying its truth claims and ends up eliminating the distinction of knowing and its object on which its constitutive opposition of consciousness depends.[22]

Hegel's contribution to the theory of consciousness is rather to be found in his systematic philosophy of mind, whose abbreviated treatment of psyche, consciousness, and intelligence offers a too ignored antidote to the reigning dogmas of modern philosophical psychology. Given the schematic character of Hegel's contribution, it does not provide anything like a complete and adequately argued account. Nonetheless, it leaves us with the challenge of completing Hegel's unfulfilled project of conceiving the totality of mind, encompassing consciousness together with the psyche and intelligence.[23]

---

22. For a critical thinking through of Hegel's *Phenomenology* that demonstrates how the work achieves its propaedeutic purpose of overcoming the opposition of consciousness through an immanent critique of that opposition, see Richard Dien Winfield, *Hegel's Phenomenology of Spirit: A Critical Rethinking in Seventeen Lectures* (Lanham, MD: Rowman & Littlefield, 2013).

23. I have attempted to address this challenge in three works, *Hegel and Mind: Rethinking Philosophical Psychology* (Houndmills, UK: Palgrave Macmillan, 2010), *The Living Mind: From Psyche to Consciousness* (Lanham, MD: Rowman & Littlefield, 2011), and *The Intelligent Mind: On the Origin and Constitution of Discursive Thought* (Houndmills, UK: Palgrave Macmillan, 2015).

Chapter 8

HEGEL AND THE ORIGIN OF LANGUAGE

The Puzzle of the Origin of Language

The origin of language presents a daunting puzzle due to two key features of discursive intelligence that have won widespread recognition.

First, language and thought are necessarily ingredient in one another. There can be no thinking that does not employ language anymore than there can be linguistic activity that does not involve thought. Individuals may think without communicating, but any thought unexpressed to others is still realized in interior monologue, using words. Conversely, any partaking in language employs meanings that transcend the particularity of imagery and engage thinking. Discourse always has some conceptual content, even if linguistic expression is restricted to individual commands or designation by proper nouns. Every command expresses something that can be performed by others in different circumstances, just as every proper noun refers to something with a reidentifiable selfhood extending beyond a point in space and a moment in time. Universality always enters into language, requiring more than images for its expression.

Secondly, although individuals may think in solitary monologue, no one can discourse inwardly or outwardly unless the meanings invoked have been established in actual interaction with others. Any intelligent individual may create a sign by associating some intuited content with a general representation, abstracted from multiple intuitions and images. Yet even when an individual recollects such an association, that semiotic connection cannot be assured any commonly apprehended significance unless individuals recognize one another making that association. The same proviso applies to any further modification of the content of signs or of their relationships in expressions. Without any intersubjective validation of the bearers and ordering of linguistic meaning, words and propositions cannot attain their own universal, communicable significance, rendering thinking impossible.

Together the unity of language and thought and the intersubjectivity of meaning seem to leave the origination of language an unfathomable mystery. After all, how can individuals engender discourse if all they have to rely upon are pre-linguistic, pre-conceptual resources, such as intuition, recollection, and imagination? How can they possibly institute, let alone recognize intersubjectively valid meanings and syntactic rules?

Any attempt to evade the looming difficulty through divine intervention only begs the question. No monotheistic god can gift language to humanity, for how could such a deity think or communicate without first acquiring thought and language in engagement with others? Alternately, no plurality of deities could circumvent the challenge to mortals, for any immortals would face the same conjuncture of thought and language and the intersubjectivity of linguistic usage. The gods would already have had to solve the same problem that we mortals confront at the origin of our discursive humanity.

The same would apply to any extraterrestrial intervention, whose eliciting monoliths might teach able humanoids to speak but would still leave in mystery how its makers generated their own language.

Any appeal to the blind chance of natural evolution provides no more illumination. All this does is acknowledge the contingent emergence of a species being whose biological endowment enables it to converse. Admittedly, the first intelligent animals to engage in linguistic interaction must have been born with the requisite biology enabling them to generate the rudiments of language, as well as learn preexisting language once there is a linguistic community within which to be raised. Further, that this occurs through natural selection is hard to deny given species reproduction, mutation, and a struggle for existence. Nonetheless, that evolution engenders the enabling biological conditions for discursive individuals does not itself determine what psychological process necessarily enters into the origination of language and then into learning as well as into the collective alteration of the discursive practice in which individuals find themselves. An animal species may evolve with a biological "language faculty" giving its members the cognitive and sensorimotor potential to discourse and, with it, the potential to generate and communicate new words and an infinity of discursive expressions.[1] What, however, must take place for those animals to progress from having the potentiality to think and speak to the actual enacting of discourse? How do those living minds

---

1. Chomsky frequently invokes such an infinitely generative biological "language faculty," most recently in his 2013 Dewey Lectures. See Noam Chomsky, "The Dewey Lectures 2013: What Kind of Creatures Are We?," *Journal of Philosophy*, vol. 110, no. 12 (December 2013): 647, 651, 672.

which are sufficiently endowed ever first found a particular language without being raised in a preexisting linguistic community?

The common experience of childhood language learning perennially surmounts the different challenge of acquiring language and thought from exposure to individuals who already converse. The very unfolding of that process casts in doubt that individuals can just be born as interlocutors, ready to speak without further ado. Rather, the originators of discourse must somehow put their maturing psychological endowment to work and thereby take the first step to founding language. Yet, how can this possibly occur? How do the founders of language, who have not yet begun to converse, move from imagery and dumb signaling to thought and verbalization?

The task of linguistic origination would be hopelessly demanding if it required speechless individuals to institute collectively from scratch the vocabulary and grammar of a real language. Grammatical rules are too complex to be known or consciously followed by any but a professional linguist. For just this reason, the natural learning of language by children in a linguistic community does and must occur without need of any conscious knowledge of grammatical structure. That structure can hardly be an object for collective invention by individuals who have yet to converse as well as think in inner monologue.

What removes this forbidding difficulty is similar to what overcomes the implausibility of random mutations generating anything as hugely complex as a multicellular organism, let alone a rational animal. If evolution required generating a new animal species through blind contingency building upon nothing but the most minimal life form, evolution would stall before the same infinitesimal probability of a monkey banging out *Finnegan's Wake* at a typewriter. Whereas the proverbial monkey always begins typing on a new blank page, evolution proceeds from an emergent organism, already embodying the cumulative results of prior mutations and natural selection.[2] Each step along the evolutionary path can involve just one minute alteration, which builds, however, on all that went before. What is produced from every engagement of blind chance mutation thereby has a feasibly reduced scope. The same is true of whatever accident may precipitate the transition from inorganic process to life. The origination of life need only consist in the emergence of the simplest autopoietic entity.[3] All that need emerge is the most elemental prokaryote

---

2. Hans Jonas points this out in *The Phenomenon of Life* (Evanston, IL: Northwestern University Press, 2001), 42–44.
3. See Evan Thompson, *Mind in Life: Biology, Phenomenology and the Sciences of Mind* (Cambridge, MA: Harvard University Press, 2007), 91–118, for an account of the minimal structure of the autopoiesis of life.

cell, containing chemicals whose reactions, regulated by an enclosing cellular membrane, result in the renewal of those same reactions while reproducing the selectively permeable boundary enabling them to continue without being dispersed or interrupted by extraneous chemical processes.

Analogously, the origination of language need not and cannot consist in the invention of a full-fledged grammar and vocabulary from no prior linguistic materials. Instead, the genesis of language can feasibly proceed with the collective institution of the most basic linguistic factor. Then, further development can proceed upon the acquisition of that primary linguistic heritage by individuals who are raised in a community that uses that factor, wielding with it the generative power it possesses for freely producing new expressions. These individuals can then supplement and modify that minimal language element, once more doing so in rudimentary ways that are acquired by each subsequent generation through the natural learning process made possible by their common genetic endowment. That inherited so-called "language faculty" allows maturing individuals to acquire the prevailing linguistic competence as well as to enrich further its verbal repertoire and syntax without any formal study of vocabulary or grammar. Not until a linguistic science has emerged may any member of the emergent linguistic community have conscious knowledge of the grammatical complexity of their shared language.

The Three Dogmas Barring Comprehension of the Origination of Language

Although this incremental process promises to engender an initial genuine language, the very first step along the way remains blocked by three dogmas dominating much contemporary philosophy of mind. These are the dogmas of mind/body dualism, of the identity of mind and consciousness, and of the discursive character of all consciousness.

The dogma of mind/body dualism, which sets mental reality apart from physical reality, renders inscrutable any theoretical and practical interaction of the two domains it demarcates from one another. This is equally true of the offshoots of dualism, the monisms of idealism and materialism, which retain the incompatibility of mental and physical realms but deny the existence of one while affirming the solitary actuality of the other. On either account, the incommensurability of the mental and the physical leaves inexplicable how individual minds can exist for one another and engage in any communication, let alone express any mental content in an intuitable sign. Without minds having individual bodily realizations with which to express mental activity, the very possibility of linguistic interaction is removed. To the extent that thought and language go together, Descartes' "notion" of a solitary immaterial thinking thing is something of which it is impossible to be certain.

The common identification of mind with consciousness equally precludes any genesis, let alone any actuality of language. This is not just due to consciousness being the form of mind that opposes itself to a world from which the conscious ego is extricated, operating with a subject–object opposition where every mental determination is treated as being of something independently confronting conscious awareness. When that dualism is made the exclusive shape of mind, both the preconscious psyche and intelligence are precluded. The preconscious psyche relates to its mental contents as modifications of its own embodied subjectivity, feeling its own feelings. Through the repeated act of its own self-feeling, the psyche modifies its own subjectivity, forming habits, building universal modes of motility and sensitivity in which the opposition of consciousness is not yet at hand. This permits mind to engage in unconscious activities while its conscious attention is focused elsewhere. Without such unconscious habituation and the trove of internalized feelings it embodies, no individual could possess the memory and habits of linguistic practice, without which vocabulary and syntax could neither be learned nor repeatedly employed in the solitude of inner discourse or in the motor skill of outer communication.

On the other hand, language is unrealizable without intelligence, which supplements the psyche and consciousness by apprehending its mental modifications as being both mind's own subjective determining and the determinations of objectivity. The most elemental realization of linguistic activity requires individuals to be aware of intuitable signs and intuitable relations of signs, apprehending them as both products of discursive subjects and determinations of intersubjective and objective meaning. The oppositional cognition of consciousness cannot grasp both subjective and objective sides that must be associated together for language and thought to operate. Consciousness just confronts objects, without apprehending the subjective mental acts by which it does so. Only the subjective/objective awareness of intelligence can wield the discursive facility to comprehend its linguistic expressions to be products of mind that no less are about something else.

Further, if all consciousness were discursive, then no individuals could be conscious, let alone self-conscious, without already employing concepts and judgments, which equally involve language. Kant and his followers uphold this dogma, presuming that unless representations are connected by concepts rooted in the forms of judgment, representations cannot convey anything objective nor fit within the unity of self-consciousness.[4] The identification of

---

4. This, of course, is the whole point of Kant's "Transcendental Deduction of the Categories."

consciousness with discursive rationality bars the possibility of not only consciousness and self-consciousness for dumb animals and prediscursive children but of both the origination and the learning of language. Individuals who lack consciousness and self-consciousness cannot be aware of the communications of others let alone of their own expressions. How then could anyone emerge from a pre-linguistic condition to linguistic and conceptual competence?

Among historical figures, Hegel stands out for repudiating the three dogmas that obstruct the path to any understanding of the origin as well as of the learning of language. He recognizes that mind is a living reality of an embodied animal self and that mind is not just conscious but involves a preconscious psyche and intelligence. Moreover, Hegel recognizes, contrary to Kant and his followers, that consciousness has a nondiscursive actuality that both phylogenetically and ontogenetically precedes linguistic intelligence. Dumb animals, young children, and adult individuals who could inaugurate language can all be conscious and self-conscious. They can be conscious because what suffices to engender the opposition of consciousness is habit formation and the expression of feeling. These psychological developments together detach the feeling self from the domain of its sensations, which the disengaged mind now registers as a unitary objectivity it confronts.[5] No apprehension of concepts is required, which would incoherently presuppose linguistic interaction. The same can be said of the constitution of self-consciousness in the interaction of desiring conscious selves. As Hegel delineates in his mislabeled "master-slave dialectic," they encounter a recognition of their own desiring selfhood in the expressed desire of the individual with whom they interrelate, without having to speak or think.[6]

The Origin of the Basic Element of Language

For language to originate, a plurality of individuals who lack words and concepts must somehow employ their prediscursive physiological and mental endowments to establish the minimal threshold of discourse, at one blow creating the most basic actuality of thought and speech. As prerational animals, the prospective members of the first linguistic community can be granted a psyche that feels its own feelings and through repeated feeling acquires habituated sensations and motor skills, a consciousness that perceives things with

---

5. For further discussion of this point, see Richard Dien Winfield, *The Living Mind: From Psyche to Consciousness* (Lanham, MD: Rowman & Littlefield, 2011), 125–41.
6. How this is so is analyzed at length in Winfield, *The Living Mind*, 191–221. See also, Richard Dien Winfield, *Hegel and Mind: Rethinking Philosophical Psychology* (Houndmills, UK: Palgrave Macmillan, 2010), 59–77.

properties and understands dynamic relations without yet conceiving laws or universals, and an intelligence that has intuitions, represents them in recollected images, produces new imagery from its recollections, and associates all these mental contents in the inner world of its imagination.

Hegel sketches the first psychological development that paves the way for the transition to thought and language. This consists in the process of semiotic imagination, whereby an intelligent individual generates a sign.[7] The mental construction of the sign consists in an act of intelligence that operates without any intrinsic relation to the mental activity of others. Indeed, without this solitary psychological production, the intersubjective engagement in language would not be possible.

Sign production must be distinguished from symbolization. In producing a symbol, an intelligent individual associates an image with a general representation, where some aspect of the former's content is intended to convey some aspect of the content of the general representation. The symbol symbolizes a general rather than unique representation because only a generalized content can be repeatedly invoked as the same. A symbol, like a sign, has this repeatable reference, which is what allows for its communicability, since others can only apprehend the same mental content if that content is a "token" of a multiply instantiated representation. The general representation itself consists in an association of an image with a plurality of images that share the content of that image. To have a general representation, an individual must employ imagination to keep in mind the plurality of recollected images that intelligence associates to a single image that is apprehended to present something they have in common. That common content is not a concept proper but a pictorial image. Consequently, the production of a general representation can precede discursive rationality, for which it provides an indispensable mental prerequisite.

Since both the symbol and the general representation it symbolizes are images, they each contain a manifold pictorial content, which leaves ambiguous what the symbol is conveying. The ambiguity is not total, because what the symbol symbolizes is a content contained in both the symbol and the general representation with which it is associated. Accordingly, when the individual produces a symbol, that individual must also choose which aspect of the symbol's imagery as well as which aspect of the general representation to associate. That selection, however, is not itself present in the symbol or in the general representation it conveys.

---

7. See G. W. F. Hegel, *Philosophy of Mind: Part Three of the Encyclopaedia of the Philosophical Sciences (1830)*, trans. William Wallace and A. V. Miller (Oxford: Oxford University Press, 1971), 457–60, 210–18.

Sign production goes one crucial step beyond symbolization. Semiotic imagination associates an intuitable content with some general representation where, unlike symbolization, the association is completely independent of any shared imagery. The intuitable content figures as a sign because it connotes a general representation with which it is associated solely by the act of intelligence, with complete indifference to how the sign's imagery may otherwise be related to what it means. The sign is an image which intelligence apprehends to signify a general representation with no constitutive pictorial relation to it. As such, intelligence knows the image to be a sign only insofar as it is equally aware of the association it makes between that sign and what it signifies. Although semiotic imagination still employs imagery, it is completely free in how it associates an intuitable sign with some general representation. No inspection of the given content of a sign can disclose its meaning, for that meaning is a creation of intelligence and can only be perceived by simultaneously apprehending the act of semiotic imagination. Here for the first time, intelligence expresses a meaning that is completely independent of the given imagery of its vehicle of expression. The meaning may still be linked to a general representation that presents a shared pictorial content, but the sign provides mind with a tool for freely rising beyond the given confines of received intuitions.

This freedom reaches its negative acme in what Hegel describes as mechanical semiotic or verbal memory, where the mind autonomously recalls signs in an order indifferent to the meanings they convey.[8] Mechanical verbal memory operates on the basis of the mind's recollection of individual signs, whose association of an intuited content and a general representation is internalized and made available for recall. Once this internalization is at hand, intelligence can then recall signs at will and associate them with one another. Of course, once signs are associated by mind, that association itself can be internalized and recollected. The recollection of associated signs takes the form of a rote, purely mechanical memory insofar as the recollected ordering of signs is completely external to their own image content, as well as to that of the general representation they otherwise signify. Mechanical semiotic memory is duly celebrated by Hegel as a liberation of intelligence from representation, bringing mind to the threshold of thought and language.[9] Even though such recollection may appear to be utterly meaningless and seemingly mindless, it completes the negative emancipation from representation by setting the recollected signs free from their last remaining connection to imagery—that of the general representations they signify when they are first baptized as signs. To

---

8. Hegel, *Philosophy of Mind*, 463, 221–22.
9. Hegel, *Philosophy of Mind*, 464, 223.

move from the negative freedom of mechanical semiotic memory to the positive freedom of discursive rationality, intelligence must proceed to associate signs in such a way as to give them determinate meaning.

Hegel is ready to identify signs as names without, however, immediately connecting them with linguistic interaction or conceptualization.[10] The individual intelligent mind can baptize names of its own simply through its own activity of associating an intuitable image with some general representation irrespective of any pictorial tie. These names are produced subjectively and as such they have no intersubjective validity or any intrinsic conceptual character.

Their lack of intersubjective validity is evident in how the association of sign and signified remains confined to the apprehension by the individual name producer of the mental association that individual makes between that name and the general representation to which it refers. That connection cannot be grasped by others by inspecting the content of the sign or of any general representation, which only becomes perceivable by others after having been externalized in some intuitable factor. So long as the semiotic connection remains an individual, subjective act, communicable intelligibility is lacking. Even for the individual who makes that subjective semiotic association, nothing in that individual act or its repeated recollection can ensure that the connected terms have any nonarbitrary tie that can distinguish "proper" from "improper" use and ensure that that connection be upheld from one moment to another. This is why there can be no "private" language, for no individual subjective semiotic association can have an abiding unequivocal meaning for others or for the individual who independently produces signs.[11]

Moreover, the production of names by the individual intelligence does not yet have any genuine conceptual content since what they signify are general representations, which remain shared imagery rather than imageless thought. General representations lack conceptual universality precisely because they consist in common image contents, which as such are indefinable. At most they comprise the family resemblances with which Empiricism confuses thought by reducing concepts to shared imagined contents that have been abstracted from experience.

---

10. Hegel, *Philosophy of Mind*, 462, 219–20. As Hegel notes, "Language here comes under discussion only in the aspect of a product of intelligence for manifesting its ideas in an external medium" (Hegel, *Philosophy of Mind*, 459, 214).
11. For the classic statement of the argument against private language, see Ludwig Wittgenstein, *Philosophical Investigations*, trans. G. E. M. Anscombe (New York: Macmillan, 1958), §259–74, 92e–95e.

On both counts, semiotic imagination's production of names does not constitute the emergence of language and it would be a mistake to condemn Hegel for here reducing language to the ostensive reference of naming.

Instead, what Hegel here provides is the elemental semiotic factor which individuals can and must possess *before* acquiring thought and language. Once individuals have given themselves this psychological product they are in a position to interact in terms of the commonly intuitable expressions they give to their signs in the face of commonly perceivable objects. Only by having produced signs beforehand do they have something to "triangulate" in the intersubjective process of baptizing a communicably intelligible name, where individuals recognize one another associating the same name with the same sort of object and sustain that practice.

Of course, such "triangulation" can by itself only provide a naming of empirically given resemblances represented by general representations rather than concepts.[12] Interacting individuals can mutually signify similar objects with similar signs, but these intersubjective associations only apply to contingent collections of shared observations.

Nonetheless, words that begin their linguistic career as signifiers of empirically abstracted commonalities can eventually come to signify conceptually determinate factors, exhibiting the logical connections of universality, particularity, and individuality with which judgment and syllogism can operate. Vygotsky describes this transformation as a key part of the language learning process of children, who begin by using words to describe contingent groups of things devoid of logical relations but later come to employ the same words to signify definable meanings subject to conceptual relationships. What allows

---

12. For this reason, Davidson's claim that "triangulation" ensures that conceptual determination, intersubjectivity, and objectivity go together would only apply when the meanings at stake are concepts, not just general representations, and the objectivity in question is not just commonly observed appearance but an intrinsically determined totality. See Donald Davidson, *Subjective, Intersubjective, Objective* (Oxford: Oxford University Press, 2001), 129–30. Significantly, Davidson acknowledges "a prelinguistic, precognitive situation which seems to me to constitute a necessary condition for thought and language" and first describes triangulation in terms that he explicitly applies to dumb animals, writing, "it is the result of a threefold interaction" where,

> Each creature learns to correlate the reactions of other creatures with changes or objects in the world to which it also reacts. One sees this in its simplest form in a school of fish, where each fish reacts almost instantaneously to the motions of others. This is apparently a reaction that is wired in. A learned reaction can be observed in certain monkeys which make three distinguishable sounds depending on whether they see a snake, an eagle, or a lion approaching. (Davidson, *Subjective, Intersubjective, Objective*, 128)

children to move from preconceptual to conceptual use of names is exposure to the discourse of adults who use the same names to refer to logically determinate groups, under which fall some if not all of the same things to which children originally associated those names.[13]

The original move from words to language and concepts obviously cannot rely upon such exposure. Instead, it depends upon individuals supplementing their original "triangulation" of communicable names with the further steps that engender the grammatical being of language, without which thought is impossible. Hegel has little to say about these moves, but his analyses of semiotic imagination and mechanical verbal memory provide the psychological processes that must be enlisted.

The Move from Names to Discourse

The grammatical being of language adds to names two fundamental modifications that make discourse possible. These are the intersubjectively recognized ways in which new meanings are determined through specific types of syntax, that is, relations of words and of modifications of words within these relations. Crucial to how these grammatical processes enable thought is that both involve a freedom of intelligence where the relations and modifications of words are open to infinite realizations. With such limitless procreative potential, these grammatical structurings in no way limit what words can be employed and what meanings can be expressed. They instead imply general forms of declensions and syntactical orderings to which every possible word is subject, no matter what it may be.

Hegel's account of the subjective production of signs already exhibits how intelligence is able to make any intuitable content a sign and to make any putative sign signify any general representation. Since general representations are themselves freely abstracted from intuitions and images, they are themselves indefinitely multiple. Further, mechanical verbal memory exhibits how intelligence can repeatedly relate signs in any connection it pleases, without being bound by the given determinations of their intuitable content. On top of this, intelligence can produce new signs to signify any of the infinitely possible relations of signs that semiotic imagination can form.

Consequently, grammatical alterations and relations of words cannot restrict what intelligence can signify. Given this open generative character of grammar, language cannot in any way undercut the freedom of thought that must employ verbalizations for its inner or outer expression.

---

13. See Lev Vygotsky, *Thought and Language*, trans. Alex Kozulin (Cambridge, MA: MIT Press, 1986), 92, 110–24.

Any such restriction is epistemologically incoherent. If language were to condition what can be known, there would be no way to know unconditionally of language's alleged privileged foundational role or of anything else for that matter. The supposed conditioning character of language would render all knowledge claims relative to that particular linguistic framework, including knowledge of what that framework is itself.

Nonetheless, even though grammar cannot juridically determine knowledge and thought, the employment of grammatical process makes it possible for words to have a significance based solely on their relation to one another. This feature is what lets intelligence wield the positive freedom to establish meanings independently of received intuitions.

Propositions provide a basic linguistic relation in which the relation of words signifies a specific meaning of its own. The words in a proposition do not just figure as symbols or signs of one another. Rather, their propositional connection comprises a new meaning irreducible to that which they already contain. As Hegel observes in his discussion of judgment in the *Science of Logic*, propositions, as a grammatical form, do not necessarily involve any conceptual determinations. They can connect words on the basis of empirical contingencies that are singular in nature, such as that, "'Aristotle died at the age of 73, in the fourth year of the 115th Olympiad.'"[14] Propositions, however, can be judgments, in which words convey conceptually determinate connections, where individuals and particulars are determined by universals. Significantly, individuals who first employ propositions devoid of conceptual relationships can construct judgments without need of employing words and grammatical forms that they have not already mastered. The same words and syntax can be used to make the objective conceptual specification of judgment.

The situation is no different in the construction of the linguistic expression of syllogisms. Although propositions that are not judgments can be linked together without drawing any inference, the same words and grammatical forms can be used to form a syllogistic series of judgments that determine individuals by a universal through their particularity. Moreover, the same words and syntax that are used in mere propositions or formal syllogistic inference can be used to group judgments into systematic philosophical argument, such as Hegel pioneers, which overcomes dependency upon given premises and forms of inference by thinking through conceptual self-development.

These moves are indicative of how word production and syntax offer enabling conditions for the engagement of autonomous reason.

---

14. G. W. F. Hegel, *Science of Logic*, trans. A. V. Miller (New York: Humanities Books, 1976), 626. See also *Science of Logic*, 410.

How then, can individuals, who have come to name things in an intersubjectively recognized way, develop the declensions and syntactical relations of words with which propositions, and then judgments, syllogisms, and systematic philosophical argument can be stated and thought?

The process of language development is necessarily incremental.[15] The addition of each new word requires its own recognition process by a plurality of interlocutors. So, too, does the introduction of every word that involves modifications and relations of words, such as adjectives, verbs, adverbs, pronouns, and quantitative expressions. All these can only be employed on the basis of the established usage of the words to which they relate. The accumulated succession of "triangulations," where individuals together perceive how expressions are commonly employed with respect to commonly observed phenomena, can only secure further linguistic development provided it is internalized and habitually renewed by each generation of the persisting linguistic community. The whole process may be gigantic in scope and complexity, but its incremental character permits each advance to be a minimal addition that can be built upon by individuals who learn whatever linguistic practices have so far emerged by growing up within the community that uses them. This allows for a gradual cumulative development, where additions to vocabulary, including words that signify relations of words, provide an ever-widening resource for employment in syntactical usages that themselves are very gradually invented, modified, recollected, and learned. The inherited endowment of intelligence with the capability for semiotic imagination provides all that is biologically and psychologically necessary for the process to unfold and build upon itself. Since each incremental change is a matter of convention, whose transformations take place in historical time, the rise of language can far outpace any biological evolution.

Although the process of language development is endless, the rise of thought that accompanies it reaches a stage at which full conceptual competence is achieved. Once grammar has provided the syntax for the conceptual determinations of judgment, syllogism, and systematic argument, autonomous reason has all it needs to express itself. New conceptual content can always be added, but thought, now enabled to be self-determined, is no longer limited by any external factors.

---

15. Davidson, who asserts the holistic character of mind, denies any gradual emergence of thought and language (see Davidson, *Subjective, Intersubjective, Objective*, 124, 126–27). What he fails to recognize is that even if beliefs and conceptual meanings are holistically interconnected, they can arise in different stages, acquiring newly modified significance as the context of which they are part itself alters in the course of psychological and historical development.

Even though language cannot juridically determine thought, the different stages of linguistic development can still affect how far thinking can progress. This is possible, however, only at the most primitive levels where word forms and syntax have not yet provided the grammatical tools for full-fledged conceptual determination. Once a language has developed the grammar for propositions, its participants can take the leap from general representation to thought. At that point, language leaves thought free to set its own limitations, that is, its own self-determinations. It no longer matters whether one speaks German, Greek, Hindi, Swahili, Chinese, or Navajo. So long as language has developed into propositional discourse, its users can think without conditions. In principle, they will be able to share those thoughts with those of the users of any comparable language, be it terrestrial or extraterrestrial. Translatability is guaranteed, for, unlike poetry, thought cannot be tied down to any particular verbal expression.

Chapter 9

THE LOGIC OF RIGHT

Philosophy, Logic, and Ethics

Truth and right are fundamentally tied to self-determination.

The quest for truth cannot free itself of opinion unless it liberates inquiry from the hold of given opinion and validates all its claims through its own independent labors. Philosophy must wield an autonomous reason, free in both the negative sense of overcoming dependence upon presuppositions and the positive sense of determining what its own method and subject matter should be. As such, philosophy cannot begin with any determinate claims about what is or about knowing. It must start from utter indeterminacy and generate from that presuppositionless commencement determinacy that is not grounded on any given or given procedure of specification. This indeterminate commencement allows philosophy to be a theory of determinacy, accounting for determinacy without begging the question by beginning with some given determinacy. Moreover, since philosophy develops determinacy as something generated in its own presuppositionless process, it develops self-determined determinacy. Philosophy thus begins as a development of self-determination per se.

To do so, however, philosophical investigation cannot begin by examining anything distinct from its own thinking. Any inquiry that addresses a topic different from its own knowing is doubly conditioned and relative. On the one hand, such an investigation must take its method for granted since it investigates not its own thinking but something distinct from method. On the other hand, such an investigation must presuppose the boundaries of its subject matter, since it only addresses something different from its method by confronting a topic with a given content distinguishing it from the thinking that addresses it. Hence, any investigation that begins by distinguishing its method from its subject matter, or its knowing from its object, is relative to both the given method it employs and the given determination of its topic. Philosophy can overcome this dual relativity if it overcomes the opposition of knowing and its object. This is why philosophy must begin with logic, whose thinking of thinking proceeds upon the elimination of the distinction of method and subject matter. Logic is equally autonomous in the dual sense that it proceeds without any given method or subject matter and instead generates both at once in thinking thinking. As such, logic, with which philosophy must begin is autonomous reason. Instead of beginning with any given determination of knowing or its object, logic must establish what thinking is in the process of thinking thinking. Beginning with neither any predetermined method nor subject matter, logic can only be a logic of self-determination, a logic in which determinacy is established without taking any determinacy for granted, a logic which overcomes all dependency upon foundations, a logic which thereby can validly think valid thinking.[1]

The legitimacy of conduct involves a very analogous centrality of freedom. Conduct cannot be valid unless it liberates itself from the domination of given authority and overcomes the divide between what confers legitimacy and what possesses legitimacy. So long as putatively valid conduct owes its validity to a separate foundation, that privileged factor must remain suspect. To be consistent with its own standard of validation, the privileged foundation must derive its validity from itself. Yet, insofar as the foundation must be self-grounding, its own legitimacy subverts the distinction between ground and recipient of validity, supplanting its own foundational structure of justification with self-determination as the only tenable substance of normativity. As such, ethics becomes a philosophy of the reality of self-determination, a philosophy of right, where right is understood as the actuality of freedom in all its totality.

Does the pivotal role of self-determination in both logic and ethics signify that ethics will exhibit the same logic as the logic of autonomous reason, whose development of self-determination per se is ingredient in logic's overcoming the opposition of subject and object with its thinking of thinking? Ethics may share self-determination, but ethics concerns the reality of self-determined *action*, not self-determination as a development of the categories of self-thinking thought. Moreover, ethics consists not in logic but in a philosophy of nonlogical reality, which may follow from the presuppositionless development of logic, but in so doing supplements logical determinacy with nonlogical categorization. On both counts, the relation of the pure logic of self-determination with the logic of the reality of freedom, the logic of the philosophy of right, is far from straightforward.

---

1. Hegel develops these arguments for why philosophy must begin as a presuppositionless development of self-determined determinacy and as a self-thinking logic in the two introductory sections of his *Science of Logic*, entitled respectively, "General Notion of Logic" and "With What Must the Science begin?." See G. W. F. Hegel, *Science of Logic*, trans. A. V. Miller (New York: Humanities Press, 1976), 43–59 and 67–78.

Hegel, who pioneers both presuppositionless logic and ethics as a philosophy of the reality of self-determination, provides us with the basic categories of logic and ethics with which to determine what the logic of the philosophy of right should be and how it relates to logic proper.

In the *Science of Logic*, Hegel presents self-determined determinacy as something that becomes thematic in the third and final section of logic, the Logic of the Concept.[2] Self-determined determinacy is shown to be nothing other than the determination of the concept as such, that is, the universal. The universal differentiates itself in particularity and in so doing determines nothing but itself, thereby attaining a completely self-originating character, comprising individuality. Although the concept exhibits self-determined determinacy in the process whereby the universal entails particularity and individuality, it still arises from two preceding logical developments, unfolding, respectively, the Logic of Being and the Logic of Essence. The Logic of Being accounts for how indeterminacy gives rise to determinacy, which, through its own development, renders its own immediate givenness something posited or mediated by an underlying essence. The Logic of Essence then develops all the two-tiered relationships whereby a determiner determines some determined determinacy. That development achieves closure when what determines and what gets determined become indistinguishable. This yields self-determined determinacy, not as something that owes its self-determined character to itself but as something that immediately results from the elimination of the difference between determiner and determined. Hegel recognizes that self-determination cannot be immediately given. Instead logic must move from indeterminacy to determinacy, which the relation of determiner and determined incorporates and presupposes. Only with determinacy and determined determinacy at hand can self-determination obtain the factors it needs for its own constitution. Even though self-determined determinacy is what it determines itself to be, it cannot begin its self-determining activity without these enabling conditions, determinacy on the one hand, and determiner and determined determinacy on the other.

This dependency upon enabling conditions applies as much to the reality of self-determined conduct as it does to the logical development of the concept. As Hegel points out in the introduction to the *Philosophy of Right*, the ethics of self-determination has its only deduction in the prior philosophical development of the real preconditions of conduct.[3] This "deduction" is supplied by the systematic philosophies of nature and of "subjective spirit"

---

2. Hegel, *Science of Logic*, 575–97.
3. G. W. F. Hegel, *Elements of the Philosophy of Right*, trans. H . B. Nisbet (Cambridge, UK: Cambridge University Press, 1991), 2, 26.

which develop the conceptually determinate reality of the biosphere in which animal life can develop to the point of providing individuals with theoretical and practical intelligence. This work of nature and psychology provides all that is required for conduct, that is, self-determined willing, to take place. Significantly, these natural and psychological enabling conditions in no way determine what conduct should be. Precisely because nature and mind are the enabling conditions for all conduct, they are completely neutral with regard to what distinguishes that conduct which is right from that which is wrong. This neutrality is necessary for the very possibility of normativity in conduct. Otherwise conduct would be juridically conditioned by antecedent factors. That would reinstate the incoherent framework of foundational justification, which ethics overcomes as a philosophy of right, of the reality of freedom. The reality of self-determination is determined in and through itself and for just this reason the philosophy of right can have no juridical foundations. This absence of prior legitimating principles has mystified legions of thinkers trapped in foundationalist dogmatism. They wonder whether the philosophy of right can be an ethics at all, since all it does is determine the reality of freedom, without appealing to any separate standards of validity.

This independence from the heteronomy of external grounding is basic to the logic that properly informs ethics. Hegel broadly identifies ethics as consisting in the Idea of Right, that is, the Idea of the reality of self-determined willing.[4] The Idea is the proper subject matter of each and every part of philosophy, from the logic with which philosophy must begin through the philosophies of nature and of mind that follow. In each case the Idea consists of the unification of concept and objectivity in which truth resides. Objectivity, unlike appearance or existence, does not rest upon some undisclosed ground but is determined in and through itself, as should be the proper object of true knowledge. The concept, as exhibiting self-determination, is precisely suited to lay hold of that which is independently determined. Thanks to the concept's fundamental autonomy, conceptualization can grasp a subject matter as it is determined in and through itself. The form of representation, by contrast, represents given intuitions and recollected images. Representational cognition always reflects upon given contents, modifying them in terms of the forms of its understanding. What representation apprehends is always a mere given appearance, which its general representations may correctly fit, but never know to be what is true in itself. Ethics properly develops the *Idea* of Right because this consists in presenting the conceptually determinate, self-constituted objectivity of freedom. The *Philosophy of Right* conceives its subject matter by allowing the "*Sache selbst*" to unfold in its own structural objectivity.

---

4. Hegel, *Elements of the Philosophy of Right*, 1, 25.

This requires a purely conceptual development, freely following the immanent unfolding of the concept of right. Does this signify that the logic of the philosophy of right will mimic that of logic proper?

In considering this question, we must recognize that it is not meta-ethical in character. Meta-ethics proceeds upon the logical positivist dogma that reason is empty and cannot generate any content of its own. On this impoverished basis, thinking can only be analytic, at most confirming the consistency of given content in accord with the principle of noncontradiction, but never establishing the truth of any such content. The logic of thought can then only be formal, mapping a thinking whose form is always distinct from its content, which must be received from some other source, such as experience or linguistic usage. Meta-ethics presumes that the logic of ethics is equally formal, specifying a form of ethical reasoning that can be determined without specifying the particular content of ethical values. In other words, meta-ethics presumes that the logic of ethics can be identified without distinguishing between right and wrong, as if one could distinguish the ethical from the nonethical without distinguishing what is ethical from what is unethical. Such formalism is precluded by the concrete logic of self-determination. Since the "form" of self-determination, namely the unity of the self, is the very content it determines itself to have, the logic of freedom, whether purely logical or ethical, cannot be an external form, indifferent to what it orders. As self-ordering, self-determined determinacy has a form that is pregnant with a content of its own. This means that the logic of right is uniquely tied to the one and only content of the reality of freedom. Since ethics *is* the philosophy of right, meta-ethics is as much a fraud as formal logic's pretention to have anything to do with philosophical thinking.

Nonetheless, this does not preclude asking whether the reality of free willing shares the same concrete self-ordering form as the pure logic of autonomous reason. Hegel might appear to draw a strict connection between the two from the very start of ethical investigation. In the introduction to the *Philosophy of Right*, he introduces his concept of the free will by sketching out how the will achieves self-determination by exhibiting universality, particularity, and universality.[5] The will first of all displays the negative freedom of universality by being able to abstract itself from any given end and instead pursue some other goal. This abstract universality, Hegel notes, must be supplemented by particularity, for unless the will makes a particular choice, it fails to *determine* its self. Finally, the will must not succumb to external dictate in the particular determinacy it gives itself. Rather, to be free, the will must remain at one with its self-determining self in engaging in a particular action, and to the extent

---

5. See Hegel, *Elements of the Philosophy of Right*, 5–7, 37–41.

that it does so, it unites its particularity with its universality, thereby exhibiting individuality.

Does this connection signify that the *Philosophy of Right* begins with the same logical development as the Logic of the Concept, which starts by conceiving universality, particularity, and individuality? Moreover, should we expect that the unfolding of the structures of right will map onto the progression of the rest of the Logic of the Concept, with judgment and syllogism being followed by the forms of objectivity and then the logical determinations of the Idea?

Two important factors weigh against any close correspondence of ethical and logical development. The first concerns the general relation between the self-ordering of logic and the development of the nonlogical part of philosophy, or what Hegel calls *Realphilosophie*, to which belongs ethics, that is, the philosophy of right. The second concerns how the self-determination of the will fundamentally differs in structure from the self-determination of the concept per se.

Logic per se versus the Logic of *Realphilosophie*

The self-development of autonomous reason achieves closure when logic completes its valid thinking of valid thinking, which culminates in the so-called Absolute Idea, where the entire logical development is methodically recapitulated as the self-constitution of logical science. Once this culmination is achieved, the totality of logical determination has come into *being*. This addition of the form of being to the Absolute Idea constitutes something that is irreducible to any logical determinacy, since it incorporates all the logical categories within its form. Insofar as the emergent being of the Absolute Idea is the least determinate qualification that could be added to logical totality, it comprises the minimal determinacy of what is extralogical, providing the starting point for *Realphilosophie*, arriving at something beyond logic without illicitly introducing any putative "given" content. This minimal threshold of nonlogical determinacy can be described by Hegel as the self-externality of the Absolute Idea[6] since it consists of nothing but the totality of logical determinacy as immediate, as beyond its own self-mediating, self-constitution. Any further development of nonlogical determinacy must proceed upon this minimal self-external totality, which Hegel appropriately identifies with space,[7] the most basic factor of nature that all further natural realities incorporate.

---

6. Hegel, *Science of Logic*, 843–44. See also, G. W. F. Hegel, *Philosophy of Nature*, trans. A. V. Miller (Oxford: Oxford University Press, 1970), 247, 13–14.
7. Hegel, *Philosophy of Nature*, 254, 28.

Although the Idea, that is, the conceptually determinate objectivity, of nature will constitute itself from this structural starting point, the development of nature cannot consist in a simple application of the succession of logical categories to the completed Absolute Idea. Nature cannot consist in such a "development" for that would involve an external application of the logical ordering to the antecedently given logical totality. Although being may indeed immediately be nothing, and nothing and being may comprise becoming, their transitions are not that of a logical totality to which being has been added. Space can yield time and then matter and motion insofar as each stage along the way builds upon the entirety of what has heretofore been provided, without the contribution of any further content or the application of any categories to some given content by an external *deus ex machina*. The ultimate ordering principle of the development of nature will consist in the natural totality that arises when all natural relationships have come into being in their structural unity.

This totality, which consists of the natural universe that has become a biosphere, then provides the starting point for the development of the non-natural reality of the "psychozoids," the rational agents that animal life makes possible. Here, on the basis of the psychological reality of intelligent individuals, the threshold of ethical reality emerges. At each stage in the development leading up to this enabling platform for self-determined willing, what determines the succession of real factors is something more specific than an application of particular logical categories to the absolute Idea. Once space has provided nature a minimal nonlogical realization, what orders the ensuing development are two converging considerations. On the one hand, each subsequent development will build itself from nothing more than what has already emerged and, on the other hand, the unfolding that proceeds will determine itself to be the development of the totality whose self-constitution brings that realm to closure. Space will therefore be not a determination of and by the Absolute Idea but rather the most rudimentary feature of a universe that exhausts its natural possibilities by being the biosphere of animal life.

Similarly, that biosphere will turn out to be the incorporated threshold on which rational agency constitutes its historical world, culminating in the cultural achievement of philosophy, by which the totality of reality comes to contain that which knows it in its whole truth. Accordingly, to comprehend the "logic" of right, it will be necessary to focus on the structural interrelationships of the different spheres comprising the reality of freedom, in light of the natural and psychological materials that provide the enabling conditions of ethics. That this involves more than applying the logical ordering of categories is reflected in the second factor that bars any simple parallelism.

Self-Determination in Logic versus Self-Determination in Ethics

This second factor consists in the key difference in the self-determination of the concept and the self-determination of the will. Unlike the concept, the free will inextricably involves the interrelationship of individuals.

The logic of the concept begins by developing universality, particularity, and individuality without reference to any plurality of individuals.[8] Hegel presents universality, followed by particularity, and then by individuality, indicative of how the particularization of the universal does not presuppose a plurality of differentiated particulars, that is, individuals. Instead, universality, poised to determine itself, differentiates itself as particularity per se, which gives rise to individuality only *after* particularity affirms its unity with universality. Only once universality and particularity take on individuality in their contrast with one another does the concept divide itself into a plurality of individuals, setting the stage for judgment.

By contrast, the will achieves self-determination only by participating in an interaction of right, in which the self-determination of one individual is interdependent upon the self-determination of others.

Hegel's application of the categories of universality, particularity, and individuality to the self-determination of the will might suggest that an individual can act autonomously without interacting with any other agents. Simply by having the capacity to choose, the individual can wield the universality of negative freedom, deciding which end to pursue without being bound to any given goal. Moreover, by making a choice, irrespective of relating to others, one can exhibit the particularity of giving one's will determinacy. What, however, can enable that particular choice to exhibit universality and provide for the individuality of volition? What can allow the will to give itself a determination that is its own, rather than being a content given *to* the will by external circumstance or given inclination? How can the choosing will escape being bound to options mandated not by will but by outer or inner conditions? How can choice escape remaining a slave to contingent externality and subjective desire?

---

8. Admittedly, in Judgment, the factors of the concept will be determined by one another in relationships that involve a plurality of individuals, but in the preceding account of the concept, individuality as such is determined through nothing but universality and particularity. For a detailed discussion of these logical developments, see Richard Dien Winfield, *From Concept to Objectivity: Thinking through Hegel's Subjective Logic* (Aldershot, UK: Ashgate, 2006), 67–105 and Richard Dien Winfield, *Hegel's Science of Logic: A Critical Rethinking in Thirty Lectures* (Lanham, MD: Rowman & Littlefield, 2012), 207–60.

So long as the individual wills monologically, that is, without interacting with other agents, the choice it makes fails to achieve self-determination on two fundamental counts. On the one hand, the individual does not determine the identity of its own agency. Rather than individuating the self that wills, the single agent instead wields a faculty of choice that is given antecedently to every decision it makes. Since that faculty is the enabling condition rather than the product of every choice, it is not a product of willing. Rather than being an artificial agency, it is a natural will, comprising an inherited capacity that is merely a potential whose actualization adds nothing to its defining character. The natural agency of the monologically choosing will is thus not self-determined, but given independently of willing, as a psychological endowment that comes into being through the natural maturation of the individual.

Furthermore, the faculty of choice fails to determine not only the form of its own agency but also the content of what it chooses. The individual agent may wield the negative freedom, the abstract universality, of deciding which goal to pursue, but the faculty of choice does not itself supply the options among which it can decide. The faculty of choice is formal, having no intrinsic content. What it chooses are ends that must be found outside the will itself—ends given by such independent factors as external circumstance and internal drives and representations. Instead of achieving self-determination, the natural will employs a faculty of choice that leaves it unable to determine by itself either the form or content of its volition. Who the agent is and what the agent wills are both heteronomous, determined not by willing but by other factors, be they objectively external or subjectively psychological. This double conditioning is why Socrates in Plato's *Republic* declares the very idea of self-rule, that is, self-determination, to be unintelligible. After all, Socrates observes, how can any individual be both agent and patient at once? How can the isolated agent possibly will its own character when it must employ itself to determine itself?[9]

What overcomes the otherwise insoluble enigma of self-determined willing is the intersubjective practice of rights. Individuals, who by nature are endowed with the faculty of choice, can use their natural wills to achieve self-determination provided they interact with one another in function of determining both the form and content of their respective agencies. They are able to do this in the most basic way by embodying their wills in separate objective realizations that they mutually recognize to be the actualizations of one another as self-determined persons. Through such reciprocally coordinated willing, they establish for one another a type of agency that comes to be in and

---

9. Plato, *Republic*, Book IV 430e–431a in Plato, *Complete Works*, ed. John M. Cooper (Indianapolis, IN: Hackett, 1997), 1062.

through their interaction, an interaction in which they will both who they are as self-determined individuals and what they will to do so. Their interaction establishes an agency whose identity is defined by the recognized embodiment it gives itself rather than by any features given independently of their willing. Further, what each individual thereby wills is an embodiment of that agency, which, as its self-determination, is defined not by any given features of that embodying factor but by the recognition that it actualizes the self-determination agency that wills it as its own realization. Since each participant can determine itself only by facilitating in its counterparts the same type of willing that it itself engages in, each partakes in a universal, lawful willing. This lawful willing is an exercise of right because it is a recognized self-determination that is shared by all participants in their interaction.

These mutual features are minimally exhibited in the self-determination of individuals as persons, that is, as owners. One cannot determine oneself as an owner without having the exclusive embodiment of one's will recognized as such by others who have established their own domain of ownership in some other exclusive embodiments. To give oneself the character of being an owner, one relies upon nothing other than embodying one's will in some factor that is acknowledged by others to be one's exclusive domain, acknowledged by their refraining from infringing upon that property. Nothing about one's natural identity renders one an owner. No matter what may physiologically, psychologically, or culturally individuate one from others, unless one wills an embodiment that is recognized by others, one cannot distinguish oneself as an owner. Similarly, no given feature of the factor that becomes property makes it something owned. Only the recognized presence in it of the will of the person renders it property. This is what allows the acquisition of property to be a self-determination, for what individuates the agent as an owner is determined through the coordinated willing of the mutually recognizing individuals rather than by any antecedently given features of those individuals or of the factors they appropriate. To be an owner, one must abstract from all features by which one is individuated by nature or external circumstance and acquire an identity determined through nothing but the convention of property ownership consisting in the coordinated acts of will in which one participates. To be an object of property, by the same token, a factor must figure as a pure receptacle for the embodiment of the will. Its identity as an object of property is determined solely by that embodiment and only insofar as that is the case can the factor be the vehicle for the self-determination of the individual as an owner.

Although both person and property realize self-determination by obtaining an individuation produced by the coordinated choices of the participants in the exercise of property right, the most elementary and primary actuality of self-determination consists in the acquisition of a very specific type of property, without whose appropriation no other property can be obtained or relinquished, nor any other exercise of right can be had. This form of property is that of the agent's own body, which every person must be recognized to exclusively own before that person can engage in any further acts of self-determination. Self-ownership of one's body is primary because unless one is recognized to be the exclusive proprietor of one's facticity, nothing one does can count juridically as one's own deed. Instead, one has the status of a mere factor, susceptible of appropriation by the will of another, who is responsible for whatever the enslaved individual causes to happen. Only once individuals mutually recognize one another as having taken exclusive ownership of their respective bodies can they take further actions that can be attributed to themselves. For this reason, one's ownership of one's body has the unique character of being inalienable. One cannot transfer ownership of one's body to another because to do so would be to annihilate the entire actuality of one's self-determined embodiment, leaving one incapable of retaining the status of recognized person.[10]

This primacy of self-ownership renders property right equally primary in the reality of freedom. It does not, however, make property right a first principle of ethical construction, as social contract theory believes. If property right were made a determining foundation of all further ethical validity, it would confer validity upon other institutions and activities which would thereby be conditioned on property right instead of being self-determined. In order for any further conduct to be autonomous, property right must enter in not as a determining principle but as an elementary ingredient in an exercise of freedom that contains but is irreducible to property relations.

In developing the Idea of Right, Hegel properly begins with property right and unfolds property relations in the order of their self-constitution.[11] First comes the original acquisition of property, which starts with the mutual recognition of individuals as persons who have taken exclusive inalienable ownership of their respective bodies. With this primary property at hand, agents who have freely individuated themselves as self-owning persons can now make the next logical move in extending their freedom. This consists in taking ownership of other factors by recognizably laying their will in them, be it by physically seizing them, altering their form, or marking them. In each case, these actions take ownership of alienable property only by being recognized by other individuals who have correlatively determined themselves as persons. Once this has occurred, persons are able to use their property and then to alienate their alienable possessions either in full or for limited use.

---

10. See Hegel, *Elements of the Philosophy of Right*, 47–48, 67, 78–79, 97.
11. Hegel, *Elements of the Philosophy of Right*, 40, 70.

Since ownership is a self-determination on the part of the owner, alienation of property can only involve a transfer of title if the receiving party wills to acquire the object or limited use of it. Hence, all transfer of property consists in a relation of contract, where persons agree to accept property, either with an exchange of property or of use of property, or without exchange, as in gift contract where only one party receives ownership or use.[12] Logically enough, only once the acquisition, use, and alienation of property have been developed can the violation of property right occur in its full totality of nonmalicious and malicious wrongs. Moreover, only with the determination of wrong does the task of righting wrong arise in the way that property relations allow. These structural implications dictate how the Idea of the first, primary sphere of right must be developed.

Where, however, should the logic of right lead after property relations have been thought and realized? The precarious situation in which the righting of wrong finds itself on the basis of property relations indicates that the reality of freedom cannot consist just in the practice of property relations. Since persons have choosing wills they can always enter into disputes in good faith concerning the boundaries of their ownerships, disputes for which the plurality of persons offers no recognized authority to adjudicate conflicts. Further, persons can always choose to violate the property of others maliciously, leaving others in the predicament of having to determine what wrong has been committed and what punishment and compensation are warranted, under conditions where none have any authority to take coercive actions without risking accusation of committing new wrongs of their own. This difficulty suggests, as it did to social contract theorists confronting the insecurity of liberty in the "state of nature," that further institutions of right must be enacted to uphold property. If, however, normativity consists in self-determination, any further institutions that secure property right must involve an irreducible freedom of their own. Further, the connection between any such institutions and property relations must be determined by an exercise of freedom, for otherwise the different spheres of right will be ordered by a power external to self-determination, leaving the totality of conduct under heteronomous control.

These considerations dictate that property right should be supplemented at least by an encompassing sphere of right in which individuals codetermine the whole reality of conduct in which they participate. In addition to property relations there ought to be self-government, where individuals will themselves as citizens who exercise self-rule and thereby determine how their political activity presides over their nonpolitical freedoms. This presents a mandate not unlike the two-tiered framework of social contract theory, which places

---

12. Hegel, *Elements of the Philosophy of Right*, 80, 110–12.

property relations under the governance of a civil administration of law that provides legal regulation and enforcement of property rights. The difference here is that the upholding of property relations should take the form of an institution of political freedom, not just an enforcement of civil legality, which may or may not involve self-government.

Hegel, however, does not restrict the Idea of freedom to a two-tiered structure of property relations and self-government, where individuals determine themselves as persons and citizens. Instead, he offers a threefold division of self-determination into the abstract right of property relations, the moral domain of conscientious subjects, and the institutional reality of ethical community, which itself contains the three spheres of the emancipated family, civil society, and self-government.[13]

Is the Threefold Division of Abstract Right, Morality, and Ethical Community Valid?

Is this division valid and comprehensive, and are the major subdivisions within each its three domains proper and exhaustive? The broad logical terms with which Hegel distinguishes the three spheres of abstract right, morality, and ethical community do not immediately exhibit the necessity of the division. Property relations are characterized as a form of self-determination in which the will obtains its free actuality in given external facticity. By contrast, in morality, the will achieves self-determination through subjective determinations that ought to be realized by conduct that is valid insofar as it reflects them. Finally, in ethical community, agents determine themselves through membership in existing associations where their freedom has an objective existence that contains the subjective activity by which it is realized. One is tempted to observe that abstract right presents self-determination in the form of the given determinacy of the Logic of Being, that morality presents self-determination in the form of the reflected, determined determinacy of the Logic of Essence, and that ethical community presents self-determination in the form of the self-determined determinacy of the Logic of the Concept. Even if this is the case, one may question why this need be and how it uniquely identifies the exhaustive division of the Idea of right, that is, of the reality of freedom.

Support for these divisions can be sought on an alternative, if complementary logical basis. The delineation of the spheres of right can be judged in terms of the two correlative provisos that govern the self-constitution of any independent totality: namely, both as conceived and as internally structured, a free-standing totality should involve a development in which each of

---

13. See Hegel, *Elements of the Philosophy of Right*, 33, 62.

its prior divisions presupposes nothing of what is found in those divisions that follow upon them, whereas those successive formations should have their sufficient enabling conditions in those preceding structures which they equally incorporate.

These dual considerations are amply satisfied by Hegel's threefold development of abstract right, morality, and ethical community. To begin with, the self-determination of persons presupposes nothing but a biosphere and the existence therein of a plurality of rational animals that are able to interact in terms of their respective choices. On the other hand, individuals can engage in none of the self-determinations of moral subjects or members of ethical community unless they have determined themselves as property owners. Otherwise, they lack recognized self-ownership, without which no further exercise of right can be had.

Moral self-determination, for its part, requires a plurality of property owners, whose actions are their own responsibility and not that of some master. On the other hand, individuals do not need to belong to any ethical community to exercise their moral freedom. Indeed, moral autonomy is characterized by a subjective determination where conduct must draw its bearings from the internal purposes, intentions, and conscience of the individual rather than from the institutional practices in which they may be embroiled. Whereas membership in family, civil society, or state is not an enabling condition for interacting with others as morally accountable subjects, acting on conscience requires turning inward for guidance, which is precisely where one is left when ethical community provides no unequivocal normative direction.

Further, the three subdivisions Hegel ascribes to morality exhibit these dual provisos of systematic unity.[14] The first exercise of moral freedom, where moral subjects hold each other accountable only for that part of their actions that are prefigured in their purpose, does not depend upon the other two aspects of moral freedom, the right of intention and welfare and the right of conscience to determine the good. Rather, both of these latter aspects of morality presuppose that individuals interact in recognition of their morally circumscribed responsibility for only that part of their conduct that they do on purpose. Only once this is done can moral subjects proceed to attribute responsibility to the ramifications of what they do on purpose in function of the intentions that give the motive for their purpose. This right of intention necessarily follows upon the right of purpose since it refers explicitly to the intended consequences of what is done on purpose. The right of intention, however, does not depend upon conscience, for recognition that moral subjects be held responsible for the consequences they intend does not itself

---

14. Hegel, *Elements of the Philosophy of Right*, 114, 141.

involve the additional consideration of whether their intentions and purposes are good. On the other hand, moral self-determination with respect to purpose and intention provides all that is necessary to exercise the freedom of conscience, where moral subjects hold one another accountable for acting on purposes and intentions that conform to a good they independently determine. Moral subjects can only act conscientiously if they already interact in function of their right to be held responsible for what they do on purpose and what they intended to result from their moral deeds. On this basis, conscience need only employ its choosing will to determine which purposes and intentions will realize a good that is not yet at hand but should be objective. The whole actuality of morality thus involves the sequential self-constitution that Hegel presents.

Nonetheless, does participation in ethical community depend upon moral accountability in addition to recognition as a property owner? It is not hard to see that individuals who determine themselves as persons and moral subjects are fully able to enter into matrimony and establish an ethical household, from which they then can enter into the social interdependencies of civil society, and from there, into the activity of self-governance.

Yet does the functioning of ethical community necessarily require that its members hold one another accountable as moral subjects? Consider what it would mean to be an individual whose moral accountability is not recognized. Although one might not be treated as a slave, one would have no positive rights or duties, including any positive welfare, extending beyond ownership. One would be a mere person, restricted to a minimal autonomy that cannot make any further purposes or intentions its normative concern.

Can individuals with no moral rights of purpose, intention, and conscience still exercise their ethical rights of household, social, and political community? Persons can observe the negative, prohibitive rights of property ownership without concerning themselves with purpose, intention, and conscience. Respecting ownership does not involve the inner, subjective aspects of conduct but only the external actions that honor or infringe upon the property of others. Motive plays a role solely in determining punishments for perpetrators of malicious wrong. By contrast, in each and every sphere of ethical community, the realization of right includes the subjective activity by which it is achieved. Spouses exercise their household rights and duties not just by respecting property but by taking a positive interest in the household autonomy and welfare they share. That conscientious ethical commitment is a constitutive ingredient in the domestic association their actions aim to sustain. The same role for moral agency applies to civil society, whose members pursue self-selected particular ends that can only be realized by enabling others to do the same. Unless market participants and legal subjects aim at upholding the particular right and welfare of one another, they cannot interact in terms of market interdependence, civil legality, and the public securing of economic well-being. Although civil society provides an institution in which particular interests can legitimately be pursued, that normatively *civil* pursuit is predicated upon it being a right that all members of society can exercise. For this reason, acting only as a property owner without moral consideration is not compatible with exhibiting civil rectitude. Nor is the exclusive restriction to property right that libertarians endorse compatible with political freedom. Self-government depends upon citizens acting with a patriotism consisting in making the good of the body politic one's individual purpose and intention.

In each case, ethical conduct incorporates moral subjectivity, but clothes it in an institutional framework that overcomes the dilemma that haunts conscience as it operates outside of ethical community. Conscientious moral subjects hold each other accountable for acting with purposes and intentions that are good, where each is responsible for determining what counts as good. The good should be objectively valid, but since morality has only the subjective resource of conscience to determine what the good should be, what one conscience determines to be good can always conflict with what another prescribes. This discrepancy confronts moral subjects with the dilemma of either respecting the conflicting conscience of another while ignoring one's own conscience or following one's own conscience while disregarding that of others. In ethical community, by contrast, the good one pursues is neither something yet to be realized nor subjectively determined. Rather, in exercising the role to which membership entitles one, each individual acts to fulfill a good that is both already actual in the institution in which they participate and commonly pursued by all its members. Since every exercise of ethical conduct sustains the institution to which its members belong, no one exercising their household, social or political rights will pursue an end that violates the corresponding rights of their counterparts. Citizens, for example, may use their political prerogatives with different views on what will uphold the totality of freedom, but so long as they act within the constitutional limits of self-government, they will not prevent others from exercising their political rights. However citizens disagree, their constitutional political involvements will continue to sustain the body politic as an institution of self-rule realizing their shared political freedom.

Are Family, Civil Society, and the State the Exhaustive Differentiations of Ethical Community?

Hegel's broad division of the Idea of Right into spheres of abstract right, morality, and ethical community may therefore fit the logical demands of systematic unity, but can the same be said of his division of ethical community into the three institutional domains of the family, civil society, and the state?

Admittedly, Hegel fails to consistently develop the full content of these three ethical spheres. Unable to free his conception of holdovers of the premodern arrangements of his day, he leaves key features of each ethical sphere structured by factors extraneous to self-determination. In the family, Hegel restricts marriage to a monogamous heterosexual relation in which the male spouse lords over the female spouse as household manager and exclusive representative of the family in civil society and the state.[15] In civil society, he compounds the heteronomy of gender disadvantage by substituting estates for economic classes[16] and corporations for social interest groups.[17] Thereby he lets hereditary relations determine social function and opportunity, while allowing the natural subsistence of a peasantry to intrude upon the social interdependence of market freedom. These hereditary and natural dependencies carry over into Hegel's determination of political institutions, doing so on the backs of the corporations and estates he inconsistently foists upon civil society. Instead of conceiving the legislature as a representative assembly in which all citizens have equal political opportunity, Hegel adopts an estate assembly, allowing estate distinctions to ground political privileges.[18] Finally, he undercuts self-rule by endorsing the hereditary reign of a constitutional monarch.[19]

All these violations of self-determination can be overcome without undercutting the basic division between family, civil society, and state offered by the *Philosophy of Right*.[20] What allows this is that Hegel firmly differentiates the three ethical spheres in terms of the character of their ends and the scope of their association, neither of which have any necessary connection to the heteronomous holdover traditions he fails to discard. The end of family ethical community is the codetermined joint private good of the household, an end that is common to its members, but particular in scope, since the family

---

15. Hegel, *Elements of the Philosophy of Right*, 165–67, 206–7.
16. Hegel, *Elements of the Philosophy of Right*, 202–5, 234–37.
17. Hegel, *Elements of the Philosophy of Right*, 250–54, 270–72.
18. Hegel, *Elements of the Philosophy of Right*, 300–14, 339–52.
19. Hegel, *Elements of the Philosophy of Right*, 279–80, 316–22.
20. This is substantiated in the four books in which I have remedied the shortcomings in Hegel's account of ethical community: *The Just Family* (which reconstructs the family as an institution of self-determination), *The Just Economy* and *Law in Civil Society* (which together reconstruct civil society in accord with right), and *The Just State: Rethinking Self-Government* (which reconstructs the institutions of political freedom). See Richard Dien Winfield, *The Just Family* (Albany: State University Press of New York Press, 1998), *The Just Economy* (New York: Routledge, 1988), *Law in Civil Society* (Lawrence: University Press of Kansas, 1995), and *The Just State: Rethinking Self-Government* (Amherst, NY: Humanity Books, 2005).

is one domestic union among indefinitely many others. Civil society, by contrast, entitles the pursuit of ends that are particular, but its association is universal in scope since market interdependence, as well as the conventions of civil law and the public administration of welfare, extends as far as there are individuals who interact in terms of self-selected particular interests. Political association aims at the universal end of freely ordering the totality of freedom over which it presides, but unlike civil society, the state can have a particular boundary limited by other states.

Is ethical community properly divided into these three ethical spheres? Is the reality of ethical self-determination exhausted by the willing of ends that are universal but limited to an association particular in scope, ends that are particular but pursued through a global association, and ends that are universal but advanced by a particular totality of freedom? It might seem that this division covers all the possible permutations with two exceptions: an ethical community whose ends are particular and whose association is particular and an ethical community whose ends are universal and whose association is universal.

The former option, however, is already contained within civil society in the association of social interest groups, characterized by Hegel as corporations. The members of social interest groups pursue a shared particular interest by making a common front in relating to other groups whose particular interests are different from theirs, but must be accommodated in order to satisfy the former's interests.

The latter option is also already contained in the threefold division of ethical community, in this case within political association, which may be universal both in end and in scope. Although the state can be one among others, there is nothing about political unity that requires that it be a particular state confronting others in international relations. Contrary to Carl Schmitt, for whom political association depends upon a friend–foe opposition,[21] what define political association are its self-ruling reflexivity, autonomy, supremacy, and the universality of its ends, all of which are secured through the domestic subordination of all other spheres of freedom under the sway of self-government.[22] Self-government can proceed without the state having any other states with which to contend. In principle, the state could be global or a solitary body politic with no relations to any other.

What validates family, civil society, and self-government as necessary and comprehensive realizations of ethical community is the systematic unity they

---

21. See Carl Schmitt, *The Concept of the Political*, trans. George Schwab (New Brunswick: Rutgers University Press, 1976), 26.
22. For further analysis of these four cardinal features of political association, see Winfield, *The Just State*, 129–32.

exhibit. The emancipated family does not itself incorporate any civil or political relationships, but without household freedom, neither civil nor political self-determination can be realized. This is not because every civilian and citizen must be married or raised in a family, since individuals can certainly exercise their social and political rights even if they are single and have been brought up in public orphanages. Rather, the emancipated family serves as a structural prerequisite of civil society and self-government because if household emancipation has not been achieved, heteronomous family organization will impede the equal social and political opportunities of family members. Any deficit in household codetermination will prevent competent adult family members from being able to participate in civil society and politics on an equal footing with their household counterparts.[23] Similarly, civil society does not itself involve political relationships, which is why individuals may exercise their social as well as household rights in conditions where self-government is lacking. Nonetheless if equal social opportunity is unrealized, relations of social domination will prevent individuals from having equal opportunity to engage in self-rule. For this reason, the social emancipation provided by a civil society that regulates market activity through civil law, private social interest group activity, and the public administration of welfare is a structural prerequisite for political self-determination.

Indeed, precisely because self-government cannot operate unless household and civil rights are guaranteed, the actuality of political freedom necessarily ensures that the totality of prepolitical freedoms is realized and sustained within the state. Only with self-government crowning the system of self-determination can the specter of political oppression be removed and all rights be adequately upheld. This truth provides the logical capstone of the development of the Idea of Right.

---

23. Moreover, since normativity consists in self-determination, there can be no legitimate excuse for not leaving room for a type of self-determination that is compatible with the other institutions of freedom.

Chapter 10

A DREAM DEFERRED: FROM THE US CONSTITUTION TO THE UNIVERSAL DECLARATION OF HUMAN RIGHTS

Rights and the Constitution

A constitution should authoritatively state the rights whose recognition, exercise, and enforcement build the secure reality of the political, social, household, moral, and property freedoms in which valid conduct consists. These rights are properly inalienable fixtures of a just community and they should be constitutionally protected from violation and repeal.

The crowning institution of right is the sovereign self-governing state, whose own freedom cannot be maintained if citizens are subordinate to another power beyond their political control. Nonetheless, the supreme autonomy of self-government does not make problematic upholding the nonpolitical rights of property owners, moral subjects, family members, and participants in a duly civil society. This is because individuals cannot wield their equal political opportunity as self-governing citizens unless their other rights are respected.

First and foremost, the property right of all individuals must be upheld for the simple reason that we cannot exercise any further rights if the inalienable ownership of our own body is not respected. If, instead, self-ownership is not universally recognized, at least some individuals are subject to appropriation by some master, to whose will everything they do is attributable. Nothing they undertake will count as their own deed and they will lack any independent freedom that others need respect.

Similarly, we cannot enjoy any conscientious participation in public life unless we recognize one another to be morally responsible. Only then will we be in a position to hold one another accountable for what we do on purpose and for those consequences we intended. Those deprived of recognition as moral agents will forfeit their dignity, without which their privileged counterparts are at liberty to treat them as disposable means serving the purposes of others.

Without recognized moral agency, one loses any chance to participate freely as member of a family, a civil society, or a self-governing state.

So too, if spouses cannot exercise equal rights to codetermine their joint household property and welfare, those who are dominated by their partner will be unable to participate equally independently in society and politics. Those who lord over their spouse in the family will have a privileged say on the allotment of household duties, as well as direct by whom and how the family interest will be represented outside the home. The household master will be the gatekeeper of any opportunity of the dominated spouse to work, engage in social advocacy, or engage in political activity. Without household codetermination, social and political participation becomes a privilege instead of a right.

Finally, if social opportunity is unequal, those who are socially disadvantaged will lack sufficient resources and time to participate in self-government on a par with those who enjoy social privilege. Those wielding significantly greater wealth and social dominance will be able to pressure those who depend on them, as well as have greater ability to influence political opinion and run for office.

In sum, unless all prepolitical rights are upheld, citizens cannot exercise equal political freedom and self-rule will revert to domination by some privileged faction over others. Consequently, self-government never needs to be compelled externally to recognize and enforce the property, moral, family, and social rights of its citizens. In order for citizens to govern themselves, they must at the same time secure their nonpolitical freedoms. Only then can they wield the equal political opportunity that allows rule to be self-government rather than dominion of one group over another.

Accordingly, a proper constitution must not only authoritatively formulate the political rights and duties of its citizens. It must also authoritatively mandate the nonpolitical rights without which political self-determination cannot take place.

All these rights should be determined in a manner that prevents their constitutional repeal. Otherwise, the commitment to their preservation is uncertain. This imperative to maintain the incorrigibility of basic inalienable rights was recognized by the writers of the constitution of the postwar German Federal Republic. They had witnessed how the Nazis were elected into office constitutionally and then used constitutional powers to revoke amendable democratic provisions of the Weimar Republic Constitution. To prevent any such abominations in the future, the new German Federal Republic Constitution contained a special section of fundamental rights, whose contents were immune from amendment.

Although true basic rights deserve unbending protection, corrigibility should apply to those positive mandates of the constitution that specify details of self-government that have no necessary rational specification. These include such determinations as how many members a legislature or supreme court should have and how long terms of office should be for legislators, supreme court justices, and the chief executive.

The Narrow Focus of the US Constitution

The US Constitution satisfies some but not all of the fundamental requirements that a proper constitution should fulfill.

On the one hand, the US Constitution does not protect any of our basic rights from repeal through constitutional amendment. *Article V: The Amendment Process* allows all constitutional statutes to be revoked through amendment with two exceptions, one timeless and one temporary.

The timelessly protected rule is stated in Section 3.1 of *Article I: the Legislative Branch*, which stipulates, "the Senate of the United States shall be composed of two Senators from each State."[1] *Article V: The Amendment Process* safeguards this section by mandating that "no State, without its Consent, shall be deprived of its equal Suffrage in the Senate." This provision can hardly be an inalienable basic right, since the equal representation of states violates the political equality of the citizens inhabiting states of very unequal population.[2]

The temporary limit on amendment applies to constitutional statute applying to the international slave trade. The relevant section of Article V reads as follows: "Provided that no Amendment which may be made prior to the Year One thousand eight hundred and eight shall in any Manner affect the first and fourth Clauses in the Ninth Section of the first Article." The first clause of Article I, Section 9, reads, "The Migration or Importation of such Persons as any of the States now existing shall think proper to admit, shall not be prohibited by the Congress prior to the Year one thousand eight hundred and eight, but a Tax or duty may be imposed on such Importation, not exceeding ten dollars for each Person." The fourth clause of Article I, Section 9, reads, "No Capitation, or other direct, Tax shall be laid, unless in Proportion to the Census or Enumeration herein before directed to be taken."[3] The

---

1. All citations of the text of the US Constitution and its amendments refer to the text as reprinted in Akhil Reed Amar, *America's Constitution: A Biography* (New York: Random House, 2005), 479–99.
2. The permanent maintenance of this political inequity was, of course, the express aim of the agrarian, less populated colonies who made sustaining their disproportionate influence a condition for joining the "more perfect" but still imperfect union of the United States.
3. Akhil Reed Amar notes, "Article V gave the international slave trade temporary immunity from constitutional amendment, in seeming violation of the people's

immutability of basic rights is hardly served by the temporary immunity of the international slave trade to constitutional amendment. It rather represents a capitulation to a political conjuncture that limited what constitutional text could be ratified. The temporary nature of the hold acknowledges the transient character of this compromise, which is not the case with the permanent immunity to amendment uniquely applied to the equal representation of states in the Senate.

One might hope that our constitution's balance of powers could compensate for the absence of any immutable fundamental rights by preventing any one branch of government from violating constitutional statute with impunity. Not only must the Senate and House of Representatives concur to pass legislation, but no adopted bill counts as law until the president signs on or his veto is overridden by a two-thirds legislative vote. Even when presidential vetoes are overruled by legislative supermajorities the Supreme Court can still invalidate legislation by judging it to be unconstitutional. This final remedy, however, depends upon bringing cases to court. One can imagine situations when the immediate application of a law might inflict fatal damage upon the democratic process and even disable the procedures of judicial review. The balance of powers might then fail to impede the hegemonic assertions of the legislative branch.

Although these features may threaten firm commitment to almost any constitutional content, our constitution does lay out important features of the basic structure of a representative democracy and the political roles its citizens are entitled and obliged to perform. Does the constitution, however, contain sufficient specification of the prepolitical rights on which self-government depends? Let us briefly survey the Preamble, Articles, and amendments to see whether our constitution covers the ground it should.

The Promise of the Preamble

The Preamble to the US Constitution proclaims that "We the people of the United States [...] do ordain and establish this Constitution for the United States of America" to "form a more perfect Union, establish Justice, insure domestic Tranquility, provide for the common defence, promote the general Welfare, and secure the Blessings of Liberty to ourselves and our Posterity."

What rights does this proclamation promise? Establishing justice and ensuring peace and security seems to protect the basic rights of person

---

inalienable right to amend at any time, and came close to handing slave states an absolute veto over all future constitutional modifications under that Article." See Amar, *America's Constitution*, 21.

and property from violations due to fraud, theft, and malicious as well as nonmalicious injury and damage. Promoting the general welfare might offer some further blessings of liberty for ourselves as well as for future generations. To determine what these blessings are, however, we need to identify what interests should be satisfied to realize the welfare that is general, rather than particular. Is this a matter of providing equal satisfaction to the particular personal wants of everyone or a matter of realizing interests that are not personal but collective in character? By itself, the Preamble offers little guidance.

The *Declaration of Independence*'s proclamation of the inalienable rights to "life, liberty, and the pursuit of happiness" is similarly vague. The right to life and liberty might signify recognition solely of property right, which includes honoring one's prerogative to dispose of one's property as one sees fit as well as protecting against infringements upon one's property, including the body that is each person's uniquely inalienable object of ownership. Property in one's body is inalienable because a person has no recognizable juridical reality left if someone else takes ownership of that person's entire physical being. Nothing a slave does or suffers counts as the slave's own responsibility or wrong but rather counts as the responsibility of or wrong to its owner. Respecting each person's body as an inalienable property, as well as the basis of all exercise of property right, can also extend to a right to subsistence, that is, to life as a biological and psychological endowment. Property right, however, provides no basis for extending the "right to life" to any further level of subsistence that might involve a conventional standard of living and the resources providing equal opportunity in society and state.[4] Liberty, however, might also apply to the right to submit to no government to which one has not given one's consent, in due homage to the social contract argument that roots political authority in an exercise of property right, namely contractual agreement.

As for happiness, Aristotle had classically noted that everyone seeks happiness, but that there is controversy over in what it consists. Happiness might appear to be the fundamental end of conduct since individuals all seek happiness for its own sake and appear to subordinate all other affairs to achieving happiness. As Aristotle noted, if the value of conduct is sought in the ends one seeks, all action will be in vain if all ends are merely means to something else. Then one can never find anything worth doing, since the reason for doing each deed will lie in something whose own value depends on

---

4. This is why Friedrich A. Hayek, who embraces the libertarian limitation of right to property rights, acknowledges the right to subsistence but decries any attempt to redistribute property to maintain a conventional standard of living. See Friedrich A. Hayek, *The Constitution of Liberty* (Chicago: University of Chicago Press, 1960), 285–87.

something else, generating an endless regress of aims in need of justification. Unless one can locate an end that both is for its own sake and that for which all other ends are pursued, conduct will lack any legitimate goal. It is not enough for there to be ends sought for their own sake, for individuals would have no basis for selecting between such aims if none served as a master end, subordinating all others to its own realization. Only if an end can be a highest good, sought for its own sake and uniquely serving as the ruling end to which the pursuit of all aims is directed, can conduct have a sovereign goal, by means of which the value of all pursuits can be measured.[5]

Happiness may appear to possess both sides of the highest good, being sought for its own sake and being that to which all other pursuits are subordinate. Nonetheless, the difficulty of identifying its content sets the stage for the political thinking that inspired the founders of the US Constitution. A highest good cannot be a product of action because no product can both be of value in itself and be that which subordinates all affairs to itself. Works of fine art may have a value that is not instrumental, which is why we display them in museums and prohibit anyone from putting them to use. Nonetheless, works of fine art are not just one in number, nor do they operate as the end to which all other affairs are subsumed. Only an *activity* that is performed for its own sake and subordinates all other activities can qualify as a highest good. As Aristotle recognized, this master activity, subordinate to no other and ruling over all affairs, is none other than sovereign political conduct.[6] Identifying the highest good with political activity, however, has a suspect formality, because any successfully ruling power will qualify as the highest good in virtue of reigning supreme over everything else. There will be no way to distinguish between good and bad regimes and right will collapse into might.

If one regards the Aristotelian project of ethics as a science of the highest good to be inherently problematic, it is tempting to see the sole alternative to be the very situation from which liberal political thought pursues its two fundamental variants: utilitarianism and social contract theory.

In the absence of a highest good it appears that individuals are set free from any rational direction to aim at fulfilling a particular end. With reason failing to prescribe a master end, individuals seem to be at liberty to decide for themselves which goals to pursue. Insofar as a highest good alone allows for ends to have their value ranked by reason, it is no longer possible to distinguish

---

5. Aristotle, *Nicomachean Ethics*, Book I, Chapter 2, 1094a18-23, Chapter 7, 1097b1–7, in *The Complete Works of Aristotle—Volume Two*, ed. Jonathan Barnes (Princeton, NJ: Princeton University Press, 1984), 1729, 1734.
6. Aristotle, *Nicomachean Ethics*, Book I, Chapter 2, 1094a26-1-94b12, in *The Complete Works of Aristotle—Volume Two*, 1729–30.

the relative merit of individuals by what desires tend to govern their conduct. Since all desires are of equal value and character can be considered to reside in what dispositions one has established through the habits of one's conduct, no one's character can be judged superior to anyone else's. In other words, with the repudiation of a highest good, we are left free and equal in merit by nature.

Aristotle would regard the absence of a highest good as the triumph of nihilism, where individuals are left at license to do anything since no ends can be shown to be inherently meaningful. Liberalism, however, regards this outcome as a positive mandate to affirm liberty as the one and only principle of conduct.

Liberty versus Self-Determination

The principle of liberty is interpretable in two ways, one that gives rise to utilitarianism and another that gives rise to social contract theory.

The simplest, most direct avenue involves understanding liberty to be the freedom of desire, where, in the absence of a highest good mandated by reason, we are all at liberty to pursue any desire we choose. Understood as a principle guiding all conduct of every agent, the liberty of desire mandates that all desires are of equal legitimacy and that no individual's desire satisfaction has more value than that of anyone else. Since the absence of a rational ranking of desires precludes any qualitative orderings, the only basis for privileging one course of action over any other is the quantitative evaluation of how much it contributes to the aggregate desire satisfaction of individuals in general. What matters is not how much my *own* desires get quenched but how much *aggregate* desire is satisfied. Given the parity of all desires and of all individual happiness in the face of the absence of a highest good, making the liberty of desire the principle of conduct amounts to promoting the happiness of all, understood to consist in maximizing desire satisfaction in general.

The "pursuit of happiness" to which the Declaration of Independence refers can be associated with this utilitarian principle of the freedom of desire. There is, however, one basic problem, which leads the promoters of the principle of liberty to cease interpreting it as the freedom of desire and instead to construe it as the liberty of person and property, from which social contract theory proceeds. Desire is subjective, changeable, and contingent. What one individual desires may conflict with the desire satisfaction of any other, just as what one desires at one time may conflict with what one desires at another. Due to these vagaries, liberty of desire cannot function as a principle that determines any objective course of action. The utilitarian calculus, which purports to rate prospective conduct and institutions according to how they impact upon aggregate desire satisfaction, can never provide any reliable guidelines. Instead, the contingency of desire and desire satisfaction frustrates any attempt to make the liberty of desire a workable principle of ethical evaluation. Any injunction to promote the pursuit of happiness must have a more determinate concept of freedom.

Property right, the right of owners to dispose over their recognized possessions and, above all, over their inalienable right to their own body, serves as a superior principle of liberty for two reasons. First, unlike the freedom of desire, the right of property has an objective character that allows owners to exercise their prerogatives to use and preside over their property without entering into conflict with others. Whereas desire satisfactions can always conflict, one's prerogative over one's property does not intrude upon that of any other owner insofar as ownership is exclusive and distinct. What legitimately belongs to one owner does not belong to another and so long as owners operate within the boundaries of their property, their freedoms as owners stand in harmony. Secondly, the right of property can operate as a principle from which other institutions can be legitimated because ownership is basic to any further exercise of freedom. Without recognition as owner of at least one's own body, one cannot count as the author of any of one's actions, which otherwise are open to ownership by another. For this very reason, no practice involving self-determination can operate without incorporating recognition of the basic property rights of its participants. Property relations, for their part, can function so long as individuals mutually acknowledge one another as having exclusive ownership of some domain, minimally involving their own bodies. As a consequence, individuals can stand in a so-called "state of nature," where they recognize one another as owners, not slaves, without yet being subject to any other legitimate power. Admittedly, they may disagree in good faith over the boundaries of their property and the terms of contracts they have entered, as well as suffer malicious violations of their person and property. By themselves, owners lack any authoritative power to adjudicate property disputes and right wrongs that may occur. Consequently, they may then proceed to contract with one another to establish a public administration of justice to which they agree to submit to uphold their respective property domains, which otherwise lack an objectively recognized safeguard. In so doing, they wield their own property right to set up a public order whose validity rests in its service as a means to guarantee person and property from both nonmalicious disputes and criminal violations. This recipe for a civil administration of justice issuing from social contract is the logical outcome of advancing liberty as a principle rooted in property right.

Social contract theory fits well the *Declaration of Independence*'s demand that legitimate government have the consent of the governed. What it does not provide, however, is sufficient means to legitimate *participation* in representative democracy. As Thomas Hobbes and John Locke both recognized, the social contract imperative for founding political authority upon the consent of the governed does not require that the established government be democratic in form. Citizens can voluntarily contract to submit to a monarchy or an oligarchy just as well as to a democracy.[7] Consent is not the same thing as participation in self-rule. If the end of social contract were the realization not of property rights but of a distinctly political freedom consisting in the institutional practice of self-government, representative democracy would be legitimate as an end in itself. Instead, social contract establishes government as a means to an end that is given prior to political association. The body politic then amounts to an instrument for upholding something different from itself. Accordingly, the mere existence of a type of government neither coincides with the achievement of its legitimating end nor constitutes the exclusive means for achieving that purpose. For this reason, Locke acknowledged that the civil government arising from social contract might end up violating the property rights for which it was instituted. Citizens would then have to judge for themselves when they needed to ignore the commands of their deviant regime.[8] Hobbes knew that this right to rebel was inherently problematic, for it undermines the public authority of civil government by making it subordinate to the private judgment of each individual. As Hobbes pointed out, that throws individuals back into a state of nature, with no authoritative government to which one could appeal to adjudicate disputes and to judge and punish malefactors.[9]

This quandary reflects a fundamental legitimation problem that haunts the appeal to liberty as a principle of right. The problem is basic to foundational justification, which grounds normative validity in a privileged factor, the foundation of normativity, distinct from what it validates. Foundational justification is all too familiar and commands a pervasive hold on most discourse addressing what is true, right, or beautiful. Ordinarily, when justification is at issue, one seeks a reason to justify what is to be held true, right, beautiful, or otherwise normative. As distinct from what it legitimates, this reason operates as a *juridical* foundation. A *causal* foundation is responsible merely for the *existence* of what it founds, leaving undetermined whether its effect has normative standing. By contrast, a *juridical* foundation confers *legitimacy* upon what it

---

7. Thomas Hobbes, *Leviathan*, ed. C. B. Macpherson (Harmondsworth, UK: Penguin Books, 1968), 239; John Locke, *Second Treatise on Government*, ed. Thomas P. Peardon (Indianapolis, IN: Bobbs-Merrill, 1952), Sections 131–32, 73–74.
8. Locke, *Second Treatise on Government*, Sections 240–42, 138–39.
9. Hobbes, *Leviathan*, 231, 365.

justifies. In so doing, the juridical foundation confers normative validity upon something other than itself, just as what it certifies to be valid owes its legitimacy to something distinct from itself. The problem with foundational justification is that when the authority of its privileged foundation is called into question, that foundation can be justified on its own terms only by undermining the defining divide between what confers and what enjoys validity. Since foundational justification mandates that validity derives from the privileged foundation, that foundation can only be justified by itself. Then, however, what determines validity and what is determined to be valid are the same. Contrary to the two-tiered framework of foundation and the founded, the foundation's own validity ceases to rest upon something else and the erstwhile foundation ceases to validate something other than itself. In becoming self-referentially consistent, foundational justification ends up supplanting itself by rendering self-determination the very substance of normativity. This result is inescapable, for any attempt to ground validity in what is determined by something else ends up invoking a foundation whose own legitimacy cannot be established on its own terms without reinstating the exclusive normativity of self-determination.

Is the principle of liberty immune from the dilemma of foundational justification? After all, many identify liberty with freedom and self-determination. The problem is that when one advances liberty as a *principle*, it serves as a privileged foundation from which legitimate conduct and institutions are to be derived. The *principle* of liberty cannot then escape the foundationalist dilemma. As the foundation of right, the principle of liberty functions as a procedural principle, postulating a form of willing that confers legitimacy upon whatever follows from its exercise. The principle of liberty determines not itself but the derivative institutions that result from its operation. Consequently, liberty as principle is not self-determined, but a determiner of something else, which is itself not self-determined but determined by a distinct determining factor.

Can liberty claim any authority, without exhibiting the self-grounded foundation-free character of self-determination? The avatars of the various foundational appeals to liberty operate as if it were self-evident that the failure of a principle of a highest good confers exclusive legitimacy upon liberty. Admittedly, if reason cannot prescribe a highest good, there is no way to rank the given content of ends, the desires for them, and the habitual dispositions directed at them. Without a highest good, our wills may no longer be bound by reason to pursue any particular end. Nor may anyone claim more merit than anyone else on the basis of a character defined in terms of dispositions to aim for certain ends. This outcome does not eliminate the challenge of nihilism, which Aristotle held to follow from a failure to arrive at a highest good.[10] After all, even if no ends have any a priori value, this does not oblige individuals to respect the liberty of others. One can equally follow the siren of nihilism and lawlessly oppress anyone else.

Only the foundation-free, self-grounding character of self-determination escapes this outcome, for self-determination has a positive character of its own exclusive to normative validity.

To grasp the reality of self-determination and what it constitutes as the proper subject matter of ethics, it is crucial to recognize how liberty as principle is not self-determined but a determiner of something other than itself, which is not self-determined, but other-determined. These two correlative sides of the foundational operation of liberty as principle define the character of both the civil government that derives from social contract and liberty as a form of willing.

The civil government that issues from social contract is not self-determined and thereby for its own sake but rather a derivative instrument for upholding the liberty from which it follows. This derivative, instrumental character is what robs civil government of any intrinsic connection to self-rule and leaves the authority of its rule subject to question, given how a means to an end need not serve that end since it is not the end itself.

For its part, the liberty that legitimates institutions distinct from itself is not self-determined but an exercise of a faculty of choice whose form and content are both extraneously given. Liberty is an endowment of the self that an agent must possess in order to make any choices whatsoever. For this reason, liberty, as a faculty of choice, cannot be a product of willing. Since choosing any end depends upon prior possession of liberty, liberty is not "artificial" but given by nature. As the natural enabling condition of all willing, choice is necessarily formal. It has no connection to any end in particular, for it is operative in selecting whatever end is chosen. For that very reason, the ends of liberty are not given by the faculty of choice but must be found independently in given desire, external circumstances, or the edicts of reason, whose ability to prescribe ends is precisely what liberalism denies in turning to liberty as the principle of conduct.

To be self-determining, the will must determine both its own form and content, instead of letting them be given independently. The self-determining will must determine the form of its own agency, which must therefore be a product of its volition. The genuinely free will determines in some respect both *who* the agent is and *what* the agent wills. The form of the self-determined will must therefore be a non-natural, conventional agency, determined in the

---

10. Aristotle, *Nicomachean Ethics*, Book I, Chapter 2, 1094a18–23, in *The Complete Works of Aristotle—Volume Two*, 1729.

very willing in which it is exercised. This does not mean that the self-determined agent has no natural faculty of choice or any natural individuation. Every agent must have by nature the liberty to choose as well as an individual body and individual psyche given independently of its self-determined agency, without which no conduct is possible. Nonetheless, in being self-determined, the autonomous individual must give itself a non-natural individuation by means of willing ends that are not given independently of its own volition. These requirements cannot be satisfied by a single individual acting upon external nature or upon itself. In any solitary action, an agent wields a given faculty of choice, pursuing ends defined by its desires, outer circumstance, or rational reflection.

In Book IV of the *Republic*, Socrates points to the insoluble dilemma self-determination poses for the individual, considered by itself. Socrates notes that self-rule is inconceivable, for how can the same individual be both patient and agent at once, acting upon and being acted upon in one and the same action? The only solution Socrates can see is to divide the soul into a ruling part and a subservient part, foreshadowing the division of the Polis into a ruling class of guardians acting upon the subject class making up the rest of the body politic.[11]

What Socrates, as well as classical liberalism, ignores is how self-determination consists in an interaction of a plurality of agents with one another, in which they exercise rights that provide them with a conventional agency that aims at ends specific to the practice of each form of right. Property right, as we have seen, is the most basic mode of self-determination because unless agents recognize one another as exclusive owners of their own body, nothing they do can count as their own responsibility. Agents determine themselves as owners through the coordinated acts of will by which they recognizably embody their volition in some external factor that gives their freedom a recognized objectivity that is compatible with the recognized objectivity that other owners give their own self-determination as property owners. Although they each must have a natural individuality, including their body and psychological endowment as a unique choosing self, they give themselves a new individuated conventional agency as a particular owner, individuated by the factors in which they recognizably embody their will. Whereas each owner's body is uniquely inalienable, since no owners can retain their self-determined agency if their body becomes completely subservient to the will of another, every other factor of which they take ownership can be alienated by recognizably

---

11. Plato, *Republic*, Book IV, 430e–431, in Plato, *Complete Works*, ed. John M. Cooper (Indianapolis, IN: Hackett, 1997), 1062.

withdrawing their will. Others can then take ownership of the alienated factor by recognizably embodying their will in that entity.

Although the self-determination of individuals as persons, that is, owners, must be incorporated in all further forms of self-determination, this does not make property right the determining foundation of other forms of freedom. Instead, these other types of self-determination retain their autonomous character by incorporating ownership as an enabling constituent that leaves undetermined the additional types of self-determination building the totality of freedom.

This nonfoundational relation is exhibited in the next most minimal form of self-determination, moral accountability, where individuals interact with one another by determining themselves as moral subjects. Individuals acquire the artificial agency of moral subjectivity by recognizing one another to circumscribe the scope of their responsibility in function of the purposes and intentions with which they act. Moral subjects must acknowledge their respective status as owners of their own body in order to hold one another morally responsible only for that part of what they cause to happen that they did on purpose and for that part of the consequences of their actions that they intended. Because property owners can always dispute the boundaries of their property and the terms of contracts they enter, as well as commit malicious wrongs intentionally violating the property of others, persons find themselves in the moral predicament of having to take the initiative to bring right into being with the personal responsibility of determining where the good resides. This conscientious action has inherent dilemmas of its own. Because conscience is a subjective, yet other related agency, moral subjects may find that what their conscience determines to be right purposes and intentions may conflict with the consciences of other moral subjects. Moral subjects then face the predicament of either holding fast to their own determination of the good while denying the validity of the conscience of others or alternately recognizing the conscience of others at the expense of transgressing their own.

To solve this quandary requires a different type of self-determination, where agents interact by assuming roles whose characteristic ends are inherently coordinated so as to reproduce the association in which those roles operate. This institutional freedom is the framework of ethical community, wherein individuals exercise rights of membership in an association that their freely chosen ends uphold so long as they fulfill their roles in respect of the corollary rights of their fellow members. Whereas moral subjectivity falls into conscientious conflict by aiming at a good that is not at hand but must be subjectively determined, the members of ethical community act in respect to an existing association that their roles reproduce. The most basic form of ethical community, which does not contain any other, but all others may incorporate, is the emancipated household, where spouses unite to codetermine a joint private domain, consolidating their alienable property and managing together their combined household welfare. By wedding the private domains of its spouses, the ethical family can readily be the arena in which children are born and reared in function of the ethical imperative that parental care enable children to achieve autonomous maturity. What gender and sexual orientation spouses have is irrelevant to exercising the household codetermination of spouses or the ethical charge of parenting.[12]

The rights and duties of spouse and parents, however, remain in jeopardy unless family members can earn a sufficient livelihood, as well as benefit from the public institutions that provide legal enforcement of their rights, including the adjudication and protection of not just their joint property but also the welfare of spouses and children. This challenge is partly at stake in the second form of ethical community, comprising a legitimately civil society whose members determine themselves as autonomous economic agents and legal subjects. In the ethical community of civil society individuals interact in terms of self-selected particular interests that can only be satisfied by enabling other participants to satisfy self-selected particular interests of their own. These other-directed self-selected interests are not natural wants but socially determined needs for commodities, whose satisfaction takes the form of an exercise of right, where market participants satisfy their own need for what others have to offer under the condition of providing them with what they are willing to obtain in return. Although market interaction always operates in terms of this reciprocity of commodity exchange, the establishment of money and profit seeking enterprise produces a competitive dynamic that requires firms to grow in order to survive, leading to a polarization between employers and employees with very different economic opportunities. Together with the contingencies of market activity, this polarization puts the equal exercise of economic freedom in jeopardy, requiring private and public interventions to secure equal economic opportunity, on which family welfare also depends. The private interventions involve the activities of economic interest groups, such as trade unions, business associations, landlord and tenant organizations, and consumer federations. The public intervention partly involves a civil administration of law, to protect the person and property of commodity owners and the family rights of spouses, parents, and children.[13] Public intervention also consists in a civil administration of welfare remedying market failure

---

12. For a systematic development of family self-determination, see Richard Dien Winfield, *The Just Family* (Albany: State University Press of New York Press, 1998).
13. For a systematic development of the civil administration of law, see Richard Dien Winfield, *Law in Civil Society* (Lawrence: University Press of Kansas, 1995).

by enabling all able members of civil society to exercise their economic self-determination and earn a conventional living sufficient to support themselves and their dependents.[14]

These basic imperatives of the ethical communities of family and civil society are preconditions for the ethical community of political freedom because unless the family and social rights of individuals are secured, these individuals cannot wield equal political opportunity to engage in self-government. Disadvantage in the household and society will block some citizens from being able to participate on par with those who enjoy household and social advantage. Individuals determine themselves as free citizens by participating in democratic rule, exercising political rights that can only be wielded within existing democratic institutions, whose own continued existence depends upon the ongoing unimpeded political self-determinations of its citizens. Unlike civil society, whose members pursue self-selected particular ends in a web of interdependence of global extent, the ethical community of political freedom consists in engagements in self-rule where citizens act in pursuit of universal aims, lawfully governing the whole order of the body politic, which may be a particular state in relation to others. Since political autonomy rests upon household and social autonomy, which themselves depend upon the recognition of moral accountability and property right, the reality of political self-determination inherently incorporates the realization of the other forms of self-determination.[15] The universal aims of political self-determination therefore encompass securing property, moral, household, and social rights in conformity with self-government.

This is why a constitution that ignores family and social rights puts democratic freedom in jeopardy. It is also why classical liberal theory, with its truncated construal of freedom, is inadequate to justify the institutions of self-determination for which self-government provides the sovereign capstone. A theory of freedom that limits autonomy to property right and morality cannot support a republic, but better suits the license of the Roman Empire, where freedom is limited to property right and everything else is subject to the whim of the emperor.

How then, does the US Constitution stand with respect to the constitutional securing of the prepolitical rights on which political freedom depends?

---

14. For a systematic development of economic self-determination and the private and public interventions required to uphold economic freedom, see Richard Dien Winfield, *The Just Economy* (New York: Routledge, 1988), and Richard Dien Winfield, *Rethinking Capital* (Houndmills, UK: Palgrave Macmillan, 2016).
15. For a systematic development of political freedom, see Richard Dien Winfield, *The Just State: Rethinking Self-Government* (Amherst, NY: Humanity Books, 2005).

The Limitation of Rights in the Articles of the US Constitution

Prepolitical Rights in Article I

The constitution begins in Article I by specifying the organization, qualifications, and functions of the legislative branch of government. Unlike the Articles of Confederation, Article I mandates a bicameral legislature empowered to make law on behalf of the citizens of the United States that is binding for all the member states.[16] Instead of being an advisory body of a loose confederation dependent upon the indulgences of each state, "Congress," Section 8 specifies, "shall have Power To lay and collect Taxes, Duties, Imposts, and Excises, to pay the Debts and Provide for the common Defence and general Welfare of the United States." The British Parliament met behind closed doors, had no fixed sessions, and filled its lower house with members representing districts of greatly different populations.[17] By contrast, Article I requires Congress to open its proceedings to the public, have regular elections with fixed terms for its legislators, and, in the case of the House of Representatives, allot legislators to districts of equivalent population, duly registered by census every decade. All these innovations are important mainstays of representative democracy.

Still, they make little mention of the property rights, family rights, or social rights on which equal political opportunity depends. This "omission" is of positive significance, for it signifies that the legislature will carry out its lawmaking activity without being bound by any distinctions of property ownership, kinship relations, or social position and wealth.

Unlike the Articles of Confederation and many of the State Constitutions,[18] Article I attaches no property qualification to holding office in either the House of Representatives or the Senate, other than having the status of a free person. That status rests upon recognition as the owner of one's own body. Without that basic recognition one cannot exercise any rights whatsoever. Instead, one is subject to enslavement, where everything one does is the responsibility of one's master. So basic is this status of free personhood that Article I can pass over it while citing citizenship, appropriate residency, and minimum ages as primary requirements for legislative membership.

---

16. See Amar, *America's Constitution*, 57–58, for a discussion of the key differences between the "old Congress" of the Articles of Confederation and the "new Congress" as empowered by Article I of the Constitution.
17. Amar, *America's Constitution*, 75, 82, 84.
18. Amar, *America's Constitution*, 66.

Admittedly, the absence of particular property qualifications for federal legislative office is qualified in two respects, both qualifications of which have proven to be transient.

On the one hand, although Article I does not require federal legislators to own any alienable property in specific kind or amount, those who choose congressional representatives and senators may still be subject to property qualifications of their own. Since the states retain the authority to regulate federal elections, for some time many states were able to impose property requirements without which citizens could not cast a direct vote for their House representatives nor for the state legislators who originally chose Senators. Moreover, some states made holding state legislative office contingent upon ownership of a certain amount of landed property.[19] These vestiges of oligarchic restriction on voting for and holding federal legislative office eventually withered away before the XVII Amendment (1913) provided direct election of Senators.

On the other hand, the notorious Section 2 of Article I makes slave ownership in each state partly determinative of the number of its House representatives and the amount of federal taxes levied on its taxpayers. The key text reads: "Representatives and direct Taxes shall be apportioned among the several States which may be included within this Union, according to their respective Numbers, which shall be determined by adding to the whole Number of free Persons, including those bound to Service for a Term of Years, and excluding Indians not taxed, three fifths of all other Persons." This measure enhances a state's representation in the House by the amount of slave ownership of its free inhabitants.[20] Citizens who live in states with less slaves have comparatively fewer legislators to vote for, indirectly imposing a property qualification upon them. Emancipation has since eliminated this oligarchic deformation.[21]

Two further features of Article I leave kinship relations with no role to play in the qualifications for legislative office, while expressly restraining them from wielding any influence in government.

First, the age requirements for holding office as a House Representative and as a Senator are both set higher than the voting age. Section 2 requires a Representative to be at least 25 years old, whereas Section 3 requires Senators

---

19. Amar, *America's Constitution*, 66.
20. Of course, if the slave states had emancipated their slaves, the number of adult male slaves would have counted integrally in the calculation of congressional representatives, and not by the fraction of 3/5.
21. As Amar observes, "Nowhere else did the federal Constitution concede so much political power to property per se." See Amar, *America's Constitution*, 93.

to be at least 30 years old. Both of these measures aim at preventing young men of privileged families from having immediate access to office on the strength of their family ties. Instead, the higher age requirements give individuals time to prove their mettle through their own accomplishments and win office on that basis.[22]

Second, Section 9 undermines any role for hereditary succession by prohibiting any "Title of Nobility" to "be granted by the United States." Family ties are not to intrude upon the workings of legislation, nor, for that matter, upon any other functions of government.

Social position and wealth go equally unmentioned in the specification of House and Senate qualifications. Nonetheless, an important measure prescribed by neither the Articles of Confederation nor the contemporaneous state constitutions prevents the wealth of legislators from conditioning their ability to hold office.[23] Section 6 mandates that "The Senators and Representatives shall receive a Compensation for their Services, to be ascertained by Law, and paid out of the Treasury of the United States." Since national legislative work is geographically dislocating and time consuming, without mandatory compensation no one can afford to hold House or Senate office who does not possess independent means. Giving legislators a livable salary thus destroys an important root of oligarchy. Paying legislators, however, does not remedy the problem of how running for legislative office may require putting livelihood aside and mobilizing sizable private resources that hardly every individual possesses.

The only other occasion in the sections of Article I where issues concerning nonpolitical rights arise is in the mandates for what congressional legislation may address. Section 8 of Article I implicitly bears upon property, household, and social rights by permitting Congress to shape taxation, handle national debt, and provide for the "general welfare." What is the content of the general welfare and what instruments of nonpolitical freedom are to be supported by taxation and public financing is, however, left unspecified.

Section 8 does go on to authorize Congress "to regulate Commerce with foreign Nations, and among the several States, and with the Indian Tribes." Although this so-called "commerce clause" need not and was not intended to be restricted to economic relationships,[24] it leaves undetermined what rights,

---

22. See Amar, *America's Constitution*, 70–71, for a discussion of this intent of the Congressional age requirements.
23. Amar discusses how this represented a departure from the practice of state legislatures and the Congress under the Articles of Confederation in *America's Constitution*, 72–73.
24. Amar points out how the narrow economic interpretation of the "Commerce Clause," which has come to prevail in contemporary jurisprudence, was by no means its original meaning. As Amar writes, "the broader reading of 'Commerce' in this clause would

economic or otherwise, are to be protected and promoted by this regulation. Nor does it explain why any such rights would only deserve protection as they apply in international and interstate relations. Any prepolitical rights properly involve interactions that do not depend on relations *between* nations or states (i.e., provinces). Instead, the rights of individuals in family and society should hold sway just as well *within* states and nations.

Further measures of Section 8 do provide and safeguard some of the national financial, transportation, communication, and technological resources serving the "general welfare." These include provisions

> to establish an uniform Rule of Naturalization, and uniform Laws on the subject of Bankruptcies throughout the United States; To coin Money, regulate the Value thereof, and of foreign Coin, and fix the Standard of Weights and Measures; To provide for the Punishment of counterfeiting the Securities and current Coin of the United States; To establish Post Office and post Roads; To promote the Progress of Science and useful Arts, by securing for limited Time to Authors and Inventors the exclusive Right to their respective Writings and Discoveries.[25]

All these endeavors can aid national economic development. Nonetheless, what are the economic rights of the members of the body politic? Are they adequately addressed simply by having national government erect and protect public goods serving all economic agents, not only in commerce with other nations and between states but within state borders? Can that be enough for individuals to gain a decent livelihood, provide for their families, and be equipped to participate equally in the political life of the nation?

The closing words of Section 8 might provide some additional leeway by empowering Congress "to make all Laws which shall be necessary and proper for carrying into Execution the foregoing Powers."[26] Is, however, this "necessary and proper clause" sufficient to guarantee the household and social rights on which political freedom depends?

Certain strictures of Section 9 do the very opposite. They bolster enslavement by forbidding Congress from imposing "capitation" taxes on slaves, which could have driven slavery out of business, and from taxing "Articles

---

seem to make better sense of the framers' general goals by enabling Congress to regulate all interactions (and altercations) with foreign nations and Indian tribes" (Amar, *America's Constitution*, 107).
25. Amar, *America's Constitution*, 483.
26. Amar, *America's Constitution*, 110.

exported from any State," which could have been used to penalize the products of plantation slavery.[27]

Section 10 does prohibit states from imposing any "Law impairing the Obligation of Contracts,"[28] which could be seen to safeguard property rights in general. This measure does not uphold family and economic freedom, however, at least so long as household and social rights are irreducible to rights of ownership.

Prepolitical Rights in Article II

Like Article I, Article II specifies the organization, qualifications, and functions of a branch of government, in this case the executive, without explicitly addressing any prepolitical rights. Family and social relations only intrude negatively by being barred from wielding any direct influence on the selection and workings of the executive. Just as legislators are prescribed residency, citizenship, and age requirements without reference to property and kinship, so the requirements for chief executive (at least 14 years residency within the United States, natural born citizenship or citizenship at the time of the constitution's adoption, minimum age of 35) do not include any property qualifications or family linkages. Once more the elevated age requirement works against dynastic privilege by giving candidates time to prove themselves before the electorate. Similarly, just as compensation for legislators permits them to hold office without need of private wealth, so the pay for president ensures that riches need not be necessary to devote full time to the demands of the highest executive position.

A certain illicit property does wield its privilege in the selection of the president, as it does in the election of Representatives to the House, at least until Emancipation and the 14th Amendment made the matter moot. Article II Section 1 again gives property in slaves special political clout. By specifying that the Electoral College that elects the president allot electors to states based on the number of its Senators and House seats, Section 1 allows each state's slave ownership to enter into determining its electoral representation.

Beyond these indirect and partly transient implications, Article II leaves unmentioned the prepolitical rights on which equal political opportunity depends.

---

27. Amar, *America's Constitution*, 120.
28. Amar, *America's Constitution*, 123.

Prepolitical Rights in Article III

Article III follows Articles II and I in specifying the organization, qualifications for, the functions of a fundamental branch of government without directly addressing the family, and social rights on which political participation depends. Here what lies at stake is the judicial branch of the federal government, whose organization into federal courts and a supreme court is indicated, but whose detailed specification is left to Congress, subject to presidential veto.

Article III says nothing about the apportionment of federal judges among the different states, but leaves the matter to Congress to decide. Accordingly, the disproportionate legislative clout of slave holding states led, at least for a time, to slave states having a comparably disproportionate share of federal judgeships, as well as Supreme Court justices.[29] Although qualifications for federal judgeships do not involve any property requirement, the property most at odds with property right, slave ownership, once more wields indirect power over the selection of federal officials.

Otherwise, Article III leaves all "free" citizens, whether born or naturalized, eligible to hold federal judgeships. Moreover, just as Articles I and II provide legislators and chief executive a salaried position, so Article III guarantees federal judges paid employment so long as their tenure fulfills the "good behavior" standard. In the judiciary, as in legislative and executive office, participation in federal government need not depend upon private riches. Paid service combats oligarchic privilege, even if it leaves unanswered whether all citizens can acquire the resources they need to reach the point of standing for government office.

Besides specifying the organization, qualifications, and functions of the federal judiciary, Article III also mandates that federal criminal cases be tried with juries. Federal civil cases are left without any jury requirement, in line with the secondary treatment they are afforded by the constitution and its amendments. Civil cases, however, are of signal importance when it comes to upholding family and social rights. A constitution that fails to guarantee individuals an equal hearing, as well as legal representation, in civil litigation has not balanced the scales of justice.

Prepolitical Rights in Articles IV–VII

Article IV, which considers the relation of federal law to state and interstate legal disputes, has no more to contribute to the specification and protection of prepolitical rights than the three preceding articles.

---

29. See Amar, *America's Constitution*, 214–15.

The focus of sections 1 and 2 of this constitutional statute is on civil law, as it relates to person and property, and ensuring that states respect one another's legal proceedings, even when, as section 2 allows, a state legally protects the enslavement of some of its inhabitants.

Prepolitical rights are of no more concern to Section 3, which allows no new states to be formed out of parts or conjunctions of existing states without the consent of their respective legislatures, and ensures that "nothing in this Constitution shall be construed as to Prejudice any claims of the United States, or any particular state."

Section 4 might be thought to raise wider concerns by mandating that "The United States shall guarantee to every State in this Union a Republican Form of Government." This could and should commit the Federal government to guarantee every state the recognition and enforcement of the household and social rights without which citizens cannot equally engage in self-government. Since, however, the specification of the "republican form of government" in Articles I–III itself ignores securing the prepolitical rights enabling citizens to partake in representative democracy, section 4 does not invite the wider interpretation that should have been made explicit in the foregoing articles.

Article V, which addresses the procedures of constitutional amendment, has one part that, as earlier noted, bears indirectly upon issues of household and social right. This is the provision that "no Amendment which may be made prior to the Year One thousand eight hundred and eight shall in any Manner affect the first and fourth Clauses in the Ninth Section of the first Article." This edict imposes a temporary ban on any measures that would jeopardize the slave trade by limiting the "Migration or Importation" of "such Persons" or by any "Capitation, or other direct, Tax" that might threaten the economic viability of slavery. Temporarily contravening the family and social rights of the enslaved, Article V has nothing positive to offer for securing the prepolitical rights other than the transience of its collusion with the most basic violation of personhood.

Article VI restricts itself primarily to emphasizing the integrity of national commitments and the sovereignty of federal political action. Declaring that "all Debts contracted and Engagements entered into, before the Adoption of this Constitution, shall be as valid against the United States under this Constitution, as under the Confederation," Article VI proceeds to reiterate the supremacy of federal governance, stating that "this Constitution and the Laws of the United States which shall be made in Pursuance thereof; and all Treaties made, or which shall be made, under the Authority of the United States, shall be the supreme Law of the Land." Article VI does, however, add one provision that touches upon the freedoms of civil society. This is its final provision that "no religious Test shall ever be required as a Qualification to any Office or public Trust under the United States." Although this does not incur any positive household or social rights, it does prevent any particular religious group from wielding political privilege and thereby undermining the social autonomy of individuals in civil society.

The silence of the constitution on all the other prepolitical enabling conditions of political freedom is sealed with Article VII, which quickly closes with a final formulation of the ratification procedure for "the establishment of this Constitution."

Prepolitical Rights in the Bill of Rights

Our survey of the seven Articles of the US Constitution has confirmed that none offer any positive enunciation of the household and social rights on which free citizenship rests. Does the Bill of Rights provide the needed supplement to remedy this fundamental omission?

The first amendment directly secures basic opportunities for the exercise of political freedom by barring any "establishment of religion," guaranteeing "freedom of speech, or of the press," ensuring "the right of the people peaceably to assemble, and to petition the Government for a redress of grievances." All of these rights can serve to buttress prepolitical rights insofar as political action provides the ultimate instrument for legislating and enforcing family and social freedoms. Religious freedom and freedoms of speech, assembly, and petitioning do not of themselves mandate to what ends these pillars of political freedom will be used. As our history has shown, the formalities of political freedom can be observed while leaving family welfare and social independence in jeopardy. So long as this is the case, religious freedom and freedoms of speech, assembly, and petitioning can be the vehicles of a creeping oligarchy, where household and economic deprivation impair equal political participation.

The second and third amendments, which bear upon the right "of the people to keep and bear Arms" and bar peacetime quartering of soldiers "in any house, without the consent of the Owner," may incidentally affect household welfare and economic well-being. However, providing for "a well regulated Militia" and prohibiting intrusive billeting of soldiers hardly ensure that the family and social rights of individuals are recognized and enforced.

Amendments IV through VIII all concern rights of civil legality, focused on protecting person and property, rather than the wider rights of family welfare and social independence. Article IV protects individuals from searches without warrants, whereas Article V requires indictment by civil Grand Jury in nonmilitary cases and wards against double jeopardy, self-incrimination, appropriation of private property for public use without just compensation, and deprivation of "life, liberty, or property, without due process of law." The life and liberty in question are those of legal owners, whose freedom fits the confines of social contract. Article VI upholds the corresponding legal rights of a person in criminal prosecution, guaranteeing "speedy and public trial, by an impartial jury of the State and district wherein the crime shall have been committed," with due notice of accusations, confrontation with accusing witnesses, and "compulsory process for obtaining witnesses in his favor, and [...] the Assistance of Counsel for his defense." Article VII extends the right to trial by jury to "suits at common law, where the value in controversy shall exceed twenty dollars." Finally, Article VIII prohibits "excessive bail," "excessive fines," or "cruel and unusual punishments." Although these articles stipulate formal norms for both criminal cases and common law suits, they do not address the material issues of what entitlements, beyond those of person and property, should come under judicial enforcement.

The only amendment of the Bill of Rights that might bear upon other prepolitical entitlements is the concluding Amendment X, which reserves to the States or the people "the powers not delegated to the United States by the Constitution, nor prohibited by it to the States." Since the constitution has not guaranteed any specific rights pertaining to the household or the economy, Amendment X could represent a blank check on which to lay claim to all those prepolitical rights without which self-government cannot operate. Yet, in the absence of further precisions, it is only a blank check, with no determinate commitment.

Prepolitical Rights in the Other Amendments

The remaining amendments have so far failed to overcome the constitution's limited reach as a bulwark of freedom.

Most have no bearing upon the problem. Amendment XI addresses the limits of federal judicial power in respect to suits between individuals of different states or different nations. Amendment XII recalibrates how the Electoral College selects the president and vice president. Amendment XVIII introduces direct election of Senators. Amendment XVIII introduces the prohibition of "intoxicating liquors," which Amendment XXI repeals. Amendment XX alters the starting date of presidential and legislative terms. Amendment XXII limits presidents to two terms. Amendment XXIII gives the District of Columbia voting rights in the Electoral College. Amendment XXV details procedures for replacing the president due to death, resignation, or unfitness. Amendment XXVI lowers the age requirement for voting to 18 years. Amendment XXVII prevents any change in the compensation for Senators or Representatives until after an intervening legislative election.

None of these amendments contribute to upholding the household and social rights on which equal political opportunity depends.

By contrast, Amendments XIII, XIV, XV, XVI, XIX, and XXIV do have some bearing upon family welfare and social opportunity but primarily by removing the barriers to legal and political equality that slavery and women's disenfranchisement comprised.

The Thirteenth Amendment's abolition of slavery and involuntary servitude, "except as a punishment for crime whereof the party shall have been duly convicted," does rescind these flagrant violations of property, family, and social right, but it does not lift the barriers to household and economic opportunity that confront otherwise emancipated members of civil society. Free status may enable individuals to exercise property rights, autonomously marry and rear children, and enter the market as owner of at least their own labor power, but emancipation does not further secure family or social welfare.

The same can be said of Section 1 of the Fourteenth Amendment's prohibition of any state abridging the "privileges or immunities of citizens of the United States" or of depriving "any person of life, liberty, or property, without due process of law" or of denying "any person within its jurisdiction the equal protection of the laws." So long as laws restrict themselves to mandating respect for property, civil legality, and the formal process of self-government, Section 1 offers no guarantee for family well-being and economic independence.

The Fifteenth Amendment may prohibit the United States or any state from denying or abridging the right to vote of any citizen "on account of race, color, or previous condition of servitude" and thereby grant all male citizens formal political equality. Nonetheless, reaffirming the universal right to vote does not itself guarantee the household freedom and social opportunity on which equal political participation depends.

The Nineteenth Amendment's enfranchisement of women similarly lifts a final barrier to formal political equality. It still does not guarantee that household rights are enforced and that the economic welfare of individuals and households is sufficient to enable them to engage in political activity on an equal footing with others.

Amendment XXIV does attempt to remedy one way in which poverty, and particularly race-based poverty, can be used to obstruct equal political participation. The 24th Amendment does so by guaranteeing that "the right of citizens of the United States to vote" in federal elections "shall not be denied or abridged by the United States or any State by reason of failure to pay any poll tax or other tax." This prohibition of poll taxes may indeed free the right to vote from having costs that weigh differently upon citizens relative to their wealth. Admittedly, by enabling individuals who were too poor to pay poll taxes to vote, the 24th Amendment may facilitate their new political voice to influence legislators to better address family and social welfare. It does not, however, directly stipulate or enforce the social rights to economic independence and security, which go well beyond making voting payment free.

The 16th Amendment, by contrast, does provide an instrument for directly addressing some of the obstacles to economic opportunity. By empowering Congress to "lay and collect taxes on incomes, from whatever source derived, without apportionment among the several States, and without regard to any census or enumeration," this amendment offers a means of both raising public revenue and reducing income inequalities that may threaten family welfare and stifle equal opportunity in society and politics. Amendment XVI does not specify what household and social rights any income tax might serve. More is needed to secure the prepolitical foundations of democratic freedom.

Is the US Constitution Incomplete?

In the several centuries since the ratification of the US Constitution, most attention has fallen on exposing and remedying the inconsistent interpretation and enforcement of the civil and political rights it mandates. Although the Constitution does not itself distinguish between the entitlements of men and women, nor assign property qualifications to any office, nor limit free status by any racial or ethnic identification, the constitutional order it founded began by extending full civil and political freedom only to white men with a certain amount of property. The founders and their immediate successors took for granted that only adult males could fully participate in civic and political life. They failed to guarantee non-white free men the right to vote and run for office throughout the union. They allowed state laws to impose property qualifications on both voters and office holders. And, of course, they tolerated the enslavement of blacks. Nearly two and a half centuries of various civil rights struggles have ensued, seeking to fulfill the universal entitlement basic to the meaning of civil and political right. Thanks to constitutional amendments, statutory reforms, and judicial decisions, gender, race, and wealth have largely ceased to exclude individuals from the formal exercise of their civil and political freedom. The strictures of the constitution have gained a much more consistent realization than the founders either desired or anticipated.

Nonetheless, the very triumphs of civil rights movements have made it more and more evident that even a consistently interpreted and enforced constitution is insufficient to uphold political freedom and the prepolitical freedoms on which it depends. Far from fulfilling the Preamble's promise to "establish Justice," "promote the general Welfare, and secure the Blessings of liberty to ourselves and our Posterity," the constitution has presided over a nation of rampant social disadvantage, threatening the family welfare and political equal opportunity of its citizens. The United States has become the most economically unequal developed nation, where the most wealthy 1 percent hold as much wealth as the bottom 90 percent, where a quarter of the population has zero or negative net worth, where almost half our children grow up in poverty, where social mobility is less than anywhere else in the developed world. Families suffer malnutrition, homelessness, and substandard housing; public schools are failing while higher education is increasingly unaffordable; and health care remains a privilege rather than a universal right. Meanwhile, the full-time job, to which all too many benefits remain tied, is under growing assault from automation and the explosion of the "gig" economy, where internet connectivity is allowing employers to farm out more and more work to freelancers, with no guaranteed hours or benefits. Powerful interests are flooding the political process with money, while most citizens find themselves lacking sufficient resources to exercise their right to run for office.[30]

FDR's Call for a New Social Bill of Rights

Facing an earlier incarnation of this abiding predicament, Franklin Delano Roosevelt warned in 1944 in his final State of the Union Message to Congress that the constitution was in need of supplement.

> This Republic had its beginning, and grew to its present strength, under the protection of certain inalienable political rights—among them the right of free speech, free press, free worship, trial by jury, freedom from unreasonable searches and seizures. They were our rights to life and liberty. As our Nation has grown in size and stature, however—as our industrial economy expanded—these political rights proved inadequate to assures us equality in the pursuit of happiness. We have come to a clear realization of the fact that true individual freedom cannot exist without economic security and independence.[31]

---

30. For a powerful examination of these social inequalities, see Andy Stern, *Raising the Floor: How a Universal Basic Income Can Renew Our Economy and Rebuild the American Dream* (New York: Public Affairs, 2016).
31. All citations of Roosevelt's January 11, 1944 "Message to the Congress on the State of the Union" are taken from the text contained in *The Public Papers and Addresses of Franklin D. Roosevelt: 1944–45 Volume*, compiled by Samuel I. Rosenman (New York: Harper, 1950), 32–42. The "second Bill of Rights" is on page 41.

Roosevelt thus called for "a second Bill of Rights under which a new basis of security and prosperity can be established for all regardless of station, race, or creed."

Roosevelt proceeded to enumerate eight new rights, none of which is explicitly mentioned in the constitution or its amendments. Are these eight rights valid and sufficient to secure the prepolitical independence on which self-government rests?

Roosevelt begins with a right to work, "the right to a useful and remunerative job in the industries or shops or farms or mines of the Nation." This entitlement to gainful employment is the anchor of economic independence and security, at least for those who are able and willing to take up the opportunity to work. Instead of facing indigence or the idle dependence of living on the dole, the beneficiary of this right to work can be sure of wielding the economic opportunity that the market leaves a mere possibility. How this right to work is to be enforced is left unspecified. That it provides the basic exercise of economic freedom on which family welfare and political participation depends is less uncertain and Roosevelt proceeds to underscore its fundamental service in the precisions that follow.

First Roosevelt adds to this right a qualification guaranteeing that employment be sufficient to feed and clothe individuals, as well as to allow sufficient rest and diversion to replenish breadwinners. None can exercise any of their freedoms if they cannot escape starvation, sickness, and death by exposure, and debilitating physical and spiritual exhaustion. Hence, Roosevelt calls for "the right to earn enough to provide adequate food and clothing and recreation." It is important to recognize that this right is not fulfilled by the mere provision of employment. Market conditions may be desperate enough to enable callous employers to pay workers too little to feed and clothe themselves, as well as to extend their working day beyond the point of any reasonable relief.

Roosevelt adds two further social rights that apply the general right to earn to the specific occupations of two types of nonemployees: independent farmers and entrepreneurs. On the one hand, there is "the right of every farmer to raise and sell his products at a return which will give him and his family a decent living." The market cannot itself ensure the fulfillment of this right. The prices of land, seeds, animals, fertilizer, pesticides, tools, equipment, and conveyance of produce to points of sale may all be too high for the farmer to break even, let alone earn a surplus. Moreover, no matter what costs of production may be, insufficient consumer demand may leave the farmer without the sales needed to earn any living. On the other hand, there is "the right of every businessman, large and small, to trade in an atmosphere of freedom from unfair competition and domination by monopolies at home or abroad." Left to itself, the market cannot prevent the formation of monopolies, owing to the significant barriers to entering a field of business, where overhead costs require large initial investments that cannot be recouped for some time to come. Consequently, the playing field of competition can be kept relatively equal only through public interventions that counteract and suspend monopoly formation. Insofar as monopolies undercut equal economic opportunity, constitutional stipulation and enforcement must address this problem.

Further, Roosevelt adds "the right of every family to a decent home." How can the constitution "promote the general Welfare, and secure the Blessing of Liberty to ourselves and our Posterity" if it does not ensure that every household has housing sufficient not only to maintain biological health but to enable all its members to exercise without disadvantage all their freedoms in the family, society, and state? This involves considering the due role of the home as a facilitating foundation for performing one's rights and duties as members of families, society, and the state. Accordingly, the "decent home" to which one is entitled should offer not only proper protection against the elements but sufficient space to carry on with all one's due engagements in private and public life, as well as all the utilities necessary to participate in society and politics on a par with others.

The security of a decent home and a decent livelihood do not themselves protect us from all the natural and social contingencies that jeopardize our economic security, our family welfare, and our political involvement.

On the one hand, respect for our freedoms requires that we all have access to the medical treatment we need to stay healthy and exercise our rights. Since health is the basic enabling condition for the engagement of any type of self-determination, Roosevelt adds "the right to adequate medical care and the opportunity to achieve and enjoy good health."

Even with adequate health care, however, we remain vulnerable to the economic consequences of aging, disease, accidents, and unemployment. If we cannot earn a living due to old age, sickness, accident, or unemployment, we are left without the means to provide for ourselves and our families. Hence, Roosevelt calls for "the right to adequate protection from the economic fears of old age, sickness, accident, and unemployment." Admittedly, "the right to a useful and remunerative job" and "the right to earn enough to provide adequate food and clothing and recreation" should already remove the need for income replacement when jobs are lost. With the employment right recognized and actually enforced, any individuals who become unemployed will have a job waiting for them. Replacement income will, however, be called for when old age, illness, or accident makes it impossible to continue earning a living.

One last right remains, "the right to a good education." What is a "good education" and why should we be entitled to have it? To be an endowment constitutive for equal participation in our free republic, the education in question must be crucial to exercising our various rights.

To exercise rights, we must have some working knowledge of the different prerogatives to which we are entitled and of the corresponding duties we have to respect the analogous prerogatives of others. This requires becoming informed of what rights we have as well as understanding the normative value of the rights in question. Without both descriptive and prescriptive apprehensions, we lack sufficient knowledge and motivation to observe rectitude in every sphere of freedom. The right to such education thereby provides closure to the social rights that secure our "pursuit of happiness" and underlie our political freedom.

The Additional Rights of the Universal Declaration of Human Rights

The Universal Declaration of Human Rights, adopted by the United Nations in 1948, gives international support to Roosevelt's injunction to supplement the civil and political rights of our constitution.

Thanks to the guiding spirit of Eleanor Roosevelt, who headed the United Nations committee charged with drafting the Universal Declaration of Human Rights, that Declaration incorporates all of the "economic" rights that FDR proposed in his 1944 address to Congress, while adding some further guarantees.

The Universal Declaration of Human Rights begins in its Preamble by invoking the Four Freedoms with which the Allies of the Second World War promised "the advent of a world in which human beings shall enjoy freedom of speech and belief and freedom from fear and want."[32] The rights to freedom of speech and belief echo the First Amendment of the Bill of Rights. The freedoms from fear and want, on the other hand, stand in need of clarification to determine whether they apply only to respect for person and property or extend to family and social welfare as well.

Where the Preamble clearly ranges beyond the scope of the US Constitution is in its mission declaration to be "a common standard of achievement for all peoples and all nations [...] to promote respect for these rights and freedoms and by progressive measures, national and international, to secure their universal and effective recognition and observance." This international form is only part of the story, however. The content of these internationally attested

---

32. All citations of "the Universal Declaration of Human Rights" are taken from the text as found in Johannes Morsink, *The Universal Declaration of Human Rights: Origins, Drafting, and Intent* (Philadelphia: University of Pennsylvania Press, 1999), 329–36.

rights shows itself to reach beyond that of the US Constitution once we come to the specific articles that address more than civil legality and political freedom.

Articles 1 through 12 follow the guide of the US Bill of Rights and the 14th and 15th Amendments in upholding the basic property, legal and political rights of individuals "without distinction of any kind, such as race, color, sex, language, religion, political or other opinion, national or social origin, property, birth or other status" (Article 2). Articles 13–15 address the rights of individuals to leave any country, to seek asylum from persecution, and to have a nationality of which they cannot be "arbitrarily deprived" or "denied the right to change" (Article 15). Articles 17–21 protect the basic civil and political rights to property (Article 17), freedom of thought, conscience, and religion (Articles 18 and 19), the right to peaceful assembly and association (Article 20), and the right to participation in government (Article 21).

The confines of the US Constitution and Amendments are finally breached in Articles 16, 22, 23, 24, 25, 26, 27, which contain Roosevelt's new economic rights, with a few additions.

Article 16 addresses family rights, which the US Constitution completely ignores. Article 16 confers upon adult men and women the "right to marry and to found a family," with marriage "entered into only with the free and full consent of the intending spouses," and with spouses entitled to "equal rights as to marriage, during marriage and at its dissolution." Admittedly, Article 16 leaves unspecified whether the right to marry extends to same-sex as well as heterosexual unions, but nothing about it blocks that due extension. Further, Article 16 maintains that the family "is entitled to protection by society and the State," a charge that has important implications for how family welfare and family rights and duties must be harmoniously accommodated by the exercise of social and political freedoms.

Article 22 stipulates very broadly "the right to social security" of every member of society, mandating its achievement "through national effort and international co-operation" enforcing "the economic, social and cultural rights indispensable for his dignity and the free development of his personality." What exactly are these rights and how are they at stake in "dignity" and the free development of "personality"? Is the relevant personality simply the agency of the person (e.g., property owner) or of the moral subject or does it involve the social agency of the member of civil society and the political agency of the citizen?

Articles 23–27 clarify these crucial questions.

Article 23 addresses the right to work, which is the cornerstone of Roosevelt's new economic bill of rights. This right is not an external assignment of work, as occurs under centrally managed economic organization. Rather, it involves a guaranteed exercise of economic freedom, where everyone has the right "to free choice of employment, to just and favorable conditions of work and to protection against unemployment." The choice is not to be just formally free, but must take place under conditions where the employment options offer a fair opportunity to every individual. Accordingly, the right to work entails the corollary rights of everyone "to equal pay for equal work" and "to just and favorable remuneration ensuring for himself and his family an existence worthy of human dignity, and supplemented, if necessary, by other means of social protection." Insofar as fair opportunity in employment depends upon balancing the economic power and options of employee and employer, Article 23 further acknowledges that the right to work requires enforcing everyone's "right to form and to join trade unions for the protection of his interests."

Article 24 further circumscribes the right to work, mandating that "everyone has the right to rest and leisure, including reasonable limitation of working hours and periodic holidays with pay." This right has two ethical foundations, one residing in the need to have time to spend with one's family to attend to household right and welfare, the other residing in the need to have time to engage in political activity, without which the freedom to participate in self-government becomes empty.

Article 25 concretizes Article 23's mandate for "just and favorable remuneration." It does so by guaranteeing every individual "a standard of living adequate for the health and well-being of himself and of his family, including food, clothing, housing and medical care and necessary social services, and the right to security in the event of unemployment, sickness, disability, widowhood, old age or other lack of livelihood in circumstances beyond his control." Article 25 acknowledges that this injunction requires "special care and assistance" for "motherhood and childhood," including the "same social protection" for "all children, whether born in or out of wedlock." Although Article 25 does not detail the policies all this requires, it mandates not just sufficiently fair remuneration but public provisions to ensure that no one lacks the basic physical subsistence and health care necessary to exercise their freedoms.

Article 26 complements these social guarantees by requiring that everyone should have the education needed to develop their autonomous agency and respect the rights of others while exercising their own due freedoms. Article 26 accords parents "a prior right to choose the kind of education that shall be given to their children," in function of their parental right to determine how to raise their children to autonomous independence. This right remains circumscribed by the parental duty to foster the independent freedom of children. Accordingly, Article 26 duly restrains parental license by holding that education shall strengthen "respect for human rights and fundamental freedoms," as well as "promote understanding, tolerance and friendship among all nations, racial or religious groups, and shall further the activities of the United Nations for the maintenance of peace."

Finally, Article 27 extends the rights of individuals to enjoy the fruits of culture, which warrant consideration insofar as they contribute to the flourishing of and enlightened involvement in the different institutions of freedom. Broadly speaking, "everyone has the right freely to participate in the cultural life of the community, to enjoy the arts and to share in scientific advancement and its benefits." Moreover, since cultural creation depends upon the creators receiving compensation sufficient to engage in such beneficial activity, "everyone has the right to the protection of the moral and material interests resulting from any scientific, literary or artistic production of which he is the author."

The Abiding Challenge

Although the United States has yet to enact the second bill of rights for which FDR called back in 1944, the United States did join almost all other members of the United Nations in voting for the Universal Declaration of Human Rights in 1948.[33] Obviously, our adherence to the Universal Declaration of Human Rights has not been followed by the adoption of constitutional amendments or congressional statutes that fulfill its call to enforce family and social rights. The challenge ahead requires thinking through the rights ingredient in household and social freedom and applying that philosophical knowledge to the historically given conditions in which our nation stands today. Combining philosophical principle with empirical observation, our task is to formulate the constitutional commitments and legislative measures that can supply our democracy with the realization of family and social rights on which self-government rests. This requires leaving the ivory tower of philosophical speculation behind and descending into the murky depths of our cave of historical contingency to engender a new birth of freedom, securing the economic independence and security on which our family welfares and political involvement depend.

---

33. Of the nations participating in the United Nations General Assembly vote on the Universal Declaration of Human Rights, only Saudi Arabia, the Union of South Africa, and the Soviet Union and its satellite regimes refrained from supporting its adoption.

Chapter 11

WORLD SPIRIT ON THE CAMPAIGN TRAIL IN GEORGIA: CAN THE PHILOSOPHY OF RIGHT BE A GUIDE TO SOCIAL REFORM?

Contesting the Enslavement of Theory to Practice

As citizens and philosophers, straddling history and reason, as well as persuasion and dialectic, we are easily tempted to follow Marx's 11th Thesis on Feuerbach, according to which our theorizing about the world should serve the end of changing it.[1] A whole school of philosophy has paid homage to this injunction, as if subordinating theory to practice could possibly make sense. There can be no normative critique if reason forfeits its autonomy to become subservient to anything else. Yet what could be more antithetical to the sovereignty of reason than making an emancipatory goal the conditioning telos of all understanding? If that end lords over theory, emancipation cannot itself be determined within theoretical inquiry. Instead, philosophy must accept the aim to which it should submit as an unquestionable ground whose content and authority reason can never establish. This leaves practice hopelessly dogmatic, aiming at a liberation whose character is beyond rational disputation. It can thus be no surprise that the "Critical Theorists" who have followed Marx's 11th Thesis on Feuerbach have never developed a concrete normative theory of the reality of freedom into which we are supposed to transform our world.

---

1. "Die Philosophen haben die Welt nur verschieden *interpretiert*; es kommt aber darauf an, sie zu *verändern*." Karl Marx Friedrich Engels *Werke*, Band 3, 535 (Berlin: Dietz Verlag, 1969).

From the Practical Conditioning of Knowing to the General Impasse of Transcendental Philosophy

The enslavement of philosophy to practice that follows from Karl Marx's 11th Thesis on Feuerbach more broadly reflects the general epistemological view that knowing is always conditioned by practical concerns. The leading lights of Critical Theory (e.g., Max Horkheimer, Theodor W. Adorno et al.), who follow Marx' thesis, are all students of Martin Heidegger, who advanced the existentialist dogma that the conditions of cognition lie not in some pure other-worldly, noumenal self, but rather in a concrete embodied subjectivity, very much practically entangled within the world it inhabits. Whether one characterizes that entanglement in terms of biological, psychological, or conventional constraints, the enfeeblement of reason is the same. Thought remains bound to practical demands that rob reason of the unconditioned independence that could allow for unqualified wisdom rather than relative opinion. The proponents of this disempowerment of reason incoherently purport to comprehend the practical entanglement of thought that robs reason of the autonomy on which depends the truth of their own global claims. If practice reigns over theory, as they pretend, how can their own diagnosis of the disempowerment of reason be anything more than the relative effect of some pretheoretical compulsion?

Ultimately, it makes no difference whether the conditions of knowing are attributed to a noumenal subjectivity or a worldly practically engaged self. Either route perpetrates the common defining blunder of transcendental investigation, which supplants ontology with epistemology as first philosophy. Transcendental philosophy correctly rejects starting philosophical investigation with ontology, since doing so makes direct claims about being without validating the knowing that ontology employs. Nonetheless, the transcendental turn begins equally uncritically by making direct claims about the alleged conditions of knowing without certifying its own transcendental cognition. Whether the transcendental philosopher characterizes the conditions of knowing in terms of a noumenal self, a concrete worldly subjectivity, the intersubjectivity of language, or some cultural framework, the authoritative knowing *of* these alleged epistemological foundations is taken for granted. This dogmatism is inevitable because the transcendental investigator always assumes that the knowing it scrutinizes is a knowing of an object, whereas the transcendental investigator engages in a knowing of knowing. Transcendental investigation must assume that the knowing it examines is different from the object of that knowing. Otherwise, the turn from ontology to epistemology would still be making direct claims about being, which is what the transcendental turn seeks to avoid. Due to this inherent difference between the knowing employed by the transcendental investigator and the knowing it examines, transcendental argument always takes for granted both the authority of its own cognition and the characterization it gives the knowing of objects it scrutinizes.

To overcome this debilitating discrepancy between the knowing under investigation and the knowing employed in the investigation, knowing must do its own critique. The resulting equalization between the knowing and object of transcendental investigation, however, undermines the defining difference between knowing and its object upon which rests the possibility of investigating knowing before making claims about the object of knowledge.

As it turns out, overcoming the dogmatism of transcendental inquiry leads to the same resolution as overcoming the opposition between theory and practice that bars the way to any true conception or realization of truth and right.

The Unification of Theory and Practice in Systematic Logic

Theory and practice stand in opposition so long as each lacks what its counterpart provides. Theory and practice properly aim at a unification of concept and objectivity, rather than just a correspondence of representation and appearances. Representation is always burdened with the residue of intuited content, which imagination modifies without ever freeing itself of given particulars that remain alien to conceptualization. Concepts have a content that is not alien to thought but inherent in universality. Even the most abstract universal, which inheres in multiple particulars without specifying anything more about them, has a unity that entails particularity as well as individuality. A common mark cannot retain its encompassing reach without extending to a plurality of instances, whereas these instances cannot be plural unless each is individual—a differentiated particular, not just sharing in the universal, but distinguished from its counterparts. Accordingly, conceptual thinking is not empty without intuition, but pregnant with immanent content. This makes the concept, rather than representation, the proper vehicle for grasping objectivity. Whereas appearances are relative to an undisclosed ground, objectivity is determined in its own right as a self-subsistent entity. As such, objectivity is worthy of being the object of true knowledge and the proper fulfillment of practice that aims at what is unconditionally worth achieving. Moreover, only conceptual thought possesses the immanent autonomy to lay hold of what is determined in its own right, instead of merely representing phenomena, which are conditioned by something else.[2]

---

2. For further discussion of the intrinsic connection between concept and objectivity, see "The Objectivity of Thought," in Richard Dien Winfield, *Hegel and the Future of Systematic Philosophy* (Houndmills, UK: Palgrave Macmillan, 2014), 45–56.

Both theory and practice aim at the unification of concept and objectivity, which Hegel identifies as the "Idea." Theory that is distinct from practice aims at achieving this unity in the form of a subjective Truth, where conceptual thinking confronts objectivity as given to it and modifies itself to correspond to objectivity. Although the resulting correspondence exhibits the Idea, it does so only in the arena of theory, where what undergoes alteration is not objectivity but concepts that take on the content they confront. Consequently, the truth of a conceptualization that leaves its opposing objectivity unaltered is incomplete, since such theory cannot manifest the independence of its object.

By contrast, practice that is distinct from theory aims at achieving the unity of concept and objectivity by transforming objectivity into the Good, an objectivity made to accord with conceptual determination. Once more, the correspondence of the Idea occurs on only one side—here in practice, on that of objectivity. This subverts the reality of practice. Objectivity must already contain within itself the objective process by which it develops to accord with the conceptual aim. Otherwise, the aim remains merely subjective. Yet if the development must be objective, the subjective aim seeking to realize the Good never achieves anything of its own.

In both cases, the alteration of concept or objectivity is not equally a transformation of its counterpart. The Truth of theory remains a merely subjective Idea, whereas the Good of practice remains a merely objective realization, whose process of constitution does not belong to its concept. A discrepancy haunts both theory without practice and practice without theory. The equalization of concept and objectivity in theory does not occur within objectivity, whereas the modification of objectivity through practice does not occur within conceptualization.[3]

Hegel points to the overcoming of these respective shortcomings in his characterization of the Absolute Idea,[4] which unifies theory and practice by achieving a conceptual development that is no less an objective transformation.

This unification of concept and objectivity that is no less theoretical than practical is the working of systematic logic. It equally affords philosophy a beginning that overcomes the opposition of consciousness, that is, the differentiation of knowing from its object, allowing philosophy to proceed without making any initial claims about being or knowing. The logic with

---

3. For more detailed discussion of theory without practice and practice without theory, which Hegel analyzes in the section on the Idea of Cognition in his *Science of Logic*, trans. A. V. Miller (New York: Humanities Press, 1969), 775–823, see "Truth, The Good, and the Unity of Theory and Practice," in Winfield, *Hegel and the Future of Systematic Philosophy*, 68–82.

4. See Hegel, *Science of Logic*, 824–44.

which philosophy must begin proceeds from the elimination of any distinction between knowing and its object. Logic does so by constituting a thinking of thinking, where the object of thought is indistinguishable from the thinking by which it is known. The thinking of the object is thereby the objective development of that object. Moreover, since at the outset of logic, neither the thinking nor what is thought have yet to be determined, logic proceeds with no positive presuppositions concerning subject matter or method. The constitution of the object in accord with thought and the development of thought itself here coincide in an immanent process that is entirely self-determined.

From the System of Right to the History of Right

The autonomy of logical thought has its counterpart in the autonomy of real agents whose self-determination constitutes an objective system of right in which freedom builds a second nature of its own. What is right is equivalent to the reality of self-determination precisely because only the objectivity of freedom comprises a world of convention that does not derive its character from something else. Just as logical thought unfolds without appeal to any given method or content, so the reality of self-determination is what it determines itself to be. Agents in the world do possess a given species being in a biosphere with given mechanical, physical, chemical, and ecological features, and these agents equally possess a given psychological identity that develops within a given linguistic community with preexisting traditions. Nonetheless, to the extent that agents participate in institutions of self-determination, they give themselves conventional roles in which they jointly determine the form and content of their free agency. Within the objective reality of right, agents determine themselves as owners, as moral subjects, as codetermining spouses, as interdependent yet self-directed members of a civil society, and as self-governing citizens. Through these multiple self-determined conventional engagements, agents escape all the normative dilemmas that afflict any community ordered by given foundations.

With the exception of Hegel, almost all thinkers subscribe to foundational justification, where what is true, right, or beautiful derives its normative character from some substantial or procedural ground that has the privilege of conferring validity upon what possesses validity. They ignore how any attempt to ground normativity in a privileged foundation ends up subverting itself. The privileged foundation must ground its own legitimacy to conform to its exclusive validity-conferring role. By grounding its own validity, however, the privileged foundation eliminates the difference between what confers and what enjoys validity, on which foundational justification rests. This self-elimination of foundational justification reveals that normativity must reside in what is self-determined. There can be no coherent alternative. The moment normativity is heteronomous, that is, conferred upon something by something else, the privileged foundation of normativity must found its own validity to be self-referentially consistent. This once more leaves normativity residing in what grounds itself, in what is self-determined.

For this reason, the Philosophy of Right, the philosophy of normative conduct, is none other than the Idea of self-determination, the objectivity corresponding to the concept of freedom.[5] As determined in and of itself, the objective reality of self-determination has a systematic unity that gains expression in both the development of the concept of right and the genesis of the reality of right.

To be systematic, the philosophy of right must present its subject matter in an ordering that is rooted in its content. This involves thinking first the most minimal structure of right, which contains no other forms of self-determination, but must be incorporated by all those that can follow in thought or reality.

Hegel duly recognizes property right to be the minimal reality of self-determination.[6] It consists in an interaction of individuals who possess a natural species being endowing them with a psychological nature capable of thought, language, and choice. In property right, they relate to one another by laying their distinct wills in recognizable exclusive embodiments through which they determine themselves as owners of property. This is the minimal form of self-determination because individuals must recognize one another as owners of their own bodies to be able to exercise any further type of self-determination. Otherwise, they are factors ready for appropriation by some master, to whom they and their actions belong.

Moral accountability comes next since moral agents cannot recognize one another's responsibility for what they do on purpose, with intention, and conscientiously, unless they acknowledge their status as persons, who own their own bodies.

The emancipated family follows upon property and morality for two reasons. On the one hand, the free household does not itself involve any further social or political self-determination. On the other hand, the members of the emancipated family cannot wield their autonomy as codetermining spouses and parents unless they recognize one another as persons and moral subjects, whose self-ownership and conscientious responsibility warrant respect.

---

5. Hegel correctly recognizes this in his Philosophy of Right. See G. W. F. Hegel, *Elements of the Philosophy of Right*, trans. H. B. Nisbet (Cambridge, UK: Cambridge University Press, 1991), §1, 25.
6. See Hegel, *Elements of the Philosophy of Right*, §34–104, 65–132.

The emancipated family, together with property and morality, is prerequisite for both social and political freedom. Unless the family is liberated from traditional hierarchies rooted in gender and sexual orientation, family members cannot equally exercise social and political freedom. The civil society in which individuals enjoy economic and legal self-determination follows upon property, morality, and the emancipated family, but precedes self-government because citizens cannot exercise political freedom if given privileges order their society, allowing some to dominate others socially. The self-governing state must therefore contain and uphold all the prepolitical institutions of right. Otherwise, citizens face obstacles to their political involvement that make it impossible for all to exercise political self-determination. This is why the state does not require some higher authority to compel it to uphold property, moral, family, and social rights. Unless the state sustains all prepolitical freedoms, it cannot be a self-governing polity.

The systematic unity of the institutions of right has important implications for how the reality of self-determination can come into being. This genesis is a normative history of freedom that philosophy can address. Hegel is often mistaken for a perpetrator of an a priori descriptive theory of what must happen in history. Hegel, however, like every philosopher worthy of the name, recognizes that convention is inherently arbitrary and that philosophy can never conceive what must happen in history. Instead, philosophy can conceive what the institutions of freedom are and can then consider what must happen in order for those institutions to come into being. This normative history of freedom follows the conception of all the spheres of right, as it does in Hegel's *Philosophy of Right*,[7] and has as its prescriptive end none other than the realization of those institutions of self-determination. There is no descriptive necessity that right come into being or remain in place. Both natural and conventional occurrences can preclude or destroy the institutions of freedom. Nonetheless, the normative, prescriptive history of freedom can have some descriptive application when property, moral accountability, the emancipated family, civil society, and self-government have factually arisen to some recognizable degree. In his *Lectures on the Philosophy of History*, Hegel carries out just such an application. He begins by making the corrigible empirical judgment that the Protestant Reformation, the Industrial Revolution, and the French Revolution exhibit how the institutions of right are in fact coming into being in modern times. Hegel then proposes that we look back at recorded history and reinterpret it, in light of the normative conception of the *Philosophy of Right*, as a history of freedom, showing the empirical genesis of right.

---

7. Hegel presents his normative "World History" as the concluding section of the Philosophy of Right. See Hegel, *Elements of the Philosophy of Right*, §341–60, 372–80.

What, however, should we do practically when we find ourselves standing within this history? We may be conversant with the Philosophy of Right and understand what are the institutions comprising the reality of self-determination, but how can we use this philosophical conception to guide our practice?

This is not a question of bringing the institutions of freedom into being in a world devoid of right. If that were our predicament, we would be in a purely moral situation, where we aim to generate a good that is not yet at hand and that depends wholly on our initiative for its determination and emergence.

Nor are we in the revolutionary position of founders of a state, who must bring into being a new constitution of freedom in its entirety. The foundation-free character of the reality of self-determination signifies that there can be no privileged procedure that must be followed to confer validity upon the institutions of right. What makes the structures of self-determination valid is not how they arise but that they are institutions of freedom, conforming to the concept of the system of right. Since self-determination consists in relations of right, which are not particular privileges but inherently universal and lawful modes of freedom, they are susceptible to and deserve constitutional enactment and protection. A constitution, however, cannot come into being through constitutional means, any more than institutions of right can arise through an exercise of the freedoms in which they consist. The founding of a constitution can occur in manifold ways, none of which consist in an act of self-determination. The act of constitution-making produces a constitutional order that does not yet exist and therefore does not contain the activity by which it is founded. It lacks the reflexivity of self-determination, whereby the agent determines not just the content but the form of its own agency.

Constitution-making, however it transpires, must take into account the systematic interconnection of the different spheres of right. This is something that bedeviled Napoleon, when, impersonating "World Spirit on horseback,"[8] he tried to impose a new modern constitution upon premodern tradition-bound Spain.[9] No unilateral political enactment, however, can make a constitution. The body politic is not an artifact, arising when form is imposed upon inert matter by an external artificer. The reality of freedom is a system that cannot exist unless its constitutive members know and will the rights they exercise. Moreover, as Hegel well knew, democracy cannot be imposed upon a community that has yet to undergo a religious reformation allowing for freedom of conscience and a secular space for self-government. Nor can individuals participate as citizens of a free state if they are trapped in patriarchal

---

8. See Hegel's letter of Niethammer, October 13, 1806, in *Hegel: The Letters*, trans. Clark Butler and Christine Seiler (Bloomington: Indiana University Press, 1984), 114.
9. See Hegel, *Elements of the Philosophy of Right*, Addition to §274, 312–13.

households subjugating women or laboring in premodern societies in which birthright obstructs economic opportunity and equality before the law. New constitutions can be instituted thanks to foreign intervention, as done successfully in postwar Germany and Japan, which both quickly embraced the most emancipated institutions they had ever had. Despite their preceding postmodern tyrannies, where privileged particularity overrode the universality of right, these nations had religious cultures, family relations, social institutions, and underground political traditions that could quickly facilitate widespread engagement in civil society and democratic government. The fiery unconditional surrender of the old regimes did not leave behind a vacuum but a phoenix awaiting reanimation.

Today, many of us stand not in a revolutionary situation, where founding a new constitution is the order of the day, but in a situation calling for reform, where right has a significant institutionalization, but one that is flawed and incomplete. How can the Philosophy of Right guide our efforts?

The Philosophy of Right's Challenge to the US Democracy

The challenge facing citizens of the United States today is of key importance, because of both the global military, economic, scientific, and cultural power of the United States and the influence of its constitution, which is the oldest continuously operative one in the world.

The US Constitution is also one of the briefest constitutions in existence. This brevity reflects the narrow range of its provisions, which leave unaddressed many of the forms of self-determination that the Philosophy of Right specifies. The US Constitution exhibits the influence of the classical liberal social contract tradition upon its founders insofar as its constitutional statutes delineate little more than the basic property and civil legal rights of its citizens, together with their political freedoms within its representative, majoritarian democracy. Totally absent from the US Constitution is any mention of the distinctly household and social rights of its citizens and residents.

The problematic consequences of these omissions have come to the fore at three crucial junctures in US history.

First, soon after the conclusion of the Civil War, when the defeated seditious Southern states were still occupied by the Federal Army, the newly freed slaves put forward two demands. In every liberated Southern state, they called for the distribution of land to themselves to provide for their economic welfare and for free public education so that they could benefit from the schooling of which they had been deprived. They recognized that it was not enough to obtain the status of free individuals who had equality before the law and the right to vote and hold office, rights which had been secured by the recently ratified 13th, 14th, and 15th Amendments to the US Constitution. Without the resources for exercising their social freedom, the newly freed slaves could not escape social bondage and truly enjoy equal rights in the reunited republic. The former slaves had reason to call for 40 acres and a mule since the dearth of free labor in southern plantation society made independent farming a more likely basis for economic independence than employment.

Neither of these social rights demands were fulfilled once Federal troops were withdrawn and Reconstruction came to an end. Instead of genuine emancipation, the former slaves fell prey to a new peonage imposed by a century of White Supremacist terror enforcing the legal racial discrimination of the Jim Crow regime that stood until the victories of the Civil Rights movement.

The problems exposed by the demands of the liberated slaves did not just apply to their plight. Their general extension was highlighted in 1944, when President Franklin Delano Roosevelt delivered his last Address to Congress, declaring that the US Constitution was inadequate to realize freedom in the face of modern society and needed to be supplemented by a new social bill of rights. These rights included the right to employment at a fair wage, to food and clothing, to health care, to decent housing, and to education, none of which the US Constitution guarantees. Although FDR died before he could implement these rights, they were all enshrined in the Universal Declaration of Human Rights, drafted by a United Nations committee headed by Eleanor Roosevelt and adopted by the UN General Assembly in 1948. Although these rights were put in the new constitutions of most nations that gained independence in the subsequent wave of decolonization, they remain largely unenforced in much of the world, including in the United States, despite its ratification of the Universal Declaration of Human Rights.

The call for a new social bill of rights was renewed in 1968, when Martin Luther King launched his Poor People's Campaign. King knew that the triumphs of the Civil Rights movement, restoring legal equality and political rights to African Americans, were not enough to achieve genuine emancipation. Legal and political freedom remained all too formal if social rights were not recognized and enforced. In particular, the material right to employment at a fair wage and to equivalent income for the disabled and retired should be guaranteed to give everyone the economic independence and security on which family welfare and fair political involvement depended.[10]

---

10. As King stated less than a month before his assassination, "if a man does not have a job or an income at that moment, you deprive him of life. You deprive him of liberty. And you deprive him of the pursuit of happiness." See Martin Luther King, Jr., *The Radical King*, ed. Cornel West (Boston, MA: Beacon Press, 2015), 241.

The Poor People's Campaign's drive for a new social bill of rights fell on deaf ears and here we are 50 years later with the richest, most powerful nation in human history leading the developed world in social inequality, mass poverty, employee disempowerment, ill health, educational failure, and mass incarceration.

Can Hegel's *Philosophy of Right* offer the fundamental principles for remedying the impoverishment of freedom in the United States and other nations that follow the neoliberal reduction of self-determination to property right and free enterprise?

Admittedly, Hegel violates his own conception of household freedom by retaining patriarchal privilege and limiting marriage to heterosexual partners.[11] It is easy, however, to remedy Hegel's inconsistencies, as I have attempted in *The Just Family*,[12] and develop the conception of family self-determination that social and political relations should accommodate. Similarly, although Hegel's account of Civil Society retains feudal estate divisions and only begins to recognize the central role of capital in market relations,[13] we can correct these lapses and conceive how social freedom realizes itself in full. I have sought to do just this in three books, *The Just Economy*, *Law in Civil Society*, and *Rethinking Capital*.[14] These together provide a systematic account of civil society, which prescribes the social rights that citizens must have accommodated to escape social domination obstructing political opportunity and partake in self-government without sacrificing social opportunity. Finally, although Hegel compromises his account of political freedom by letting feudal estates retain political privileges, keeping patriarchal limitations on political freedom, and choosing the head of state by dynastic succession,[15] all these violations of political right can be remedied, as I have attempted in *The Just State: Rethinking Self-Government*.[16] In sum, the theoretical principles of household, social, and political self-determination are all available if we stand on the shoulders of Hegel and do, as theoreticians, what Hegel should have done himself.

---

11. See Hegel, *Elements of the Philosophy of Right*, §165–66, 206–7.
12. Richard Dien Winfield, *The Just Family* (Albany: State University of New York Press, 1998).
13. See Hegel, *Elements of the Philosophy of Right*, §199–207, 233–39.
14. Richard Dien Winfield, *The Just Economy* (New York: Routledge, 1988), Richard Dien Winfield, *Law in Civil Society* (Lawrence: University Press of Kansas, 1995), Richard Dien Winfield, *Rethinking Capital* (Houndmills, UK: Palgrave Macmillan, 2016).
15. See Hegel, *Elements of the Philosophy of Right*, §280–81, 300–12, 321–22, 339–51.
16. Richard Dien Winfield, *The Just State: Rethinking Self-Government* (Amherst, NY: Humanity Books, 2005).

Nonetheless, working out the philosophical conception of right is one thing, transforming this conception into a political platform to reform an existing constitutional state is another.

World Spirit on the Campaign Trail in Georgia

I have spent much of my philosophical career tackling the philosophy of right and going beyond Hegel's achievement to develop in theory the three spheres of ethical community: the emancipated family, civil society, and self-government. The results may be largely unknown, but the work is there sitting in all the great research libraries of the world.

After the presidential election of Donald Trump in 2016, I decided the time was ripe to leave the Ivory Tower and run for US Congress in the 2018 election. My aim was to use my congressional campaign to advance the agenda of a new social bill of rights, drawing upon the Philosophy of Right to formulate concrete policy solutions to the impairments of freedom in the United States.

Because the national Congress enacts legislation that applies to the United States as a whole, a congressional campaign can advance the most far-reaching policies that require implementation at the national level. These can address all the social rights that the US Constitution fails to guarantee but which the Philosophy of Right prescribes.

Today, the United States has an electoral system in which the vote of citizens in primary elections determines in almost all cases[17] who will run as the party nominee in the general election. This primary system reflects how the US political system is not a parliamentary system, where party organizations directly control candidate nominations and financing. Instead, prospective candidates can appeal directly to the electorate to win the position of party nominee and thereby determine what the party advocates. This independence, however, comes at the cost of primary candidates having to finance their campaigns without any initial support from the party for whose nomination they are competing.

My platform proposed concrete solutions to the deficits in social freedom that put our families in jeopardy and hamstring our political participation. The anchor of my new bill of social rights was a Federal Job Guarantee, which would secure the right to employment at a fair wage. Guaranteed employment is the ultimate foundation of economic independence and security in civil society, where market freedom operates, engendering a competitive system

---

17. A few states still maintain caucuses in which groups of party members meet to decide who will be the nominee.

of enterprises. Civil society offers various modes of earning of living, engendering the three class groupings of entrepreneurs, landlords, and employees who live off, respectively, profits and dividends, rent, and wages or salaries. Competition, however, makes the employee–employer relation decisive for economic security because enterprises must grow and concentrate to survive, leading to an economy where the overwhelming majority of breadwinners must seek employment from a much smaller array of employers. This imbalance in opportunity makes the right to a job at a fair wage something on which all further rights depend, to the extent that without a job or income, to paraphrase Martin Luther King, one has neither life nor liberty, nor the opportunity to pursue happiness.[18] Since the market can never ensure that all adult members of civil society have sufficient employment, our state must step in as employer of last resort and put everyone who wants a job to work. As Hegel pointed out in the *Philosophy of Right*, social freedom is not secured by giving people handouts. Instead, civil society should provide the opportunity to earn a living for everyone who is able and willing.[19] Admittedly, as Hegel noted, unemployment will only increase if the state puts people to work in undertakings that compete with private enterprise.[20] Civil society, however, is not too poor to provide for its members, since the state can offer the unemployed jobs that provide goods and services our community needs but which private enterprise is failing to provide.

A Federal Job Guarantee should involve two other measures, which I advanced. First, people should be offered work at a fair wage. A fair wage is not just a living wage, providing for basic subsistence. Such a basic income is a recipe for continued poverty and the continued fall of the share of wages in the national income as the distribution of wealth becomes more and more unequal. Instead, there should be a fair minimum wage, tied to increases in both inflation and productivity. Then everyone shares in the growth of national prosperity and enjoys the fair economic opportunity to which civil society should be committed. Accordingly, I called for a new minimum fair wage of $20 per hour, which modestly represents what the minimum wage should be if adjusted for inflation and productivity gains.[21] Secondly, anyone

---

18. See Martin Luther King, Jr., *The Radical King*, 241.
19. See Hegel, *Elements of the Philosophy of Right*, §245, 267.
20. See Hegel, *Elements of the Philosophy of Right*, §245–46, 267–68.
21. Actually, if we take the US minimum wage at its maximum real value, attained in 1968 with a nominal rate of $1.60 per hour, and adjust that figure for inflation and productivity gains, the fair minimum wage becomes more than $22 per hour. See *Huffington Post*, "Minimum Wage Would be $21.72 [in 2012] If It Kept Pace with Increases in Productivity: Study," by Caroline Fairchild, February 13, 2013; and John Schmitt, "Minimum Wage: Catching Up to Productivity," *Democracy*, no. 29 (Summer 2013).

who is genuinely disabled or retired should receive income equivalent to the fair minimum wage offered to everyone able and willing to work. This does not violate Hegel's injunction against solving poverty by putting people on the dole, for it applies only to those who are no longer able to earn a living on their own.

I further called for two key measures to balance the playing field between employee and employer. The economic opportunities of employees are progressively diminished by the concentration and consolidation of enterprises, as well as by the accelerating threats to employee solidarity entailed in globalization and the rising gig economy. To advance all interests on par in accord with the right of civil society, we need to have mandatory collective bargaining for all employees and give employees at least half the seats on the boards of directors of corporations. Otherwise, the disempowerment of employees will continue unabated and contribute to social and political inequality.

A Federal Job Guarantee, combined with a fair minimum wage and employee empowerment, can wipe out unemployment and go far toward eliminating poverty, which, as Hegel recognized, is a deprivation of not just means of subsistence but the social resources to exercise one's freedom as a family member, a civilian, and a citizen.[22] Moreover, the job guarantee can lift the fear of firing that stifles resistance to sexual harassment and discrimination at work, provide maximum buying power to enhance economic activity, and insulate the economy against recessions and depressions by maintaining full employment.

More must be done, however, to guarantee family welfare and fulfil the social rights to health care, housing, education, and legal representation. To ensure that employees can fulfill their family responsibilities without jeopardizing their careers, I called for paid emergency family leave, nine-month paid parental leave, paid one-month vacations, and the prohibition of mandatory overtime, as well as free public child care and free public elder care. To wipe out child poverty and ensure that fair minimum wages suffice to support a family, I called for child allowances of $500 per month per child. To make health care a right, I called for a comprehensive single-payer public health insurance system with no copays or deductibles. To make decent housing available to all, I called for the Federal Job Guarantee to put people to work building affordable housing. To guarantee everyone access to quality education at all levels, I called for national funding of public schools at an equal level for every child, free tuition and living stipends for attending public colleges and public technical schools, and two years of philosophy studies in every secondary school. Finally, to ensure that everyone has comparable legal representation in both

---

22. See Hegel, *Elements of the Philosophy of Right*, §240–44, 264–67.

criminal and civil cases, I proposed a public legal care insurance program. This would operate on the model of a public health care insurance program, giving individuals the freedom to seek legal services from any lawyer of their choosing while covering all costs of personal legal representation, which would be negotiated on a national level to ensure affordable legal fees.

All these measures fulfill universal social rights, on which family welfare and political freedom depend. They should not be contingent upon means tests that restrict them to the needy, dividing society into haves and have nots, and jeopardizing general support. Although these opportunities would be available to everyone, they do disproportionately benefit those whose exercise of freedom is most impaired. Nietzsche can thus claim that universal social rights represent a slave morality insofar as their enforcement most serves the disadvantaged. This, however, does not undercut their universality, as Nietzsche falsely maintains, for social rights remain entitlements for all. Moreover, where the compensations these measures provide do not offset all their costs, these expenses can be fairly funded, as I advocated, through highly graduated wealth and income taxes that target those most able to pay.

The resulting platform for a new social bill of rights concretely tackles the task, delineated in principle in the Philosophy of Right, of securing everyone's self-determination in the household, civil society, and the state. This platform should appeal to all voters, no matter what their race, gender, sexual orientation, or economic position. Instead of serving particular interests at the expense of others, the legalization of these social rights forwards the universal realization of freedom to which politics properly aims.

Could such a platform win over the voters in the conservative, largely rural, small town, 25 county 10th Congressional District of Georgia? Nearly two-thirds of its voters supported Donald Trump and his fellow Republican candidates in the 2016 election. My primary campaign, however, addressed an electorate of Democratic Party supporters who are overwhelmingly African American, although African Americans make up only a quarter of district voters as a whole. In the large university town of Athens, there is a sizable Democratic Party majority, which includes many who are not African American. Outside of Athens, however, most whites have deserted the Democratic Party, which many see as privileging the interests of minorities while ignoring those of everyone else.

I faced two opponents, one a less radical white woman who emphasized her identity as a mother, a Christian, and a small town Georgian, and the other an African American woman who entered the race at the last moment, raised hardly any money, had almost no campaign staff, and did hardly any campaigning. I focused on my social rights agenda, which I presented at Democratic Party county meetings, union local meetings, community organizations, and African American churches, as well as by door-to-door canvassing, phone calls, mailings, and advertising on some local radio stations.

Although I raised enough money and had enough volunteers to get my message out to an audience wider than that of my opponents, I was not able to make my existence, let alone my platform, known to more than a minority of primary voters. The local radio and TV stations and the dwindling newspapers simply do not cover congressional races in the 10th District and most voters do not access online social media. With poverty widespread, public transportation lacking, and many working long hours on several jobs, the majority of Democratic Party voters simply have no time or means of informing themselves of candidates and policies.

Still, most observers found the election results completely unexpected, shocking, and almost farcical. The African American candidate who remained virtually unknown and largely absent from the fray won more than 50% of the votes and clinched the Democratic Party nomination. Some speculated about fraud or Republican Party manipulation. The likely truth is that most Democratic primary voters, who are mainly African American, came to the polls with absolutely no knowledge of the three candidates for Congress. They made their decision on the basis of the names they saw, one of which seemed to be African American. Identity triumphed over policy in the absence of exposure to candidate programs. Nonetheless, a sizable minority of 10th District Georgia voters did encounter the social rights agenda, which is more than ever before. Bringing it to the center of political debate here and beyond remains a challenge facing anyone who looks to the Philosophy of Right as a guide for practice.

Chapter 12

THE CLASSICAL NUDE AND THE LIMITS OF SCULPTURE

The role of art has never been more contested than today. Whereas Plato could at least banish art from the polis with a clear idea of the rogue exile, contemporary aestheticians, art critics, and artists all seem so perplexed over the erosion and instability of aesthetic boundaries as to be unable to tell whether art has come to an end. Compounding the confusion is the uneven vitality of different arts. Whereas technological developments have spawned new arts, such as film and video, to which vast resources, talent, and attention have been lavished, older, supposedly perennial arts have languished. Does this mean that certain arts have slipped irretrievably into the past, that somehow certain media are no longer capable of giving artistic expression to the self-understanding of our time?

Sculpture might seem to be the living or, should one say, embalmed proof that if not all then at least some arts are dead. Although sculptors remain at work and political upheavals have put many a pedestal in need of a new occupant, the contemporary position of sculpture stands in stark contrast to the golden age of plastic expression, when no temple could be without its statue, no battlefield without its trophy,[1] and no artist more venerated than a Phidias or Praxiteles.

Sculpture today may still provide the two satisfactions that plastic shaping can always offer. Simply by impressing matter with its most elementary form, spatial configuration, sculpture can furnish the juvenile pleasure of seeing our imagination and agency become the master of material. And, if the joy of making mud-pies is not enough, a purely formal, nonrepresentative sculpture can always decorate, adding charm to architectural or natural surroundings.[2] But if sculpture aspires to provide a plastic expression of some

---

1. Santayana points to these instances of how it was natural for the Greeks to make statues. See George Santayana, "sculpture," *New England Magazine*, vol. 38, no. 5 (1908): 105.
2. Santayana points to these limited satisfactions as the only fruits of a purely formal, non-representative sculpture. See Santayana, "sculpture," 103.

self-understanding fundamental to modern humanity, the possibilities are less obvious. If abstract sculpture is to rise above plastic gratification and decoration, it might aim at exhibiting the sheer subjective mastery of an artistry for whom no objective configuration retains any essential significance, much as abstract painting or serial music might do. Yet when art proclaims the superfluity of every sensuous shape, can it avoid diminishing the stature of its own productions? When, by contrast, sculpture remains figurative, can it mold any form whose frozen surface gesture can be congruent with a modern subjectivity for whom an inner life of conscience, psychological reflection, and private concerns cannot be ignored?

Two complementary considerations provide keys for answering these questions as well as for assessing the whole destiny of plastic art in modernity: first, the constitutive limits of figurative sculpture, and, secondly, the celebrated perfection with which these limitations are realized in the classical nude.

The Constitutive Limits of Figurative Sculpture

Given that fine art always achieves a unity of form and content, where the individual appearance of the work is expressive of its meaning, the tangible differences in media engender the possibility that individual arts may be differently able to configure the meanings reflecting distinct worldviews and the artistic styles that correspond to them. Among aesthetic theorists, Hegel has pursued this thought most thoroughly, arguing at length that architecture is uniquely suited to the symbolic styles expressing the self-understanding of the ancient Orient; that sculpture is particularly suited to the classical style purveying the worldview of ancient Greece; and that music, painting, and literature are each privileged vehicles of the romantic style giving modernity artistic shape. Although Hegel does grant the other arts a stage in each of these styles, he views sculpture to be so fundamentally connected to the classical style as to have a development essentially undetermined by symbolic or romantic construal.[3]

To confirm whether sculpture has any such stylistic predisposition, it is first necessary to isolate the constitutive resources of its plastic expression, excluding any features that incidentally attach themselves to particular statues. Although sculpture may be polychrome, may contain verbal markings, and may by kinetic, neither graphic design, nor words, nor movement are endemic to this most basic plastic art. What is essential to sculpture is the mute, immobile

---

3. G. W. F. Hegel, *Lectures on Aesthetics*, 2 vols, trans. T. M. Knox and W. Miller (Oxford: Oxford University Press, 1975), II 708.

shaping of otherwise undifferentiated matter, independent of any of the functional demands to which architecture must submit its own arrangement of heavy masses.

Sculpture's three-dimensional molding might seem the most faithful vehicle for presenting a sensuous appearance confronting humanity with its own truth. Whereas architecture can at best provide an environment for human activities, music can only offer nonverbal alterations of sound, painting must do with the illusion of flat images, and literature is bound to words that can only communicate representations lacking actual corporeal reality, sculpture can present the real contour of human individuals. Yet, if the fundamental truths of humanity that art must address reside in ethical and religious affairs, where actions and accompanying thoughts and passions play essential roles, sculpture's restriction to the immobile, mute spatial form of the body seems especially confining.[4] Not only does the shape to which sculpture is limited comprise only one abstract aspect of the human body,[5] but it seems to exclude the most revealing sides of rational agency.

Because sculpture must always present three-dimensional shapes that stand on their own, it cannot concretely configure the surroundings of individuals in action, as painting can do through the infinite expanse of perspective, and as literature can achieve all the more fully with the resources of narrative. Hence, if sculpture is to evoke the situation of significant conduct, it must do so solely in virtue of how its figures' surface and juxtaposition reflect the context in which problems worthy of artistic treatment unfold.

Moreover, because sculpture is both immobile and mute, it must crystallize all the issues of human striving in a single, silent external shape of otherwise undifferentiated material. Although painting is similarly limited to a mute frozen moment, it can go beyond the effects of the shape and posture of figures by employing all the nuances of shade and color to communicate inner thoughts and feeling. And in contrast to sculpture's restriction to a solitary gesture, music, dance, literature, theater, and film can all use the time at their disposal to present a whole series of appearances in which the fluctuation and development of passion, character, and action can be manifest. Finally, whereas the silence of sculpture puts a muzzle upon how distinctly the thoughts, feelings, and situation of individuals can be expressed, the verbal resources of literature, theater, and film allow the greatest disclosure of the external and internal dimensions of human life.

These limitations define the possibilities that sculpture offers to artistic expression. Confined to free-standing figures, sculpture can at most suggest

---

4. Hegel, *Lectures on Aesthetics*, II 703.
5. Hegel, *Lectures on Aesthetics*, II 704.

the concrete setting of conduct as it is reflected in the placement and surfaces of its figures. Restricted to a motionless shape, sculpture can only present an isolated single moment, devoid of the progress of a living action interacting with the changing context in which it proceeds. And therein bound to one mute and colorless gesture, sculpture can only express what the paralyzed exterior of a body can convey.[6]

All these constitutive features severely challenge sculpture's ambition to provide exemplary configuration to fundamental human truths. Although a statue may utilize its frozen moment to capture a fleeting gesture or incidental situation, sculpture's inability to contrast this shape to color differentiations, verbal meanings, other temporally distanced gestures, or a concretely configured setting risks eliminating the universal significance that enables its work to be more than a gratifying entertainment.[7] Somehow, the one mute immobile figure must embody an indwelling character animated with some passion from which emanates a compelling dimension of human agency. Moreover, sculpture's suspended animation[8] must still retain the individuality of the figure, without reducing it to a metaphor or symbol, whose meaning can be just as well conveyed by some other configuration, eliminating the unity of shape and significance basic to beauty.

In a most immediate fashion, sculpture must here solve the mind–body problem, making manifest how the animating spirit of rational agency can infuse the most impoverished, minimal feature of physical externality, extension. The task might appear to have an easy solution, involving nothing more than appropriating the naturally given physique of *Homo sapiens* or of any other natural species, terrestrial or extraterrestrial, possessing rational autonomy.[9] The anatomically perfect surface of the human body may, however, just as well be the lifeless shell of a corpse, the pod of a comatose human vegetable, or the blank exterior of a human animal, lacking intelligence and will. To

---

6. Hegel, *Lectures on Aesthetics*, II 703. As Hegel observes, this prevents sculpture from presenting much that does appear on the surface of the figure, such as the trembling and twitching accompanying outbursts of anger and passion. See Hegel, *Lectures on Aesthetics*, II 715.
7. For this reason, Hegel claims that sculpture must leave the portrayal of changes of countenance to painting and other more suitable arts, focusing instead upon the universal, permanent dimension in the unity of body and spirit. See Hegel, *Lectures on Aesthetics*, II 718.
8. Santayana aptly refers to the "suspended animation" of sculpture. See Santayana, "sculpture," 110.
9. In this sense, Hegel observes that the fundamental shape for sculptural construal (the human frame) is given by nature, rather than created by sculpture. See Hegel, *Lectures on Aesthetics*, II 713.

express any unity of mind and body, sculpture must employ the aspects of physical appearance specifically communicating rational agency and subject the figure to an idealization replacing whatever natural features are incidental to the self-understanding of humanity at issue with external contours that fit its spirit.[10]

Insofar as rational agency exhibits its strivings in how intelligence and will activate the body, the plastic configuration of character and conduct must center upon the expression, gestures, and posture of the body parts specially used to communicate and act.[11] This may vary from species to species, but among humans, the expression of the face, the gesture of the limbs and erogenous zones, and the posture connecting all together have a privileged role.[12]

However these physical elements be molded, sculpture must thereby concentrate its whole significance in the single frozen moment it captures, a moment that must exhibit what is fundamental to the rational agency in whose individual configuration something of universal human importance resides. This imperative applies generally to figurative sculpture and therefore seems to be a challenge to which every sculptural style can rise. The anatomical distortions, borrowings of animal features, and exclusions of individual personality by which much so-called primitive sculpture takes its bearings seem fully able to express in one gesture a self-understanding in which human subjectivity finds its essence in natural powers external to it. So, too, the tranquil Buddhas, whose idealized visage has absorbed all individuality into a relinquishment of self to a divinity for which rational agency is an illusory epiphenomenon, seem to face no artistic obstacle in sculpture's confinement to a largely isolated, frozen figure. Nor does this limitation seem to have prevented Medieval and Renaissance sculpture from expressing a human individuality

---

10. This "idealization" may even take the ironic extreme of a prosaic naturalism in which every detail is present except for the animation of rational agency. This is the case in romantic sculpture that expresses the independence of rational agency from any sensuous configuration by vacillating between abstraction and rote immersion in the facticity of appearance. When the latter option is embraced, the human figure may be appropriated with a "fidelity" in which only the expression of character is lacking (Duane Hanson, George Segal et al.), an expression requiring some transfiguration of the immediate surface of the body.
11. As Santayana observes, "sculpture is not a matter of surfaces; the muscles [...] must first have been taught to relax or strain [...] to some purpose [...] to mean something to the beholder" (Santayana, "sculpture," 108).
12. In this connection Hegel observes that although rational agency permeates the entire body, it is primarily concentrated in the expression of the face, whereas the other bodily appendages express mind and will only through their posture. See Hegel, *Lectures on Aesthetics*, II 727.

whose own infinite worth transcends natural differences and retains an inner life whose significance is not compromised by its inability to ever be fully expressed in the external appearance of conduct. Medieval religious sculpture cannot be denied the success of shaping figures who retain individuality while giving expression to a life of the soul that transcends mundane, outer phenomena.[13] Similarly, can Renaissance sculpture be denied the achievement of configuring a human individuality confident of its universal worth and inner depth? And cannot the rote naturalism of a Segal or of a Duane Hanson,[14] exact in topographical detail but devoid of animation, employ the mechanical reproduction of the surface of persons to convey a modernist view for which every external appearance is equally indifferent to the independent freedom of individuality? Color, perspective, speech, and a temporal narrative may all be absent in sculpture, but why cannot facial expression, gesture, and the whole carriage of the body be resource enough to give expression to the widest range of styles and corresponding self-understandings?

If the above examples are to be believed, an abiding doubt can still be raised regarding the relative aesthetic perfection of the different styles of sculpture. Might classical sculpture give expression to a self-understanding so uniquely capable of exhausting itself in a plastic embodiment that the other possible styles of sculpture must fall behind in artistic rank, both in contrast to classical statuary and in comparison to the other arts in which these styles are realized? This possibility, so confidently argued by Hegel and Santayana, among others, seems completely blind to the achievement of Michelangelo, not to mention Rodin, who can hardly be faulted for the deficit in individuality with which much of the preceding gallery of statues might be reproved. Yet, even if the greatness of Michelangelo's sculpture can hold its own against anything of Phidias or any Renaissance art in other media, the possibility remains that Michelangelo's *David* (or, for that matter, Rodin's *Balzac*) has its beauty thanks to a reappropriation of classical ideals, as Hegel suggests.[15] Consequently, to

---

13. Nonetheless, Hegel claims that romantic religious sculpture ultimately amounts to an adornment of architecture, as if all it achieved was decorative charm. See Hegel, *Lectures on Aesthetics*, II 789.
14. Admittedly, Hanson relies on coloring and clothing his figures to achieve the greatest verisimilitude; nonetheless, these extra-sculptural touches remain in line with other plastic embodiments of the same agenda that photorealism pushes in painting.
15. Hegel, *Lectures on Aesthetics*, II 708, II 789. Yet, as Clark argues, Michelangelo's *David* has features that hardly fit the classical mold: "the strained, defiant neck, the enormous hands, and the potential movement of the pose" all suggest a different spirit. See Kenneth Clark, *The Nude: A Study in Ideal Form* (Princeton, NJ: Princeton University Press, 1972), 61. Rodin's *Balzac* seems even more distant, with its inner, searching gaze.

settle the issue the alleged perfection of classical sculpture must be addressed in its own right.

The Affinity between Sculpture and Classicism

If classical sculpture has an aesthetic privilege, the constitutive limits of sculpture must have some special fit with the content endemic to the classical spirit. To establish any such affinity, some determination must be made limiting what kind of rational agency is susceptible of portrayal in a purely visible and spatial shape.[16]

Because sculpture makes do solely with the bodily form of rational agency (which for us is the human figure), whatever subjectivity is meant to dwell within must spread itself out upon that entire surface, instead of focusing itself in some detached expression, as might be seen in the painterly flash of an eye. Such subjectivity cannot have a particularized emotion, as a series of actions could make manifest through the contrast of its different movements, nor comprise a character presented in all the vicissitudes of its practical engagements. Instead, the subject of sculpture is principally in repose or, at most, standing at the threshold of the first beginning of action, without any differentiated inner life.[17]

Hegel, for one, takes this spatial self-repose of the plastic figure to signify that sculpture is a medium congruent with a stage of human development where rational agency takes its essential identity to reside in its bodily existence and in a universal substance, instead of having withdrawn into a self-aware subjectivity immersed in the particular motives and convictions of its own inner life.[18] Given its limitation to a single, isolated, mute spatial form, sculpture cannot properly give expression to the dimension of subjectivity that disdains the objective, abiding, bodily manifestation of conduct, to withdraw into a world of ephemeral inclination and caprice. Instead, sculpture is fit to capture the "objective," substantial, imperishable dimension of rational agency, which is as it appears on the surface once and for all. This dimension is not devoid of self-consciousness, but the subjective element it contains does not need to be separately expressed. Rather, it is a subjectivity permeated by what is objective and substantive, enabling it to be expressed in the fixed bodily shape of rational agency that sculpture can deliver.[19]

---

16. Hegel, *Lectures on Aesthetics*, II 710.
17. Hegel, *Lectures on Aesthetics*, II 705–6.
18. Hegel, *Lectures on Aesthetics*, II 710.
19. Hegel, *Lectures on Aesthetics*, II 711–12.

If this "objective" dimension of rational agency is not merely an aspect common to each and every form of human individuality but rather the defining essence of a particular configuration of human life, then sculpture would indeed seem to be a privileged artistic vehicle for that constellation of humanity. Such an objective and substantive rational agency would be specially able to achieve an adequate self-understanding in sculpture due to several salient features.

First, by being an individuality whose own objective manifestation exhaustively contains its essential identity, this shape of rational agency would judge its mettle by how it appears for others in the public show of conduct, where what the body reveals is all that counts. While this outer manifestation includes public discourse, unexpressed feelings, doubts, convictions, and motives would not bear upon the ethical and religious concerns of an individual for whom everything merely subjective is as devoid of significance as beliefs investing divinity in subhuman forms or transcendent powers. Accordingly, rational agency would here find fulfillment in its own manifest being as a member of an ethical community, performing a public role in recognition of values already visibly embodied in the existing institutions such performance sustains. No inner tribunal of conscience would hold sway, for such an individuality would judge itself and be judged by others in respect to how adequately it fulfilled the public role that community membership involves.

Further, since each and every public manifestation of the individual is a particular phenomenon appearing to sense, the identification of value with what objectively appears entails that ethical and religious truths remain paradigmatic in character. Instead of exhibiting a universality that can be expressed solely in thought, apart from sensuous particulars, such truths must be defined by concretely given communities and exemplary figures whose identity cannot be reduced to law and abstract principle. As a consequence, such an individuality can only comprehend itself in a configuration that concentrates everything upon the particular external manifestation of the agent and locks the agent into a fixed appearance expressing the encompassing given values that are already commonly recognized and operative in the particular community and its religious pantheon. In other words, the agent in question is a plastic individual, whose character is all of one piece with its external appearance and its embeddedness in a particular public world with antecedently defined norms.

Such a shape of rational agency may well be particularly suited for sculptural embodiment, but this affinity does not immediately canonize that embodiment as either a generic rule for figurative sculpture or as an unequaled paragon of plastic art. What instead lies at hand is determining how such an individuality achieves sculptural expression. To the degree that classical art gives shape to the self-understanding of just such an individuality, this is a matter of conceiving how classical sculpture must mold the human figure to achieve the unity of form and content on which beauty in any medium rests.

Form and Content in the Classical Nude

Although classical sculpture historically does not make the nude its exclusive vehicle, the nude has a salient role, both for presenting the unity of form and content most directly and for exhibiting most starkly the elementary idealization with which classicism transfigures the human figure.

In several respects, the nude presents the most literal realization of the specific limits of sculptural configuration. Taken on its own, stripped of implements, clothing, and every other addition, the nude concentrates all attention upon the exterior of the body, as that upon which whatever is worth expression must be manifest. This surface must convey the substance of the individuality dwelling within, and do so in a single fixed configuration. These desiderata, of course, apply to any naked statue, leaving completely undetermined what type of agency is expressed and how the chosen moment relates to anything else, within or without the configured individual. Thus, although nudity *can* be a vehicle for celebrating the immediate unity of spiritual significance with the external reality of the human figure, the classical nude must involve much more than nakedness to fit the individuality of its distinctive spirit. Otherwise, it degenerates into the formalism of neoclassicism, where physical perfection gets detached from any matching spirit,[20] or into the rote reportage of naturalism, where subject matter recedes into indifference. Moreover, since the unity of body and spirit is preeminently visible in facial expression, gesture, and posture, not all parts of the body must be unclothed to give expression to that harmony of inner and outer.[21] To be a paradigm of classical art, the nude must thus not indifferently sing the body electric, even if the Greek cult of nakedness expresses the conviction that the spirit and body are one.[22] The nude must instead focus upon exhibiting the permanent, essential substance of an individual for whom everything of fundamental significance falls in the sensuous, public reality of human conduct. Consequently,

---

20. Clark, *The Nude: A Study in Ideal Form*, 26.
21. As Hegel points out, although the nudity of the statue can present how the body infused by rational agency is esteemed as the most beautiful shape, mind and will attain bodily expression primarily in the face and posture of the figure. Body parts whose nudity is not a condition for disclosing facial expression and posture need not be unclothed. Therefore complete nudity is not essential to the realization of classical sculpture, and Greek sculptors were not inconsistent in clothing most female figures. See Hegel, *Lectures on Aesthetics*, II 744–45.
22. Clark, *The Nude: A Study in Ideal Form*, 24–25.

the nude, unlike other naked statuary, must employ some distinctive stylization of bodily shape to enable these classical commitments to show themselves.[23] For this reason, Kenneth Clark can duly observe that the nude is not a subject of art, defined by a shape indifferent to meaning, but a form of art, in which the content and its treatment go hand in hand.[24]

The distinguishing features of the classical nude have been noted for centuries, but few observers have focused upon how these features are connected to the significance they express. This reflects the persisting formalism among art critics, who so often analyze style in reference to either types of configuration or types of meaning, neglecting the central aesthetic problem of how shape and significance join together. Among aesthetic theorists, Hegel has gone farthest in disclosing the unity of form and content in the classical nude, presenting a catalogue of congruencies that have found their echo, albeit in a much more limited treatment, in Kenneth Clark's analysis. If we follow in the path of Hegel and Clark, the stylization of the classical nude becomes transparent, setting the stage for considering whether sculpture is dead and sculptors in modernity are zombies.

Given how, independently of language, color, sound, and motion, rational agency can still visibly animate the surface of the body, it should come as no surprise that the idealization of the classical nude concentrates upon the face, the gesture of the limbs, and the unifying posture of the whole figure.

The face of the classical nude might seem a secondary, almost dispensable appendage, an archaic vestige peculiarly devoid of the vitality and independent spirit penetrating every other part of the body. After all, do any of the headless nudes, from the Elgin Marbles to every lesser example, seem to lose anything essential by terminating at their broken stumps? In fact, do not the complete nudes lose something by having a blank, placid, impassive, utterly shallow youthful cranium stuck above a fluid, dynamic, yet supremely controlled torso? Can any unsentimental critic escape admitting that whatever greatness the classical nude possesses begins from the neck down?[25]

Such nagging doubts are not without a basis, but they ignore precisely how the limits of the classical head are one of a piece with the beauty of the classical torso. Indeed, to discard the face and privilege the decapitated figure would be to ignore the very stylizations that bring to a head the specificity of classical individuality and its incompatibility with the modern self. Nothing

---

23. As Clark observes, the sculpting of the nude aims "not to imitate, but to perfect." See Clark, *The Nude: A Study in Ideal Form*, 12.
24. Clark, *The Nude: A Study in Ideal Form*, 5.
25. Clark not inappropriately speaks of the "expressionless, time-free pumpkins of antique sculpture." See Clark, *The Nude: A Study in Ideal Form*, 102.

confirms this unity of classical face and body better than the jarring anomaly of those Hellenistic, Roman, and modern ceremonial statues that set a portrait head on top of an ideal nude torso.[26]

To begin with, the head of the nude shares certain basic idealizations with the rest of the figure. First, the surface of the face has the same absence of blemishes, scars, wrinkles, and other irregularities to be found throughout the nude. This departure from portrait-like verisimilitude is not simply an accommodation to the technical limits of marble, for even if stone were resistant to capturing such details, the question would still need to be raised as to why stone should be chosen as a material. Yet, the facility with which classical sculptors succeed in capturing the supple flow of flesh and bone, not to mention drapery and hair, indicates that Phidias had no technical ground for not giving plastic expression to the anatomical detail of a Philip Pearlstein or Chuck Close. The abstraction from particular irregularities instead stands at one with the spirit permeating every aspect of the classical nude: the spirit that treats the externality of the body as the perfectly adequate expression of rational agency. To convey this unity, the body must be purged of every contingent detail that is indifferent to the public embodiment of mind and will. Only if rational agency were understood to have an essential inward dimension to which no embodiment would do justice could every last physical detail be left in place in testimony to the indifference and independence of individuality from every particular given.

In addition to this exclusion of insignificant physical idiosyncrasies, the treatment of the face joins that of the rest of the body in embracing a stage of physical prime where the individual has reached a healthy maturity without yet entering a period of physical decline.[27] Once more, the departure from mimetic fidelity fits the unity of body and spirit, where nothing in the exterior should be unresponsive to the aspirations of mind and will, just as rational agency should have no pathos for what cannot be realized in public action. Accordingly, from head to toe, the nude must be free of physical imperfection, as measured by the demand of giving expression to an individuality fully in control of its body and seeking no further satisfaction than what can be attained in physical exertion.

The particular molding of facial features serves the same ambition. Although contingencies of natural species and ethnic/racial subgroups play

---

26. Clark, *The Nude: A Study in Ideal Form*, 49.
27. Although the eternal youth of the classical nude might seem only apt for the portrayal of immortal gods, it equally signifies the removal of every want and need of sensuous life that an idealized identification of body and spirit requires. See Hegel, *Lectures on Aesthetics*, II 759.

a role in how face and figure get shaped, the idealization by which facial anatomy unites with a particular self-understanding involves a departure from the ethnic/racial given to which naturalism is slavishly devoted. Consequently, as much as the classical Greek nude retains features specific to the physiological particularities that may be assumed to have prevailed among the ancient Greeks, what makes the classical face aesthetically distinctive are the modifications by which the ethnographic material is transfigured for artistic ends. Here what is conceptually necessary is that the unity of body and spirit be made manifest in relation to the features of the face in the same way in which the idealizations of physical perfection apply to the overall surface and contour of the body. Insofar as different facial features play roles of varying importance to the conduct of rational agency, their shaping should here reflect the fitting of the body to the demands of mind and will. Those parts of the face that serve purely natural functions should be subordinated to those facial features that are central in discourse and action. In the case of humans, the eyes, ears, and mouth take priority as facial vehicles of conduct, and do so in the configuration that turns them away from physical necessities and orients them to human interaction. Thus, whereas animals can have snouts emphasizing the subordination of physiognomy to the natural functions of obtaining food and drink, the independent projection of nose and mouth is virtually eliminated in the classical profile, where the plane of the eyes, the forehead, the mouth, and the chin all fall in a line, whose continuity is emphasized by having the bridge of the nose come straight from the forehead, with the eyes deeply set on either side, highlighting even more the projection of the forehead.[28] Moreover, the lower lip is characteristically fuller than the upper, giving the mouth a form free for speech but not subordinated to alimentary functions like the animal muzzle.[29]

Although these stylized arrangements give emphasis to the theoretical and ethical affinities of the face, while relegating the purely natural elements to the background, two other salient features restrict the scope of mind and will in ways that frame the limits of classical individuality and set it apart from a modern sensibility. On the one hand, the eyes are left without any differentiated articulation of pupil and iris that could express the concentration of an internal feeling and conviction distinct from the general bearing of the exterior of the body, or the internal reaction of the agent to what is seen.[30] On

---

28. Hegel, *Lectures on Aesthetics*, II 727–28, II 734.
29. Hegel, *Lectures on Aesthetics*, II 736.
30. Hegel, *Lectures on Aesthetics*, II 731–33. Although, as Hegel observes, in some ancient temples certain statues had painted eyes, the *sculptural* treatment remains devoid of any plastic indication of the inner soul that a glance might unveil.

the other hand, the face as a whole is generally devoid of any expression that would reflect particular moods or thoughts or contexts of action.[31] Instead, the blank eyes and stolid cast of the face present a self-repose in which the individuality of the figure exhibits a permanent fixity of character and a lack of inner division. To a modern eye, these coordinate features give the face a lack of depth; yet this shallowness expresses precisely the unity of body and spirit, of inner and outer, of individual and given ethical community, by which the classical subject is distinguished. It is the exact counterpart of the physical perfection that pervades every other part of the figure.

From neck to toe, the same form of rational agency achieves expression. In contrast to the stiff, flattened shaping of Egyptian and archaic torsos,[32] the classical nude contrasts the line of the shoulders and that of hips in a fluid balance that expresses at one and the same time the effortless, unimpeded animation of the body and the independent repose in which that animating spirit dwells. Replacing rigid symmetry with a dynamic alternation of body planes, crystallized in the *cuirasse esthétique*, the accentuated band of muscles joining thighs and torso,[33] the classical nude remains internally balanced, so as to support and retain its own position, instead of presenting a fleeting spectacle or a contortion due to external force. Just as the face has a fixed gaze in which nothing lies hidden within or before or after, so the vital balance of the figure presents an animating spirit, fully expressing itself in the body it masters, striking an abiding pose in which its complete, universal character shines through. To avoid injecting a division of body and spirit, the posture of the figure appears unforced, as if the body assumed its own position in effortless harmony with the agency within.[34] No passage to any hereafter or any inner tension is intimated. Instead, the figure gives all that is to be had in the one frozen exterior. In this way, the resources of sculpture are fully utilized, giving expression to a self-understanding that can pack in everything it has to say in the confine of a nude statue. Whether the figure is a god, a hero, or an unheralded mortal, the type of individuality is the same and the pervading idealization of the nude can remain constant.

The result certainly has a special harmony. The classical nude gives expression to an individuality in which body and spirit can be united, because the

---

31. Exceptions to this lack of expression are found only in groups of figures, engrossed in interactions involving different responses. A good example is the father and sons of the *Lacoon* ensemble.
32. Hegel analyzes at length the distinctive flatness and rigidity of Egyptian sculpture, showing despite himself how sculpture need not be confined to the classical style. See Hegel, *Lectures on Aesthetics*, II 781–84.
33. Clark, *The Nude: A Study in Ideal Form*, 35, 40.
34. Hegel, *Lectures on Aesthetics*, II 740.

self views nothing that sets it at odds with the external, public world of conduct to be essential to its being. Inner feelings, convictions, and turmoil need not be denied. Achilles can sulk in his tent, Oedipus can be tormented by his outrages, and Socrates can doubt the knowledge of his peers. Yet nowhere is conscience given an independent standing, nowhere is rational agency determined apart from all particular embodiment, nowhere is ethical community freed of given traditions that set the stage for irreconcilable, tragic conflicts with ethical associations of competing customs. The good of the individual is still nothing but the good of the community, knowledge and virtue are inseparable, wisdom is an object of love, and truth and beauty go hand in hand.

These may be the parameters of a world to which sculpture can provide essential insight, but do they represent the only form of humanity for which sculpture can be a living art?

Sculpture and Modernity

Those, like Hegel and Santayana, who treat sculpture as a fundamentally classical art commit a basic oversight. They assume that the limitations of sculpture to an immobile spatial figure only allow for art's unity of form and content when the meaning to be shaped comprises a self-understanding that locates everything essential in the exterior of human conduct. How the classical nude achieves its exemplary melding of shape and significance, however, already suggests that other possibilities are available. For to be a vehicle of the classical spirit, the nude must idealize the human figure, removing imperfections, freezing facial expression into a depthless self-repose, posing a body in its prime in a dynamic balance. Insofar as the nude's achievement of artistic success rests on a particular transfiguration of the human form, why cannot different types of transfiguration convey different forms of individuality?[35] Gothic sculpture, for instance, must still make do with molding the exterior of frozen figures, but it can employ a stylization with a very different balance, gesture, and visage to fit an individuality whose inwardness and withdrawal beyond secular affairs take center stage.[36] Similarly, a secular romantic sculpture can discard the unblemished eternal youth of classical construal and bring back the whole gamut of the human condition, in all its imperfection and with a face and bearing evoking the inner tension of conscience

---

35. Hegel himself acknowledges these options and their historical realizations by showing how the symbolic and romantic forms of art sculpt the human figure. See Hegel, *Lectures on Aesthetics*, II 779–84, 788–91.
36. See Clark for a description of how the facial expression, gesture, and posture of Pisano's *Venus* all express an other-worldly longing. Clark, *The Nude: A Study in Ideal Form*, 95.

and personal conviction. Contrary to Hegel,[37] the particular expression of the eye, for example, can be treated in plastic terms, provided the sculptor is consistently expressing an individuality whose inner depths are not matters of indifference.

Accordingly, elevating classical sculpture, or indeed classical art in general, as an unapproachable paradigm of beauty involves the same blunder as treating the Greek understanding of tragedy as a hegemonic paradigm of ethics. The current communitarian wave leans in this direction, with everyone from Rorty to Nussbaum urging a turn away from systematic philosophy to seek instruction in art, as if the unconditioned universality of ethical principle can never be upheld because action (not to mention knowing) is always caught in overdetermined, conceptually opaque contexts, leaving agents prey to the "moral luck" of fate and the clash of irreconcilable ethical frameworks so perspicuously portrayed in the ancient epic and tragic drama. Yet just as the classical nude gives perfect sculptural expression to only a particular constellation of rational agency, so ancient literature fits but one form of individuality, that same shape of humanity in which the given particularity of the external public sphere is the exclusive and fully adequate home of mind and will.[38] If conduct were forever confined to the polis, then perhaps we would have no choice but to take our bearings from the exemplary representations of classical art. This would amount to abandoning the modern agenda of freeing conduct from subordination to particular foundations, a liberation to be positively achieved by enacting property, moral, household, social, and political relations of self-determination, where the hold of given tradition has been supplanted by the institutions of freedom. If conduct can attain such autonomy, wherein the household, social, and political associations of ethical community attain a definite structure determined by the concept of self-determination, then the truth of ethics is no longer overdetermined and only to be encountered in the sensuous exemplars of art. Then, by the same token, art will need something more than the classical style to be a living testimony to human possibilities. The examples of sculpture that have supplanted the perfections of the classical nude are harbingers of what still calls to be done.

---

37. Hegel, *Lectures on Aesthetics*, II 733. Hegel here states not just that ancient sculptors were consistent in avoiding to portray the glance of the eye but that sculpture in general cannot express the demeanor of the soul through the eyes. The former claim may be valid, but the latter is refuted by the entire history of romantic sculpture.

38. As Hegel observes, the anthropomorphism of classical sculpture is deficiently incomplete since it leaves out of account the dimension of particular subjectivity, without which the full concrete individual remains elusive. See Hegel, *Lectures on Aesthetics*, II 790.

These examples of how sculpture can accommodate a plurality of modes equally signal that the individual arts can avoid collapsing into the styles of art, averting the category confusion into which Hegel and Santayana fall by identifying individual arts with particular styles. This escape does not save sculpture from the common fate of art in modernity, where the fundamental options of style may have already been played out and where every media must struggle to prevent the arbitrariness of form and content from undercutting art's own significance. The stylistic openness of sculpture does, however, raise sculptors from the dead and bring them before the common challenge of modern art, a challenge giving figurative sculpture the task of configuring a humanity that can no longer be at home in its body.[39]

---

39. See Santayana, "Sculpture," 108, who remains skeptical of modern sculpture's prospects.

BIBLIOGRAPHY

A Sourcebook in Indian Philosophy, ed. Sarvepalli Radhakrishnan and Charles A. Moore. Princeton, NJ: Princeton University Press, 1957.
Amar, Akhil Reed, *America's Constitution: A Biography*. New York: Random House, 2005.
Aristotle, *On the Soul, Metaphysics, Nicomachean Ethics, Physics*, in J. Barnes (ed.), *The Complete Works of Aristotle*. Princeton, NJ: Princeton University Press, 1984, 641–92, 1552–728, 1729–867, 315–446.
Brann, Eva, *What, Then, Is Time?* Lanham, MD: Rowman & Littlefield, 1999.
Chomsky, Noam, "The Dewey Lectures 2013: What Kind of Creatures Are We?," *Journal of Philosophy*, vol. 110, no. 12 (December 2013).
Clark, Kenneth, *The Nude: A Study in Ideal Form*. Princeton, NJ: Princeton University Press, 1972.
Collingwood, R. G., *An Essay on Metaphysics*. Oxford: Oxford University Press, 1998.
Davidson, Donald, *Subjective, Intersubjective, Objective*. Oxford: Oxford University Press, 2001.
Deleuze, Giles, *Difference and Repetition*, trans. Paul Patton. New York: Columbia University Press, 1994.
Descartes, René, *Meditations on First Philosophy*, trans. Donald A. Cress. Indianapolis: Hackett Publishing, 1993.
Descartes, René, *The Philosophical Writings of Descartes, Volume I*, trans. John Cottingham, Robert Stoothoff, and Dugald Murdoch. Cambridge, UK: Cambridge University Press, 1985.
Foster, Michael B., "Christian Theology and Modern Science of Nature," Part II, *Mind*, vol. 45, no. 177 (January 1936), 1–27.
Hayek, Friedrich A., *The Constitution of Liberty*. Chicago: University of Chicago Press, 1960.
Hegel, G. W. F., *Elements of the Philosophy of Right*, trans. H. B. Nisbet. Cambridge: Cambridge University Press, 1991.
———, *Lectures on Aesthetics*, 2 vols., trans. T. M. Knox and W. Miller. Oxford: Oxford University Press, 1975.
———, *Logic: Being Part One of the Encyclopedia of the Philosophical Sciences (1830)*, trans. William Wallace. Oxford: Oxford University Press, 1975.
———, *Phenomenology of Spirit*, trans. A. V. Miller. New York: Oxford University Press, 1977.
———, *The Philosophy of History*, trans. J. Sibree. New York: Dover, 1956.
———, *Philosophy of Mind, Part Three of the Encyclopaedia of the Philosophical Sciences (1830)*, trans. William Wallace and A. V. Miller. Oxford: Oxford University Press, 1971.
———, *Philosophy of Nature*, trans. A. V. Miller. Oxford: Oxford University Press, 2004.
———, *Science of Logic*, trans. A. V. Miller. New York: Humanities Press, 1969.
———, *Werke 8 Enzyklopädie der philsophischen Wissenshaften im Grundrisse (1830), Erster Teil: Die Logik mit den mündlichen Zusätzen*. Frankfurt am Main: Suhrkamp, 1970.

———, *Werke 10: Enzyklopädie der philsophischen Wissenshaften im Grundrisse (1830), Dritter Teil: Die Philosophie des Geistes mit den mündlichen Zusätzen*. Frankfurt am Main: Suhrkamp Verlag, 1970.

———, *Wissenschaft der Logik: Die Lehre vom Sein (1832)*. Hamburg: Felix Meiner Verlag, 1990.

———, *Wissenschaft der Logik: die Lehre vom Wesen (1813)*. Hamburg: Felix Meiner Verlag, 1992.

———, *Wissenschafter der Logik: Die Lehre vom Begriff (1816)*. Hamburg: Felix Meiner Verlag, 1994.

Hegel: The Letters, trans. Clark Butler and Christine Seiler. Bloomington: Indiana University Press, 1984.

Hobbes, Thomas, *Leviathan*, ed. C. B. Macpherson. Harmondsworth, UK: Penguin, 1968.

Husserl, Edmund, *Cartesian Meditations: An Introduction to Phenomenology*, trans. Dorion Cairns. The Hague: Martinus Nijhoff, 1960.

Jonas, Hans, *The Phenomenon of Life: Toward a Philosophical Biology*. Evanston, IL: Northwestern University Press, 2001.

Kant, Immanuel, *Critique of Pure Reason*, trans. Paul Guyer and Allen W. Wood. Cambridge: Cambridge University Press, 1998.

———, *Metaphysical Foundations of Natural Science*, trans. and ed. Michael Friedman. Cambridge: Cambridge University Press, 2004.

King, Jr., Martin Luther, *The Radical King*, ed. Cornel West. Boston, MA: Beacon Press, 2015.

Lem, Stanislaw, *Fiasco*, trans. Michael Kandel. New York: Harcourt Brace Jovanovich, 1987.

———, *Summa Technologiae*, trans. Joanna Zylinski. Minneapolis: University of Minnesota Press, 2013.

Locke, John, *Second Treatise on Government*, ed. Thomas P. Peardon. Indianapolis: Bobbs-Merrill, 1952.

Luria, A. R., *Cognitive Development: Its Cultural and Social Foundations*, trans. Martin Lopez-Morillas and Lynn Solotaroff. Cambridge, MA: Harvard University Press, 1976.

Marx Engels, *Werke*, Band 3. Berlin: Dietz Verlag, 1969.

Morsink, Johannes, *The Universal Declaration of Human Rights: Origins, Drafting, and Intent*. Philadelphia, University of Pennsylvania Press, 1999.

Newton, Isaac, *Opticks*. Amherst, NY: Prometheus Books, 2003.

Nietzsche, Friedrich, *On the Genealogy of Morals & Ecce Homo*, trans. Walter Kaufmann. New York: Vintage Books, 1969.

———, *Twilight of the Idols / The Anti-Christ*, trans. R. J. Hollingdale. Harmondsworth: Penguin Books, 1990.

Plato, *Parmenides* and *Republic* in Plato, *Complete Works*, ed. John M. Cooper. Indianapolis: Hackett, 1997.

Rapp, Carl, *Fleeing the Universal: The Critique of Post-Rational Criticism*. Albany: State University of New York Press, 1998.

Roosevelt, Franklin Delano, *The Public Papers and Addresses of Franklin D. Roosevelt: 1944–45 Volume*, complied by Samuel I. Rosenman. New York: Harper & Brothers, 1950.

Saint Augustine, *Confessions*. Harmondsworth: Penguin Books, 1979.

Santayana, George, "Sculpture," *New England Magazine*, vol. 38, no. 5 (1908), 105.

Schmitt, Carl, *The Concept of the Political*, trans. George Schwab. New Brunswick: Rutgers University Press, 1976.

Sextus Empiricus, *Against the Logicians*, trans. R. G. Bury. Cambridge, MA: Harvard University Press, 1935.

———, *Against the Physicists, Against the Ethicists*, trans. R. G. Bury. Cambridge, MA: Harvard University Press Loeb Classical Library, 1936.

———, *Outlines of Pyrrhonism*, trans. R. G. Bury. Cambridge, MA: Harvard University Press Loeb Classical Library, 1933.

Stern, Andy, *Raising the Floor: How a Universal Basic Income Can Renew Our Economy and Rebuild the American Dream*. New York: Public Affairs, 2016.

Thompson, Evan, *Mind in Life: Biology, Phenomenology, and the Sciences of Mind*. Cambridge, MA: Harvard University Press, 2007.

Vygotsky, Lev, *Thought and Language*, trans. Alex Kozulin. Cambridge, MA: MIT Press, 1986.

Winfield, Richard Dien, *From Concept to Objectivity: Thinking through Hegel's Subjective Logic*. Aldershot, UK: Ashgate, 2006.

———, *Hegel and Mind: Rethinking Philosophical Psychology*. Houndmills, UK: Palgrave Macmillan, 2010.

———, *Hegel and the Future of Systematic Philosophy*. Houndmills, UK: Palgrave Macmillan, 2014.

———, *Hegel's Phenomenology of Spirit: A Critical Rethinking in Seventeen Lectures*. Lanham, MD: Rowman & Littlefield, 2013.

———, *Hegel's Science of Logic: A Critical Rethinking in Thirty Lectures*. Lanham, MD: Rowman & Littlefield, 2012.

———, *The Intelligent Mind: On the Genesis and Constitution of Discursive Thought*. Houndmills, UK: Palgrave Macmillan, 2015.

———, *The Just Economy*. London: Routledge, 1988.

———, *The Just Family*. Albany: State University of New York Press, 1998.

———, *The Just State: Rethinking Self-Government*. Amherst, NY: Humanity Books, 2005.

———, *Law in Civil Society*. Lawrence: University Press of Kansas, 1995.

———, *The Living Mind: From Psyche to Consciousness*. Lanham, MD: Rowman & Littlefield, 2011.

———, *Modernity, Religion, and the War on Terror*. Aldershot: Ashgate, 2007.

———, *Overcoming Foundations: Studies in Systematic Philosophy*. New York: Columbia University Press, 1989.

———, *Rethinking Capital*. Houndmills, UK: Palgrave Macmillan, 2016.

———, *Systematic Aesthetics*. Gainesville, Florida: University Press of Florida, 1995.

Wittgenstein, Ludwig, *Philosophical Investigations*, 3rd ed., trans. G. E. M. Anscombe. New York: Macmillan, 1968.

Woody, Melvin, *Freedom's Embrace*. University Park: Pennsylvania State University Press, 1998.

INDEX

Absolute 77–78, 79–80
Absolute Idea, *see* Idea, Absolute
abstract right 139–40
accident 77–78, 80–81, 85–86
Achilles 209–10
action, *see* conduct
actuality 9, 75, 79, 82–84, 89
   formal 83
   real 83–84
Adorno, Theodor H. 182
aesthetics 27–28
antinomy 64
animals 11–12, 26, 35, 38–40, 100–1,
   105, 133
appearance 76–77,
   law of 78–79, 107
architecture 198, 199
Aristotle 14, 26, 28, 59, 60–64, 65–66, 69–70,
   77–78, 92, 151–52, 153, 156–57,
   Metaphysics 61
art, fine 197, 198
Articles of Confederation 162
artifact 9, 18–19
attribute 77–78, 79–80, 81–82
Augustine 94–95
autonomy, *see* self-determination
autopoiesis 37, 42, 115–16

beauty 27–28, 75, 89
becoming 63, 66–67
being 66–67,
   determinate 67
Bill of Rights 169–70, 176, 177
biosphere 133
Brann, Eva 92–93

capital 160–61, 191
capitalism 160–61

categorical imperative 73
category 77–78
causality 26–27, 70–71, 85–86,
   blind 85, 86
   efficient 18–19, 26, 36, 47–48
   material 34–35, 36
   reciprocal 31, 70–71, 86–88
chance 82–83
change 63
character 201
chemical process 9–11, 36–37
choice
   capacity of 41–42, 134–35
Chomsky, Noam 13, 41
civil administration of justice, *see* civil
   legality
civil administration of welfare 160–61
civil legality 138, 141–42, 154, 169–70
civil government 157
Civil Rights Movement 172–73, 190
civil society 44–45, 141–42, 148,
   192–93
Clark, Kenneth 205–6
class 143, 194
   see also universality, of class membership
Close, Chuck 207
cognition 76
commodity exchange 160–61
compensation 138
computer 18–19
concept 13, 15, 20–21, 49, 130, 134
   and self-determination 15, 25, 134
conditions
   determining 16
   enabling 8, 16, 30–31, 35, 37–38, 40–41,
      104, 129–30, 133, 135, 175
   juridical, *see* foundation
conduct 128, 201

conscience 140–42, 159, 204
consciousness 39
  as discursive 118–19
  as identified with mind 117
  as non-discursive 107, 110
  as reason 108–9
  opposition of 39, 66, 103–4, 106, 109, 110
consistency 24–25, 56
constitution 45, 147, 148–49, 161, 188
  making 188–89
  of German Federal Republic 148
  of Weimar Republic 148
  of United States of America 149–50, 161, 162–73, 176–77, 189–90, 192
constitutional amendment 148–50
contingency 9–11, 83, 85
contract 137–38, 154
contradiction 69–70, 72
  principle of 18–19, 49–51, 56, 59–73, 101–2, 131
corporations 143
crime, *see* wrong, malicious
criterion 65
Critical Theory 182
culture 35, 179
cyborg 7

dance 199
Davidson, Donald 122, 125
Declaration of Independence 151, 153–55
deconstruction 1
deductive reasoning *see* logic, formal
Deleuze, Giles 51, 52, 53, 56
democracy 188–89,
  see also self-government
density 93–94
Descartes, René 75–76, 93–94, 116–17
desire 38, 100–1,
  appetitive 108, 110
  recognitive 108, 110
determinacy 30, 52, 62, 66, 68, 75–76,
  self-determined 30
  theory of 25, 127
difference 50, 69
diversity 69
divinity 7, 114
dualism
  mind-body 39, 105–6, 116–17, 200–1

economic freedom 160–61, 177–78
Einstein, Albert 92–93
electromagnetism 9–11, 36–37, 97–98, 100
emotion 11–12
empirical science 1
empiricism 32–33, 121
entropy 37, 92–93
epic 211
epistemology 47
  foundational 27–28, 47–49, 57, 58, 182–83
equal opportunity, *see* right
essence 34, 54, 63
essentiality 68–69
estate 143, 191
estate assembly 143–44
ethical community 139, 140, 141–42, 159–60, 161, 204, 211
ethics 27–28, 128, 133, 211
evolution 7, 9–12, 17, 114–16, 125
excluded, middle
  principle of 52, 63
existence 75, 76, 78–79
extraterrestrials 7, 17, 114

family 44–45, 143–45, 148, 159–61, 186–87
Federal Job Guarantee 192–95
film 197, 199
first principle 60–61
force 95–96,
  and expression 78–79, 107
  of attraction 93–94, 99–100
  of repulsion 93–94, 99–100
form and content 78–79
foundation 8, 12, 23, 76
foundationalism 27–28, 45–46, 70–71, 104, 128, 155–56, 185–86
freedom, *see also* self-determination 25, 28–29, 80–81, 87–88,
  negative 23–24, 41–42, 55–56, 127, 131–32, 134, 135
  positive 23–24, 124, 127
French Revolution 187

gender 159–60, 187
genetic engineering 7, 17
globalization 194
God *see* divinity
Good 184
  highest 151–52, 156–57

INDEX

grammar 13, 40, 41, 116, 123, 124, 125
gravity 9–11, 99–100
ground and grounded 78, 87

habit 38, 106, 117
happiness 151–52, 153–54
Hanson, Duane 200–2
Hayek, Friedrich A. 151
Hegel, G.W.F 1, 14, 16, 20, 47, 48–49, 51, 55, 59–60, 66, 75, 77–78, 104–5, 118, 129, 137–38, 184, 185–86, 191, 193–94, 197–98, 202–3,
   Lectures on the Philosophy of History 187
   Phenomenology of Spirit 8–9, 51–52, 56–57, 110–11
   Philosophy of Mind 110
   Philosophy of Nature 105
   Philosophy of Right 15–16, 55–56, 72–73, 129–30, 131–32, 143–44, 187, 191, 192–93
   Science of Logic 14, 53–54, 56–57, 68, 103, 105, 124, 129
Heidegger, Martin 182
heteronomy 24, 30–31, 34–35, 41–42, 45–46, 130, 143–44, 185–86
history 35, 133
   normative 187
Hobbes, Thomas 18–19, 44, 154–55
Horkheimer, Max 182
Husserl, Edmund 109

Idea 16, 76, 130, 145, 184, 186
   Absolute 132, 133, 184
   self-externality of 132
identity 52–53, 69
imagination
   semiotic 12, 13, 39–40, 119, 120, 123
immediacy 60, 65
imperialism 101
individuality 15–16, 33–34, 53–55,
   classical 206–7, 208–9
   modern 206–7, 208–9
indeterminacy 31, 65, 66
Industrial Revolution 187
inertia 9–11, 99–100
inference *see* syllogism
infinity
   true 20
information processing 18–19
inner and outer 78–79, 81–82

intelligence 12, 39, 109, 117
   animal 38–39
   artificial 7, 18–19
   linguistic 12
   theoretical 104
intention 44–45, 140–42
internet 7
intuition 12
irritability 11, 38

judgment 13–14, 40, 55–56, 124, 125

Kant, Immanuel 28–30, 35–36, 47–50, 57, 59, 64–65, 68–69, 72, 73, 77–78, 79–81, 84, 94–95, 104–5, 118–19,
   Critique of Pure Reason 28–30, 47–48, 77, 95–96
   Metaphysical Foundations of Natural Science 47–48, 99–100
King, Martin Luther 190, 192–93
knowing, *see* cognition
knowledge
   analytic 49–50
   synthetic a priori 49–50, 57–58, 72

language 7, 13, 19–20, 38–39, 40–41, 104
   learning of 104–5, 110, 115, 117–18
   original formation of 39, 113–16, 117–25
   private 113, 121
legality
   civil 44–45
liberalism 153, 161, 189
liberty 41–42, 153, 155–57
   of desire 153–54
life 9–11, 29, 37–38, 42, 75, 76, 89, 105
light 100
literature 25, 198, 199
Locke, John 44, 154–55
locomotion 26
logic 24–25
   formal 18–19, 24–25, 62–63, 71, 101–2
   of being 52–54, 75–77, 140
   of essence 15–16, 53–54, 68–69, 70–71, 76–78, 89, 140
   of the concept 15–16, 25, 54, 56, 71, 87–88, 89, 132, 140
   place in philosophy 24, 127
   transcendental 57
   systematic 57–58, 184–85
Luria, A. R. 13–14

machine 7, 18–19
market 44–45, 141–42
Marx, Karl 181, 182
matter 9–11, 93–94, 95–96, 97–98, 99–100, 133
measure 53–54
mechanics 9–11, 99–100
mechanism 30, 35–36, 47–48
memory 17, 38
  mechanical verbal 120–21, 123
  semiotic 120–21
metabolism 11–12, 36, 37–38
meta-ethics 131
metaphysics 47, 50–51, 56–57, 58
Michelangelo 202–3
mind 11–12, 29, 38
  animal 38–39
modality 75, 84, 87, 89
mode 77–78, 79–80, 81–82
modernity 212
monarchy 143
moral luck 211
morality 29, 44–45, 139, 140–42, 147–48, 159, 186, 188
motility 11–12, 38, 41, 100–1, 117
motion 9–11, 98
  see also locomotion
music 198, 199

name 13, 121–22
Napoleon 188–89
natural selection, *see* evolution
naturalism 205–6, 207–8
nature 35–38
  inorganic 9, 35–36
  organic 36–38
necessity 75, 79, 89
  blind 85, 89
  formal 83
  real 84
  relative 84
negation 34, 68
neoclassicism 205–6
neoliberalism 191
Newton, Isaac 94–95
Nietzsche, F. 2, 20–21, 50–52, 58, 195
nihilism 153, 156–57
nominalism 53, 88

non-contradiction
  principle of, *see* contradiction, principle of
normativity 27–28, 128, 155–56, 185–86
nothing 66–67
nude 205–6
  classical 198, 205–10
Nussbaum, Martha 211

objectivity 56, 72, 75, 76, 130
Oedipus 209–10
oligarchy 169
ontology 56–57
  foundational 47–49, 58, 65
organism 9–11, 36
  see also life

painting 198, 199
particularity 15–16, 33, 71–72
Pearlstein, Philip 207
perception 100–1, 106–7
person 136–38
phenomena 56
phenomenology 109
Phidias 197, 202–3, 207
philosophy 1, 14, 19, 23, 24, 34–35, 103–4
  analytic 50, 54
  of mind 104, 111, 129–30
  of nature 129–30
  of right 128, 131, 186, 188, 189, 192, 196
  postmodern 50, 54, 58
  Realphilosophie 132
  transcendental 29, 47–49, 77, 182–83
  without foundations 23
  systematic 110–11, 125
Pisano, Andrea 210–11
place 98
plants 11–12, 38, 105
Plato 197
  Parmenides 33
  Republic 25–26, 135
  Timaeus 8–9, 92–93
Platonism 72
poetry 126
politics, *see* state
Poor People's Campaign 190, 191
positive and negative 34, 68–70, 87

possibility 9, 75, 82–84
  formal 83
  real 83–84
possible worlds 9–11, 84–85
post-colonialism 101
Postmodernism 56
postmodernity 188–89
poverty 193–94
Praxiteles 197
property qualifications 162, 163, 172
property rights 43–44, 136–38, 153–54, 186
  as enabling condition of all other rights 44, 136–37, 147, 159
proposition 13, 124, 125
Protestant Reformation 187
psyche 12, 39, 106
  as precondition of consciousness and intelligence 106, 117
psychology 35
Ptolemy 93
public administration of welfare 44–45
punishment 138
purpose 44–45, 140–42

quality 68

race 172
Rapp, Carl 20
reality 68, 75–76
reason 1, 7, 11–12, 23, 41, 75
reciprocity 26–27, 86–88
recognition, reciprocal 42
Reconstruction 190
Relativism 1
relativity, theory of 100
religious reformation 188–89
representation 12, 130
  general 38, 119, 121
reproduction 9–12, 36, 37–38
revolution 101, 188
right 27–28, 42–43, 73, 75, 89, 137–38
  as an interaction 134–36
  as equal opportunity 42–43
  economic 165, 174–76, 177
  family 177
  genesis of 187
  new social bill of 173–76, 177–78, 190, 191, 192, 195

pre-political rights as reconditions of political rights 147–48, 161
property 42–43, 136–38
  system of 185
  to work 174, 177–78, 192–93
Rodin, Auguste 202–3
Roman Empire 161
Roosevelt, Eleanor 176
Roosevelt, Franklin Delano 173–75, 176, 178, 179, 190
Rorty, Richard 211
Rousseau, J. J 44
rule, *see* state

Sache 16
Santayana, George 210–11, 212
sculpture 197–212,
  abstract 197–98
  Classical 198, 202–5, 211
  figurative 197–98
  Romantic 202–3, 210–11
Segal, George 200–2
self-consciousness 12, 29, 39, 49, 95–96, 107–9
  and intersubjectivity 12, 108
  as nondiscursive 12, 107–9, 110
  universal 108, 109
self-determination 15–16, 31, 55–56, 80–81, 87, 131
  and normativity 28, 127, 157
  political 138–39
self-government 44–45
self-motion 26
self-ownership 136–37, 147
self-rule, *see* self-government
sense-certainty 106–7
sensibility 49
sensitivity 11, 117
sentience 11–12
Sextus Empiricus 59, 63–65, 69–70
sexual orientation 159–60, 187
sign 12, 13, 39–40, 119, 121
skepticism 1, 59–60, 63–64, 76–77
slavery 136–37, 141, 149–50, 151, 165–66, 167, 168, 171, 172
social contract 44, 138–39, 152, 153–55, 189
Socrates 25–26, 28, 41–42, 135, 209–10
something and other 34, 52

soul *see* psyche
space 9–11, 93–94, 96–97, 133
    absolute 96, 97–98
    relative 96, 97–98
Spinoza, B. 77–78, 79–80
spirit 109, 110
    subjective 109
spontaneity 29, 48–49
state 142, 143–45
state of nature 138, 154
subject 11–12, 80–81, 87
substance 31–32, 63, 79, 80, 81–82, 85–86, 87, 89
    active and passive 86–87
sufficient reason, principle of 30
syllogism 13–14, 40, 124, 125
symbol 13, 119

technology 9, 18
teleology 76, 89
    external 36
    internal 36, 37, 76
theory
    and practice 181, 183–84
thing
    and its properties 78
    in itself 29, 48–49
thinking 12, 39
time 9–11, 91–102, 133
    as rooted in mind 92, 94–96
    as rooted in motion 92–94
    historical 101
    modes of 91–92
    phases of 91–92
tragedy 211
transcendental philosophy, *see* philosophy, transcendental
triangulation 122, 123, 125
tropism 11–12, 105

truth 1, 23, 27–28, 49–50, 56, 65–66, 73, 89, 103–4, 184

uncaused cause 30, 31
understanding 49, 106–7
unmoved mover 28
Universal Declaration of Human Rights 176–79, 190
universality 15, 23–24, 32–33, 71–72, 101–2, 204
    abstract or formal 32–33, 50, 54, 101–2, 131–32
    as misidentified with essence 33, 88
    concrete 25
    of class membership 54–55, 101–2
    of genus and species 55
    of language 113
US Constitution *see* constitution, of United States of America
Utilitarianism 152, 153–54

vocabulary 13, 116
Vygotsky, Lev 122–23

welfare 164, 165
whole and parts 78–79, 88
will
    natural 131–32
    self-determined 42–43, 72–73, 131–32, 134–36, 157–58
will to power 51
Wittgenstein, Ludwig 121
Woody, Melvin 80, 85
word 13
    see also name
wrong
    malicious 138, 141–42
    non-malicious 138

www.ingramcontent.com/pod-product-compliance
Lightning Source LLC
Chambersburg PA
CBHW021140230426
43667CB00005B/196